REASONING AND COMMUNICATION
Thinking Critically About Arguments

REASONING AND COMMUNICATION
Thinking Critically About Arguments

Josina M. Makau
Ohio State University

Wadsworth Publishing Company
Belmont, California
A Division of Wadsworth, Inc.

Communications Editor: Kristine M. Clerkin
Editorial Assistants: Tamiko Verkler, Nancy Spellman
Production Editor: Jerilyn Emori
Managing Designer: James Chadwick
Print Buyer: Randy Hurst
Text Designer: Salinda Tyson
Copy Editor: Margaret Moore
Cover Designer: James Chadwick

Printed in the United States of America   19

1 2 3 4 5 6 7 8 9 10—94 93 92 91 90

Library of Congress Cataloging-in-Publication Data
  Makau, Josina M.
    Reasoning and communication : thinking critically about arguments
      / Josina M. Makau.
        p.   cm.
      ISBN 0-534-12390-2
      1. Reasoning.   2. Decision-making.   I. Title.
  BC177.M353   1990   89-37859
  168—dc20   CIP

▼　▼　▼　▼　▼　▼　▼

▼　▼　▼　▼　▼　▼　▼

To my parents
Johanna and Leon Makau

▾ *CONTENTS* ▾

▼ ▼ ▼

PART 2   Argumentation Skills

▼ ▼ ▼

PART 3 Applications

PREFACE

This book is dedicated to helping you acquire and develop organized knowledge, understanding, and skills. Most of us realize that having organized knowledge is important for resolving public policy issues, such as whether to raise taxes or regulate private drug use. Knowledge of this kind is also important in making personal decisions. Consider the highly individual decision of whether and how to plan a family. Knowledge about specific family planning options is necessary for couples facing this decision. Couples who are open to using birth control methods will find value in the knowledge *that* one method of birth control has a 94 percent rate of effectiveness combined with certain health risks, whereas a competing method has an 85 percent rate of effectiveness with virtually no medical risks. For couples who do not want to use artificial methods of birth control, knowledge *of* alternative natural methods would be more valuable. For all these couples, organized knowledge *about* alternative family planning methods plays an important role in effective decision making.

However, knowledge of this kind is not enough. Couples faced with family planning decisions need the ability to *grasp* the relevant issues. They need the ability to assess the costs and benefits of options, to predict how adopting each option will affect their lives, to discover and evaluate the values underlying their perceptions of the issues, to distinguish between their short- and long-term interests, and to determine which birth control method will satisfy these interests most effectively. In short, these couples, like all decision makers faced with difficult choices, need to acquire an *understanding* of relevant issues.

This type of understanding contributes significantly toward resolving disputes. Consider one of the couples, for example. Even after the couple acquires knowledge about their available options, the two persons find themselves disagreeing about what to do. Developing an understanding of the relevant issues will help them assess the importance of the values and interests that are tied in with adoption of each option. Thoughtful discussion and analysis of relevant issues, interests, and values will enable the couple to select the family planning option best suited to their shared values and long-term interests.

The ability to apply knowledge and understanding to the resolution of specific issues has always been vital to good decision making. Today's decision makers, however, face a burden unique to this age—the burden of information. Just one edition of the *New York Times* contains the same amount of information a person in the sixteenth century would encounter over an entire lifetime! Information specialists believe that the recent proliferation of information is likely to continue. They predict that the amount of information available to the average American will continue to double every five years.

The resulting "information overload" that occurs when people are constantly exposed to massive amounts of new information increases the importance of one's ability to *find, interpret, evaluate,* and *apply* relevant information to personal and professional problems. To make effective use of information, today's decision makers need to develop critical reading, listening, viewing, speaking, and writing *skills.* Underlying these specific skills is the more general ability to think critically.

Thinking critically about information involves careful assessment of the information's meaning, relevance, and reliability. Critical thinking involves discovering and assessing values, interests, and outcomes associated with relevant options. As such, critical thinking is a complex skill that, like other skills, requires training. Consider, for example, the ballet dancer or violin player who has no training. Or imagine trying to develop the skill of performing complex mathematical operations without proper training. Imagine a surgeon who has never practiced surgical procedures, or consider the astronaut who has never been trained to deal with weightlessness. These skills require extensive training. Similarly, development of critical thinking skills requires patient, carefully considered training.

The study and use of argumentation helps provide this training. Learning to present and evaluate arguments helps decision makers discover and assess their available options. Learning to argue helps decision makers develop the questioning habit and encourages them to carefully reconsider their ideas. Through argumentation, people are able to exchange ideas freely with each other, to evaluate those ideas, and to select from among them. In essence, argumentation enhances the ability to think freely and productively.

This book prepares you to argue with skill and to reason effectively. Developing these skills will help you make reasoned decisions in the face of complex choices throughout your lifetime. The book will also help you encourage others to understand and appreciate your decisions.

The development of these skills has the potential to significantly enrich the quality of your life. The ability to exchange ideas meaningfully, for example, will help you better relate to friends, family, and others important to you. The discovery and critical assessment of choices will help you make decisions that improve your personal as well as professional position.

Employers seek job applicants who have developed these skills. Rapid advancements in science and technology make it difficult to predict the shape of the future marketplace. Today's employers therefore are searching for people who will be able to *adapt* their knowledge and training to new contexts. And because this country's economy is becoming increasingly information-based, employers need to find people who are able both to apply critical thinking skills to information and to communicate their understanding to others.

In May, 1989, ABC News dedicated one hour to a discussion of this important topic. According to the program's announcer, "the most important work skills that a student can leave school with are powers of critical thinking." The special broadcast featured testimony from prominent business leaders such as Chrysler Corporation Chair Lee Iacocca, McDonald's Vice-President Stan Stein, Russell Corporation Executive Gene Gwaltney, and Polaroid Communications Manager Harry Johnson in support of the view that critical thinking skills will play an increasingly significant role in both hiring and retaining corporate employees. Admiral William Crowe, Chair of the Joint Chiefs of Staff, testified further that teaching Americans to think critically will be increasingly vital to our country's national security. According to Admiral Crowe, developing young people's critical thinking skills is "the priority challenge of the '90s."[1]

Former Secretary of Education William Bennett joined many of his predecessors in addressing these and related needs. He argued that institutions of higher learning should help prepare "for life, for the eminently practical tasks of living well, thinking clearly, and acting sensibly." Peter Jennings, ABC

---

1. Taken from the transcript of the ABC News Special, "America's Kids: Teaching Them to Think," broadcast May 4, 1989.

News Anchor, summed up this perspective when he noted the importance of "teaching young children how to think and thus how to succeed."[2]

The chapters that follow address this challenge. Their content is intended to help you develop both your personal and professional potential. To fulfill these goals, the book is divided into three parts. Part 1 introduces the art of critical thinking. Part 2 introduces argumentation skills. And Part 3 prepares you to apply the principles and tools of the first two parts. The final chapter provides exercises designed to help you apply your critical thinking and argumentation skills to carefully selected family life issues. Taken together, these chapters will help you acquire the knowledge, understanding, and skills needed for active and meaningful participation in today's democratic institutions and economic marketplace.

▾ ▾ ▾
ACKNOWLEDGMENTS

This book represents the culmination of fourteen years of teaching critical thinking and communication. It isn't possible to properly acknowledge all the many teachers, students, and friends who have contributed so significantly to whatever knowledge and understanding are reflected in this book.

I am deeply indebted to the teachers at Los Angeles Valley College, California State University at Northridge, and the University of California at Los Angeles and Berkeley who helped me grasp the significance of this book's subject. I am indebted too to the hundreds of students who have joined me in grappling with the issues covered in the book. Sharon Blinn, Eric Gilder, Doug Grauel, Anne Mattina, Elizabeth Nelson, and Jeanne P. Williams were especially generous in their willingness to exchange ideas.

Special thanks are also due to the many people who carefully reviewed parts of this text. Comments by Jan Fazio, Mary Garrett, Carole Pavlo, and Linda Stamps led to reconceptualizations of major portions of the text. A number of Wadsworth reviewers also provided valuable suggestions for revision. Celeste Condit, University of Georgia; Lesley Dimare, California State University, Los Angeles; Richard Katula, De Paul University; Charles Kneupper, University of Texas, Arlington; Michael Leff, Northwestern University; John Lyne, University of Iowa; Pat Marsh, California State University, Sacramento; Donovan Ochs, University of Iowa; and Beth Waggenspack, Virginia Polytechnic Institute and State University provided particularly insightful reviews. Their comments led to major revisions of previous drafts.

Thanks are also due to the book's indexer, Nancy Mulvany, and to the many people at Wadsworth who worked on this project. Senior Production Editor Jerilyn Emori, Copy Editor Margaret Moore, Editorial Assistants Tamiko

---

2. ABC News, May 23, 1989.

Verkler and Nancy Spellman, Permissions Editor Peggy Meehan, Designer James Chadwick, and Product Manager Robin Levy provided especially help-ful assistance. Above all, I want to thank the book's editor, Kris Clerkin. Her enthusiasm and support were sources of great encouragement during the book's evolution. Whatever success this book may enjoy can be attributed largely to her courage and foresight.

I also want to pay tribute to Zhivago, who left the world the summer I began work on this project. Memories of him inspired many sections of the book. I hope that he finds them to his liking, wherever he might be.

Finally, I cannot adequately express the gratitude I feel for my dear friends and family members. I am deeply grateful for their support, encour-agement, and unconditional love, without which I could not have completed this project.

THE CRITICAL THINKING PROCESS

1

An Introduction to Critical Thinking

This chapter introduces the critical thinking process. By the end of this chapter, you should have a better understanding of the nature and importance of critical thinking.

▼ ▼ ▼
WHAT IS CRITICAL THINKING?

Educator Edward D'Angelo defines critical thinking as "the process of evaluating statements, arguments, and experience."[1] Philosopher John Chaffee

---

1. Edward D'Angelo, *The Teaching of Critical Thinking* (Amsterdam: B. R. Gruner, 1971), p. 7.

adds that thinking critically involves our "active, purposeful, organized efforts to make sense of the world."[2]

The critical thinking process combines innate and learned skills. The more you engage in critical thinking, the more you will develop your natural abilities to think. As your critical thinking skills develop, you'll begin to discover new ways of evaluating what you hear, read, and experience. You'll also be likely to adopt new attitudes about many aspects of your life.

Proficient critical thinkers share at least several basic characteristics. They are committed to careful decision making. They make effective use of freedom of choice in their personal and professional lives. And they understand that exercising our liberties requires the development and use of critical thinking skills.

These skills include the abilities to ask relevant questions, find, evaluate, and effectively use relevant information, draw reasonable inferences, and evaluate inferences. One important element of this process is critical reasoning, defined by philosophers Jerry Cederblom and David Paulsen as a process "that involves looking at the *reasons* on which an opposing view is based and making an assessment of those reasons."[3]

The critical thinker is someone who has developed a refined questioning habit. Such a person regularly assesses the value of arguments and raises thoughtful questions at appropriate times. The critical thinker effectively gathers and uses information relevant to his or her professional and personal decision making. This person's decision making reflects an understanding and effective usage of principles and tools of critical thinking.

The critical thinker is also someone who effectively communicates his or her ideas. It is through communication that the critical thinker is able to subject ideas to other people's scrutiny. Effective dialogue is one of the best means for the critical thinker to raise thoughtful questions and to evaluate opposing ideas.

▾ ▾ ▾

WHY IS CRITICAL THINKING IMPORTANT?

Before we discuss these practical skills, let us address a basic question: Why is critical thinking important? Why should you make the special effort needed to acquire and develop critical thinking and related communication skills?

---

2.   John Chaffee, *Thinking Critically,* 2nd ed. (Boston: Houghton Mifflin, 1988), p. 1.

3.   Jerry Cederblom and David W. Paulsen, *Critical Reasoning,* 2nd ed. (Belmont, Calif.: Wadsworth, 1986), p. 1.

In his famous treatise, *On Liberty,* John Stuart Mill writes:

▼▼▼▼▼▼

In the case of any person whose judgement is really deserving of confidence, how has it become so? Because he has kept his mind open to criticism of his opinions and conduct. Because it has been his practice to listen to all that could be said against him; to profit by as much of it as was just, and expound to himself, and upon occasion to others, the fallacy of what was fallacious. Because he has felt that the only way in which a human being can make some approach to knowing the whole of a subject, is by hearing what can be said by persons of every variety of opinion, and studying all modes in which it can be looked at by every character of mind. No wise man ever acquired his wisdom in any mode but this; nor is it in the nature of human intellect to become wise in any other manner.[4] ▼▼▼

Mill's approach to critical thinking, listening, reading, and speaking is possible in democratic nations such as ours. We are permitted to freely form our opinions, both privately and publicly. Mastering the critical thinking skills discussed in this text will enable you to take greater advantage of the opportunities provided by our constitutional rights; you will be able to more fully and effectively use the precious rights of free expression and suffrage granted by our Constitution. You will be able to "become wise" by listening to "all that can be said" against your views and by subjecting your ideas to the view of "persons of every variety of opinion."

Critical Thinking as Fundamental to Freedom

Critical thinking requires liberty. Without the freedom to openly discuss our views, our ability to think critically would be severely limited. But the relationship between liberty and critical thinking does not end here. Not only is liberty important to critical thinking; critical thinking is fundamental to the preservation of our liberties.

Imagine a country in which citizens who have free access to information, accompanied by the rights of suffrage and free expression, choose instead simply to accept what the country's leaders and so-called authorities tell them. Although these citizens have the right to vote, they don't take the time to think about the relevant issues, and their only knowledge about political candidates comes from paid endorsements. These citizens do not think critically about the relevant issues or candidates. Nor do they question what they learn from well-trained media professionals. Instead, they let journalists, ad-

---

4. John Stuart Mill, *On Liberty* (1859; reprint Indianapolis: Bobbs-Merrill, 1956), p. 25.

vertisers, and political leaders tell them how to think and how to vote. It is easy to imagine that those in power in such a country would soon find more and more effective ways to manipulate the nonthinking masses. Before long, the people would be controlled by a small group of authorities, simply because they did not exercise their rights. They did not think critically.

Some people would argue that Hitler's Germany provides an example of such a situation. Many of the German people who originally supported Hitler were later horrified at the consequences of his dictatorship. Many of these people supported Hitler without asking important questions about his political philosophy and intellectual background. Many chose to listen only to his plans for social and economic reform. The German people had suffered from a severe economic depression. Here was a man who offered a way to end their problems. For some, this promise was enough; they chose not to consider the implications of adopting Hitler's social and economic reforms. As history has shown, the German people paid a tragic price for this choice. It could be argued that theirs was a graphic example of the consequences people may face when they fail to think critically about such an important issue.

People who think critically are able to carefully evaluate the words and actions of leaders in government and industry. Thinking critically about issues of national and international importance leads citizens to raise important questions, seek detailed information, and carefully evaluate, for example, a politician's platform or an industrialist's statements. Exercising the art of critical thinking helps protect our most cherished freedoms and encourages our country's leaders to faithfully and effectively serve their official functions.

Critical Thinking as Essential to Group Decision Making

The ability to think critically also helps group decision makers avoid serious mistakes. Jury decision making provides many good examples of this process. In the case of *People* v. *Collins,* for example, the jury mistakenly found the defendants guilty of second-degree robbery. The prosecution used circumstantial evidence to build a case on what is called "mathematical probability." Witnesses testified that the robbery in question was committed by "a Caucasian woman with a blond ponytail who left the scene accompanied by a Negro with a beard and a mustache." Janet and Malcolm Collins fit this rather unusual description. They also had no verifiable alibi for their whereabouts at the time of the crime. Based upon this circumstantial evidence, the prosecution argued that the mathematical probability that the Collins couple committed the crime was so high as to justify a guilty verdict.

The jury was impressed with this mathematical argument and found the couple guilty. Later, the California Supreme Court overruled this verdict. Justices on this high court pointed out that the lower court jury had not taken into account the possibility that "the guilty couple might have included a light-skinned Negress with bleached hair rather than a Caucasian blonde; or the driver of the car might have been wearing a false beard as a disguise; or the prosecution's witnesses might simply have been unreliable." Instead, the jury had been "unduly impressed by the mystique" of the prosecution's mathematical demonstration.[5]

Fortunately, the more adept critical thinkers on the higher court overruled the lower court's jury verdict. However, only a small percentage of cases ever find their way into an appellate court. In most instances, jury verdicts are not reversed. It is therefore crucial that jurors learn and use effective critical thinking and communication skills.

Just as many poorly made jury decisions are never reversed, group decision making in many other situations is also either not reversed or not reversible. Poor judgments in these situations can have serious and lasting negative consequences.

Yale psychology professor Irving Janis has documented a number of historical fiascos resulting from poor group decision making. He writes:

▼ ▼ ▼ ▼ ▼ ▼

Year after year newscasts and newspapers inform us of collective miscalculations—companies that have unexpectedly gone bankrupt because of misjudging the market, federal agencies that have mistakenly authorized the use of chemical insecticides that poison our environment, and White House executive committees that have made ill-conceived foreign policy decisions that inadvertently bring the major powers to the brink of war.[6] ▼ ▼ ▼

Janis goes on to show that better use of critical thinking skills probably would have prevented many of these fiascos.

The so-called Iran-Contra affair of 1987 illustrates Janis's point. In November of 1986, President Ronald Reagan told the American people and the rest of the world that the United States opposed the sale of arms to warring nations such as Iran and Iraq. At the same press conferences, the president reiterated this country's policy against trading or selling arms in exchange for hostages. Earlier, President Reagan had strongly affirmed these positions and even admonished America's allies for selling arms to Iran and Iraq.

Yet one year later, investigators uncovered evidence showing that the United States had, in 1986, sold arms to Iran in the hope of achieving freedom for hostages held in Lebanon. At first, President Reagan denied that this action constituted the sale of arms for hostages. Later, he conceded that people in his administration had violated his own publicly stated foreign policy.

---

5. People v. Collins, 68 Cal.2d. 319, Cal. Rptr. 497 (1968).
6. Irving L. Janis, *Groupthink,* 2nd ed. (Boston: Houghton Mifflin, 1982), p. 2.

Many months of investigation of this and related incidents revealed that poor organizational decision making was a primary culprit in this unfortunate chain of events. Inadequate communication between decision makers and uncritical evaluation of existing information were cited as major contributors to President Reagan's most troubling problems.

The space shuttle *Challenger* disaster of 1986 provides another example of the dangers of poor organizational decision making. On January 28, 1986, the *Challenger* was scheduled to take six astronauts and a civilian, schoolteacher Christa McAuliffe, on an exciting journey into space. Children and adults throughout the nation watched with eager anticipation as the *Challenger* left the ground—and watched with horror as the shuttle exploded in midair. After an exhaustive investigation of the circumstances surrounding this tragedy, the commission assigned to this investigation concluded that a flawed decision-making process was the disaster's underlying cause. According to the Rogers Commission, the management in charge of developing the shuttle failed to provide a well-structured and managed system emphasizing safety. Nor did the managers properly communicate information regarding possible problems to people instrumental in NASA's flight plans. And, finally, these managers ignored warnings of their company's engineers in order to accommodate NASA's public relations needs. As a result of inadequate use of critical thinking skills and poorly developed communication strategies, seven people lost their lives and a nation grieved for their loss.[7]

Critical Thinking as Essential to Professional Decision Making

Not surprisingly, critical thinking is considered vitally important in today's business environment. Business leaders have rallied behind the view that education "best serves the economy by teaching people to think, to communicate, and to understand their world." Harvard Business School now requires all first-year MBA candidates to take a course specifically designed to enhance students' abilities to think critically about the problems they are likely to encounter in the business world. The course is fittingly called "Decision Making and Ethical Values."[8]

The Educational Testing Service, this nation's primary source of testing for college admissions, recently completed an assessment of the knowledge and skills that students need to compete in today's competitive marketplace. The researchers concluded that "our nation is at an educational crossroads.

---

7. For a detailed discussion of the decision-making problems that led to the *Challenger* disaster, see James Jaksa and Michael Pritchard, *Communication Ethics: Methods of Analysis* (Belmont, Calif.: Wadsworth, 1988), pp. 120–139.

8. Hugh A. Mulligan, "Ethics Is Topic A in Every Field," *Columbus Dispatch,* April 16, 1989, p. B-1.

The success of our economy and, indeed, the survival of our democracy have become more dependent than ever before on each individual's ability to master increasingly complex knowledge and skills." According to the study, "students must become doers and thinkers."[9]

Business leaders throughout the country are openly seeking job applicants who can demonstrate the ability to think critically. Today's employers recognize that their company's success requires employees to raise relevant questions, evaluate complex information, make difficult decisions, and anticipate the outcomes of those decisions.

Today's scientists and doctors must be especially proficient critical thinkers. They are faced with complex new social and ethical dilemmas created by technological advances in the medical sciences. For example, embryos can now be produced in the laboratory, frozen, stored, and transferred from one woman to another. Should the embryo be given full rights as a person? Is it ethical to transfer an embryo from one woman to another? What should happen to embryos abandoned in freezers or left by couples who do not wish to follow through with in vitro fertilization? Should they be used for experimental purposes or be destroyed?

The Association of American Medical Colleges has addressed the challenge created by social and ethical dilemmas by generating "sweeping revisions" of its Medical College Admission Test (MCAT). The new version "emphasizes critical thinking, problem-solving, and communication, rather than rote learning of scientific facts."[10] Richard L. O'Brien, dean of the Creighton University School of Medicine, described the revised test as "a reliable tool for helping to select students who are likely to succeed in medical school."[11]

Critical Thinking as Essential to Personal Decision Making

Just as scientists and doctors must confront difficult ethical questions in their professional capacities, we must face these and related questions in our daily lives. For example, one out of six American couples who want to conceive are unable to do so without the assistance of modern reproductive technology. It is also increasingly difficult to adopt healthy infants. This problem is so serious that the Roman Catholic church published a document in 1986 prescribing appropriate decision making for practicing Catholics facing infertility. According to this essay, known as the Vatican Document, practicing

---

9.   "Students Need to Think, Study Says," *Columbus Dispatch,* February 15, 1988, p. A-7.

10.   Denise Magner, "Major Changes Set in Admissions Test for Medical School," *The Chronicle of Higher Education,* (March 22, 1989), p. 1.

11.   Magner, p. A-34.

Catholics should not make use of technology that separates love and procreation in their attempt to have children. Instead, Catholic couples suffering from infertility should seek to adopt children or simply accept their childless state. Publication of the Vatican Document has led to considerable controversy among clerics and laiety within the Roman Catholic church. This controversy reflects the seriousness of the issues facing so many people today.

Proficient critical thinking not only helps resolve such "exotic" problems but it also provides the tools needed to effectively confront more commonplace personal dilemmas. How should you spend the time, money, and other resources available to you? What job should you seek? Should you marry? Should you attempt to have children? What objectives should guide your college education? How can you best achieve your educational, professional, and personal objectives? Who should you support for Congress? How should you vote on local issues?

The ability to ask relevant questions, to find and evaluate relevant information, and to use this information to make reasonable decisions helps people deal more effectively with these and many of the other problems or issues that so greatly affect the quality of everyday life.

Yet there may be an even greater personal value to critical thinking: the fulfillment that comes from discovery and creativity. If you observe children in play, you often observe the joy they experience when they solve puzzles or learn how to resolve mysteries. The questioning habit is relatively natural to most children. Yet as we grow older, we sometimes forget the excitement that this habit can bring to our lives. Thinking critically helps rekindle the joys that come from sharing ideas, discovering new ideas, and reevaluating existing ones.

▾ ▾ ▾
DEVELOPING THE QUESTIONING HABIT

As these examples illustrate, critical thinking helps people get the most satisfaction and enjoyment out of their personal and professional lives. The discussion below introduces skills needed to make effective use of the critical thinking process.

Asking Relevant Questions

Developing the questioning habit is fundamental to thinking critically. Yet it is not enough simply to ask many questions. It is equally important to ask questions that will be likely to enhance your ability to make reasonable choices. In the following dialogue, for example, Kim asks questions that are not relevant to the subject matter. Her questions do not meaningfully contribute to the dialogue.

Darren: I think that the United States should send more money to help alleviate hunger in Third World nations. After all, we have much more food than we can possibly consume. Sometimes we even pay our farmers not to produce.

Ruth: I see what you mean, Darren. But the fact is, we don't even adequately feed our own people. Just yesterday I read an article about several severely undernourished children in Chicago.

Kim: What did the undernourished children look like? What nationality were their parents?

Ruth's observation regarding undernourished children in American cities was relevant to Darren's point regarding America's obligation to provide greater assistance to Third World countries. But it was not so clear what Kim's questions regarding the physical features and geographical origins of America's hungry children had to do with Darren and Ruth's concerns. Answering Kim's questions as she framed them would not have helped Darren and Ruth decide whether the United States should send money to help alleviate Third World hunger. In fact, Kim's questions did not contribute meaningfully to the dialogue. But suppose Kim had asked the following relevant question:

▼▼▼▼▼▼

But, Ruth, how long have the children you read about lived in America? It was my understanding that the children cited in the article had just arrived in Chicago from Third World nations and that the local authorities were making sure the children were properly nourished. ▼▼▼

Framed in these terms, Kim's question is relevant to the exchange because answering this question would contribute to a clearer understanding of the relevant facts. This question reflects a refined questioning habit.

Of course, Kim may have had this reframed question in mind all along. Suppose, for example, that sometime later in the dialogue Darren posed the reframed question about Ruth's information. And suppose that this question led Kim to utter, "That was what I was trying to ask!"

This example illustrates the important relationship between the ability to clearly and accurately communicate one's ideas and the ability to effectively use the questioning habit. As we will see throughout this text, these skills are closely related. Also directly related to these two skills is the ability to find and effectively use relevant information.

Finding Relevant Information

One of the reasons asking relevant questions is so important to critical thinking is that this process helps uncover relevant information, which is fundamental to good decision making and problem solving. Without adequate information it is not possible to think critically because, among other things, thinking functions always in a context. We think *about* something. To think about it, we must have knowledge of it.

At the same time, we need to know *how much* information is required to make a reasonable decision in a given set of circumstances. This type of assessment is an important part of the overall critical thinking process. Kristy and Tim's experience with selecting their infant's source of nutrition illustrates this part of the process.

During the first few days of his life, Kristy and Tim's fourth child did not do well on cow's milk. In response to this situation, the baby's doctor advised Kristy and Tim to give their baby a soy-based formula for the first year of his life.

Kristy had read two recently published reports which indicated that some researchers were challenging prevailing views on infant nutrition. The reports suggested that a poor early performance on cow's milk did not necessarily predict a baby's long-term predisposition toward it. The reports went on to say that some babies who initially do poorly on cow's milk later thrive on it.

Kristy and Tim knew that their baby's doctor was trained during an era when practitioners were encouraged to recommend soy-based formula for newborns who have early problems with cow's milk. They wondered how much of this training contributed to the doctor's views on infant nutrition.

Kristy and Tim recognized that if they spent many hours gathering additional information from reliable sources, they would be able to make a better, more informed choice. Yet they also realized that they had only so much time available to make their decision. With each feeding, their baby was already being given one of the available options. Furthermore, other obligations gave them only limited time to devote to doing research in order to make this decision. Among other things, their three other young children had important needs that demanded Kristy and Tim's attention.

Their first decision, then, had to be how much of their limited time and attention they should devote to pursuing more information on the topic. What would be the likely implications of adopting each of the options available to them? How much time should they devote to considering these options? Should they rely on the doctor's advice? Should they get a second opinion? Should they read more reports?

To help them make their decision, Kristy and Tim need to use certain skills and strategies that will help them quickly find reliable and relevant oral, visual, and written information so that they can make the most efficient use of the limited time available for information gathering. These skills and strategies will be discussed in Chapter 2.

In most practical contexts, relevant information significantly contributes to the quality of decision making. Whatever the source, however, it is not enough simply to find information.

Interpreting and Evaluating Information

Many people have the idea that somehow information speaks for itself. People who have this belief are often heard saying, "Facts speak for themselves" or "Pictures don't lie." Despite its appeal, this view is not warranted. Information in any of its forms must always be *interpreted* to be meaningful. Furthermore, the interpretation of information greatly determines how that information is used in the decision-making process. Legislators are especially aware of this fact. They often share exactly the same information, yet they disagree about what it means, what it entails, or what conclusions we should draw from it. They understand firsthand the central role that interpretation plays in the critical thinking process.

We all view the world with our own set of "lenses." Two people never see the same tree, plant, person, let alone event, in exactly the same way. Criminologists have known for years, for example, that no two people can be expected to provide exactly the same account of a crime they both witnessed. One person may focus on the criminal, another on the victim. One pays close attention to the getaway car, another to the bank teller lying on the floor. With only a limited capacity to "take in" the world, our lenses take in an edited version of it.

Similarly, once we have perceived a person, object, or event we further edit what we have seen. Was the cup half empty or half full? To the pessimist, it was half empty. To the optimist, it was half full. The differences in these perceptions of the same cup can be significant in the decision-making process.

These are but a few of the ways in which our lenses shape our perceptions. But today this editing process is made even more complex by the double editing process provided by the world of *videality*,[12] or the world that television and newspaper editors present to us. Because most of us learn much of what we know about the world from television and newspapers, journalists influence many of our perceptions of reality. What we know about the people of distant lands, and to some degree how much we think about them, is significantly influenced by today's journalists. Even our perceptions of the nature and scope of our own nation's problems, successes, strengths, and weaknesses are shaped in part by what we see on television and read in the newspaper. To a large degree, the world we know is the world journalists create for us; it is a world of videality.

As a blizzard descends upon Washington, D.C., for example, two newspapers might give the following headlines:

▾ The Capital Paralyzed by Killer Blizzard!
▾ D.C. Snow Gives Day Off to 300,000

---

12.   For a useful discussion of this concept, see Joseph Tussman, *Government and the Mind* (Oxford: Oxford University Press, 1977), p. 149.

These headlines might both be factually correct. Yet they would each reflect a dramatically different interpretation of the same event. Someone reading the first headline would be given a sharply different perception of the storm's impact than someone reading the second.

Advertisers, political advocates, campaigners, documentarians, and others whose job it is to shape viewer perceptions have mastered techniques for creating our images of the world. An advertising campaign produced by a public relations firm for a well-known resort provides a good example.

Carole, a photographer for the public relations firm, has been given the assignment to create a favorable image of the resort. Her job is to take photos that will highlight the resort's attractions.

As she arrives, Carole finds an area packed with tourists. All around she sees hundreds of cars in crowded parking lots and litter cans overflowing with garbage. Despite these and other unpleasant sights, Carole does capture a few beautiful scenes of trees and waterfalls with her camera. Given her purpose, Carole will neglect to take photos of the crowds, litter, and cars that clutter the resort. Her task, after all, is to present the most attractive image of the resort possible.

On the theory that "pictures don't lie," someone viewing Carole's photos may well conclude that the resort she visited was serene and beautiful. Of course, the viewer would be partially right. There was serenity and beauty to be found in the resort. But additional photos would have revealed an entirely different picture, leading the viewer to a radically different conclusion.

As this example illustrates, photos are interpretations of the physical world. These interpretations influence our perceptions of the world in which we live. To add yet another layer to this editing process, we provide our own process of interpretation to the information we are given. Facts, figures, and photos taken out of context can and often do present distorted pictures of our world.

To make best use of the information we acquire, we must first *evaluate* it. Checking the source of information, the context in which the information was acquired, and the context in which it is being presented are but a few of the methods available for evaluating information. Later chapters provide guidelines for completing this important process.

Once decision makers have acquired and evaluated relevant information, they must decide how to make the most effective use of it. They must determine, for example, what, if any, relevant conclusions should be drawn from the information. That is, they must ask what *inferences* should be drawn from the available facts.

Drawing and Evaluating Inferences

Drawing an inference involves *moving from a known or accepted idea to an unknown or unaccepted one*. Darren, Ruth, and Kim learned, for example, that two thirds of the money previously sent to Ethiopia to alleviate hunger there was diverted and used instead to perpetuate a tyrannical military regime. Based on this information, Kim infers that the United States should send no more money to Ethiopia. When Darren, Ruth, and Kim reflect critically about Kim's inference, they find its flaws.

Darren begins the evaluation process by asking whether the administrators who diverted previous money are still in power. This question prompts Ruth to argue that if there is a new group in power they may have a greater commitment to helping ensure that the allotted aid actually reaches the hungry.

At this point, Kim begins questioning her own inference. She recognizes that it is flawed in its failure to account for the reasonable possibility proposed by Darren and Ruth. And she recalls several facts that her inference fails to consider. She recalls, for example, that political conditions in Ethiopia at the time the original aid was granted required a well-stocked military to ensure that those in need would at least get one third of the aid. However tyrannical this military group was in other situations, they did make sure that one third of the aid reached the people. Ruth concurs with Kim's recollection and notes that the conditions surrounding the refugee camps housing Ethiopia's starving masses required this military intervention.

These observations reveal flaws with Kim's inference. Although these three critical thinkers might still reach the conclusion that no additional money should be sent, they would need to find better reasons to support this conclusion. Asking critical questions revealed that Kim's inference was unjustified for at least two reasons: Kim failed to account for reasonable possibilities, and she failed to account for known facts. As we will see in the chapters to follow, these are only two of the many standards against which inferences may be evaluated. For now it is important to realize that the processes of making and evaluating inferences are indispensable to the overall critical-thinking process.

In the case at hand, Kim's inference and Darren, Ruth, and Kim's evaluation of it have revealed the following: The fact that only one third of the aid actually reached the Ethiopian hungry does not, by itself, warrant the conclusion that we should stop sending aid to Ethiopia. Later, Ruth proposes alternatives to Kim's initial inference:

▼▼▼▼▼▼

Perhaps even the relatively inefficient use of the original aid was nonetheless worth our country's sacrifice. After all, although only one third of the aid reached the hungry masses, thousands of lives were saved because of it. Without any aid, these people would have died. Thus, even if our inquiry reveals that only one third of future aid will actually feed the hungry, it will still be worth sending. ▼▼▼

At this point, it is appropriate for Kim, Darren, and Ruth to begin the process of evaluating Ruth's inferences. During their inquiry, it would also be appropriate for them to present more inferences and to subject those to careful evaluation. In the ideal circumstances, Darren, Ruth, and Kim would continue their process of making and evaluating inferences until they had exhausted the possibilities and had matched their conclusions with all of the information available. Unfortunately, as we have already noted, decision makers rarely face circumstances that permit them to fulfill this ideal.

In reality, decision makers are often forced to make inferences with relatively inadequate information. In daily life, few of us have the luxury of unlimited time to find enough information to allow us to make fully informed decisions and choices. Like Kristy and Tim, most of us have many demands on our limited time.

The daily decisions we make as consumers of goods and services are particularly illustrative of the problem of limited time. We seldom have the time or energy to make exhaustive investigations about whether the "reduced" price on the name brand aspirin is a better buy than the even lower price on the generic brand. And how much time can we realistically devote to determining which of the pairs of shoes available in our price range best meets our child's needs? Or, when confronted with a one-day sale on computers, we may find ourselves forced to decide on the basis of relatively little information.

Even when we have the time and resources to acquire needed information, it is not always available. Professional policy makers often face this difficulty. Former Environmental Protection Agency Director William Ruckleshaus spoke to this problem in an interview with producers of a public television program on the problem of acid rain:

▼▼▼▼▼

By the very nature of these environmental public health kinds of decisions, we are operating in areas of enormous scientific uncertainty. . . There are so many things we don't know in these areas that it's sometimes very unnerving to try to make decisions. On the basis of the information you do have, often you simply have to make as prudent a judgment as you can.[13] ▼▼▼

Emergency squad workers work under even more extreme conditions. Their profession requires decision making based on little information, with little time for evaluation. Their abilities to quickly make good inferences often make the difference between saving a life and losing a life. In these, as in all other practical situations, decision makers must be able to make the best inferences possible under the circumstances.

---

13. Broadcast on *Nova,* the program was entitled "Acid Rain: More Bad News."

▼ ▼ ▼
SUMMARY

Critical thinking requires mastery of several related skills: asking relevant questions, finding relevant information, interpreting and evaluating information, drawing reasonable inferences, and evaluating inferences.

Critical thinking also requires the ability to effectively communicate ideas. Through effective communication, the critical thinker is able to ask relevant questions. Additionally, having a dialogue is one of the best ways to evaluate opposing ideas.

Thinking critically in group settings helps prevent errors of judgment. Juries, business meetings, and government policy-making sessions are but a few of the group decision-making situations that rely on the participants' abilities to think critically and communicate effectively.

Today's employers expect candidates to demonstrate critical thinking and communication skills. Scientists and doctors face new ethical and social dilemmas that require proficient use of critical thinking skills. And these skills are also essential to effective personal decision making.

2

Elements of Critical Thinking

Chapter 1 revealed that critical thinking requires five related skills: asking relevant questions, finding relevant information, interpreting and evaluating information, drawing inferences, and evaluating inferences. Developing these skills requires that you master the usage of certain tools, which will be discussed in this chapter. These tools—questioning skills, viewing skills, listening skills, search strategies, and reading skills—will prepare you to meaningfully explore a wide range of topics. In turn, this process of exploration will help you to fully exploit the many critical thinking opportunities you will encounter in your personal and professional life.

▼ ▼ ▼
QUESTIONING SKILLS

Asking relevant questions is fundamental to critical thinking. Throughout the chapters that follow, you will be introduced to many different types of questioning strategies. These strategies form the foundation of critical thinking. Some people have even argued that the development of a refined questioning habit is the basis of all other critical thinking skills. As you will note later in this chapter, for example, effective viewing, listening, and reading all require careful formulation of key questions. These questions guide viewers, listeners, and readers as they begin to explore their selected topics.

Chapter 1's discussion of Carole's work for a popular resort provides a good example of the importance of asking key questions. Recall that Carole was hired by a resort's public relations firm to highlight the crowded resort's few attractions. She patiently worked among the crowds of tourists and scenes filled with litter to capture a few beautiful scenes with her camera. Adept at her job, Carole was able to provide a set of photos that showed only the beauty of her client's resort.

Without asking questions, a potential resort traveler probably would accept Carole's photos as "factually correct." This same traveler would no doubt feel disappointed upon arriving at the crowded, basically unattractive resort not reflected in Carole's carefully selected display.

This traveler could have avoided his or her disappointment by asking several basic questions before going to the resort. Asking who took the photos, and with what goal, would have helped reveal the photos' questionable reliability. These questions about *source* and *purpose* would have led to the discovery that a public relations firm had hired the photographer. This discovery in turn would have helped diminish the photo display's overall credibility, thereby leading the viewer to look for additional evidence of the resort's attractiveness.

Questions about source and purpose are but two of the many investigative tools available to guide the critical thinker's listening and reading. The chapters that follow will explore the importance of asking the following questions as well:

▼ What conclusions does the artist, author, or speaker want me to draw?
▼ What support does the source give for these conclusions?
▼ Is the support relevant, reliable, and adequate?
▼ What are the assumptions underlying the author's or speaker's reasoning?
▼ Are these assumptions acceptable to me?
▼ Has the author or speaker adequately considered and presented alternative perspectives?

Developing a refined questioning habit that employs these and other questions is well worth the effort. Many serious mistakes in judgment and practice can be avoided by simply asking the right questions.

▼ ▼ ▼
VIEWING SKILLS

We've already established the importance of interpreting information. We know, for instance, that people who say "pictures don't lie" have failed to consider the fact that all images—whether televised, photographed, painted, or otherwise projected—are edited versions of the world.

Consider Sandy, a television journalist. Sandy's assignment is to cover the scene of a major plane crash. As Sandy and her camera operator approach the scene, they encounter lifeless bodies, plane wreckage, emergency vehicles, medical practitioners, aviation experts, insurance investigators, grieving families, and much more. They have been promised three minutes of air time on the evening news to present their story of the crash. What shall they present? Shall they focus on the bereaved families, the lost lives, aviation in general, the costs of such a disaster, the details of several victims' lives? Sandy and her camera operator must select what to show and how to show it. Theirs will be an edited version of the plane crash.

Viewers' perceptions of the crash will be influenced considerably by Sandy and her camera operator's edited portrayal. Film footage of real people and plane wreckage will seem to "represent reality as it is." Yet critical viewers will wonder about questions that were not answered in the three-minute portrayal of the crash. They will be sensitive to the edited nature of what they see.

Direct, live coverage of events presents a special challenge to critical viewers. For example, televised presidential debates appear to provide a complete, unedited picture of competing candidates' debate performances. Yet camera angles, lighting, and the use of other technical devices have considerable impact on the audience's perceptions of candidates. The final 1984 presidential debate between Ronald Reagan and Walter Mondale was particularly illustrative of this point.

Before the debates, the Reagan and Mondale staffs argued feverishly about lighting and camera angles. As the debate began and images were projected on the screen, Mondale's advisers were dismayed to discover that their candidate appeared tired and possibly even ill. To the auditorium audience, Mondale appeared well. But the lighting and camera angles used to televise the candidates somehow made Mondale's eyes appear puffy and worn. This led people viewing the debate in their living rooms to question Mondale's health. Given news stories about his use of medication for blood pressure problems, Mondale's televised appearance had the potential to hurt his bid for the presidency.

Critical viewers of the debate were aware of the impact that lighting and camera angles can have on televised images. They understood the mirages television can create, and they took stock of this knowledge in their evaluation of Mondale's performance.

Televised congressional hearings provide additional examples of the importance of developing critical viewing skills. During the televised Iran-Contra hearings in 1987, much public attention was given to the testimony of Lt. Col. Oliver North. Despite his repeated admission that he had lied to members of Congress, circumvented laws, and helped violate America's stated foreign policy during his tenure as a member of the National Security Council staff, North was perceived by many as a kind of folk hero. Media experts later noted that one source of the audience's affection for North was the type of image he projected on the television screen.

The congressional representatives questioning North were shown sitting high above him, looking down sternly. North in turn looked sincerely into the camera, directing his remarks to the television audience. Combined with his portrayal of himself as a martyr to President Reagan's cause, North's ability to use camera angles in this way helped him generate a warm audience response.

Camera angles affect audience responses to films as well. Media specialists note, for example, that horror films in the past were filmed from the perspective of the victim. Audiences were encouraged to identify with the victim and to feel separate from the perpetrator. Today, many horror films project a different picture. Audiences see assaults through the perpetrator's eyes. The victim is a distant person, on the receiving end of the attack. This difference of camera focus has the potential to greatly influence audience perceptions of violent attacks.

As more of what we learn and experience comes to us from televised and film images, critical viewing skills will be more important than ever. In the years ahead, we will likely be barraged with edited images created by highly skilled professionals seeking to formulate our perceptions of the world. Asking questions about the sources and purposes of these images will help you put them in perspective. Becoming visually literate by learning what you can about the technical dimensions of image creation will also be of special value.

▼ ▼ ▼
THE ART OF LISTENING

Effective listening is required to achieve several goals directly related to critical thinking. The more effectively you listen, the more successful you are likely to be at accomplishing these goals.

There are three kinds of listening skills. Each skill is tied to a separate, but related, set of goals. *Content listening* is primarily used to gather information. *Empathic listening* helps establish understanding between communicators. And *critical listening* assists in the evaluation of information and inferences.

Listening for content involves focusing on the information the speaker provides. An effective content listener is able to provide an accurate report of the speaker's message. In the example below, Diane gives a presentation to the class, followed by Frank's report of her presentation:

Diane: There are currently thirty-four persons on death row in the United States who are there for crimes committed before they were eighteen years old. Paula Cooper is one of these people. She is only seventeen years old, and this young person is in a cell waiting to die. Much of Western Europe has once again shown its moral superiority by protesting Paula's suffering. Hundreds of Germans, French, and Italians have written the judge in her case, protesting her sentence. Paula's case and others like it reflect badly on our country worldwide. It is time for us to abandon the juvenile death penalty and find a more humane alternative.

Frank: Diane has reported that there are currently thirty-four persons on death row in the United States who are there for crimes committed before their eighteenth birthdays. Paula Cooper, aged seventeen, is such a person. Hundreds of Western Europeans, aware of her case, have written protests against her sentence. Diane believes that the European protests reflect a moral superiority. She also believes maintaining the juvenile death penalty harms America's image abroad. She would like us to find an alternative to the juvenile death penalty.

Frank has provided a clear and accurate account of the facts and positions reflected in Diane's speech. He is an effective content listener. Had Frank been listening empathically, his account of Diane's presentation would have looked much different.

Listening empathically is a skill often associated with the helping professions. Counselors, clergy, and others who provide emotional help carefully attend to the feelings and personality reflected in a person's speech. These empathic listeners focus on clues to speaker intent and meaning and seek to understand the speaker's perspective.

Empathic listening is an important skill for the critical thinker as well as those in the helping professions. Simply reporting content does not, for example, always reflect an understanding of that content. Nor does content listening alone always equip the listener to contribute meaningfully to a dialogue. Suppose, for example, that Frank provides the following response to Diane's presentation:

▼▼▼▼▼▼

I really don't see the big deal, Diane. After all, we are only talking about some thirty-four people in a country of millions. Besides, Paula Cooper won't be executed. There is too much publicity surrounding her case. You really ought to calm down. ▼▼▼

It is evident in this response that Frank has not fully understood Diane's message. Listening only for content, Frank has not understood that Diane's concern goes well beyond the act of execution. She is deeply moved by what she believes is Paula's suffering while on death row. She is also intensely concerned about what she believes is a symptom of America's moral inferiority to other Western nations. Had Frank listened empathically he might have contributed the following to the dialogue:

▼▼▼▼▼▼

I understand your concern, Diane. Our moral stature worldwide is of considerable significance. And the juvenile death penalty has brought much attention to it. But have you considered alternative ways to view the case of Paula Cooper? After all, she did confess to joining three other teen-agers in stabbing an elderly Bible teacher thirty-three times with a twelve-inch butcher knife. It could be argued that the death penalty, though unfortunate, is nonetheless useful and appropriate in such an extreme and unusual case. Perhaps Cooper's place on death row will serve as an important deterrent to others considering her crime. Also, did you realize that people commit most of their crimes between ages thirteen and twenty? In light of this fact, wouldn't abolishment of the juvenile death penalty give immunity to those who commit crimes most frequently? This seems unjust. What do you think? ▼▼▼

In this response, Frank shows a sensitivity to the spirit of Diane's message. He recognizes that Diane is passionately concerned about justice and fairness. He understands the essence of Diane's presentation and empathizes with her point of view.

Because of the empathy reflected in Frank's message, Diane is more likely to think critically about Frank's questions. This openminded critical reflection will help her formulate a meaningful reply to Frank, which will in turn provide Frank with additional alternative perspectives. Thus, Frank's empathic listening has helped both Frank and Diane better prepare to make their respective judgments about the juvenile death penalty.

Critical listening—the third type of listening skill— involves both content and empathic listening skills. It requires first the ability to record the message given (that is, listening for content). It also requires the ability to understand the message and its source (empathic listening). But listening critically also involves using the tools of analysis and evaluation. Armed with knowledge about persuasion, rules of reason, principles of ethics, and the other tools discussed throughout this text, the critical listener carefully analyzes the force, validity, appropriateness, value, and ethical quality of a speaker's message.

The critical listener asks basic questions about the content of a speech:

▾ Who is the speaker and what is his or her purpose?
▾ What conclusion(s) does the speaker hope I will draw?
▾ What support has the speaker given on behalf of this conclusion?
▾ What are the assumptions underlying the speaker's message?
▾ Are these assumptions acceptable to me?
▾ Has the speaker adequately considered alternative views?

Combined with empathic and content listening, critical listening serves critical thinking goals. Together, the three types of listening skills help refine the questioning habit, provide a basis for making inferences, strengthen the process of evaluating inferences, and play an important role in finding and evaluating information.

But listening is not the only tool available to achieve these critical thinking goals. Finding written information often provides an invaluable starting point for acquiring the level of expertise needed to consider any topic. The discussion that follows will help you develop strategies to find and use various written sources.

▾ ▾ ▾
EXPLORING WRITTEN SOURCES OF INFORMATION

As with every dimension of critical thinking, developing strategies for finding relevant information is a complex process. Each topic, assignment, and question requires its own kind of search. Sometimes books provide the most useful information. Other times, journals or newspapers are the best source. In still other situations, the researcher must comprehensively search many different kinds of sources.

The nature and scope of your search for information depends in part on how much you already know about the topic. It also depends on your purpose. How narrow is the scope of your concerns? How much background information do you need to even begin your search for information? The answers to these and related questions will greatly affect the nature of your search for information.

The best place to begin your search is the library. But once you arrive there, how should you actually go about looking for the information you need? How can you most effectively use your limited time? What sources are most likely to help you?

The *search strategies* discussed below will help resolve these issues for you. With the aid of a librarian and this discussion, you will be equipped to develop search strategies tailor-made to your research needs.

Search Strategies

There are two basic types of search strategies: the *general* and the *specific*. General search strategies help you find information on general topics. They also help you determine where you will be most likely to find specific information on specialized topics. For example, if you are interested in general information about relationships between unemployment, the gross national product, taxing policies, and economic trends, you will want to use a general search strategy. This strategy will help you find general information on this topic, and help you isolate sources for each of its subtopics.

Specific search strategies help you find information on a more narrowly defined topic. For example, if you are interested in learning why stockbrokers use computers to forecast economic changes, you will want to use a specific search strategy designed to get you the highly specialized information you need.

Using Library Resources

Encyclopedias   As you begin to research your topic, you may wish to consult several encyclopedias in the reference section of the library. Encyclopedias provide overviews of topics and introduce relevant terminology.

To find your topic in an encyclopedia, you can use its index and cross references. This resource provides a complete guide to the contents of the encyclopedia. Each article has an index entry that lists other places in the encyclopedia where information on the topic may be found. The index also has entries on subjects that are covered in the encyclopedia but do not have their own separate articles.

Most encyclopedias include a bibliography at the end of each article. A *bibliography* is a reference list of sources on a given topic. Bibliographies help researchers find materials relevant to their topic. Making effective use of bibliographies requires that researchers record the following information: the author's name, with the last name first; the title of the journal article or book; and facts of publication. For each book, note the city, the name of the publisher, and the date of publication. For each journal article, record the name, volume, and date of the magazine and the pages covered by the article. Finally, for each newspaper article, write the name of the newspaper, the date, and the page.

Once you have completed this process, you will be ready to begin your search. If you lack general knowledge about your topic, you may want to turn first to the *World Book Encyclopedia*. Here you will find general information about your topic that is written in a highly readable and concise way. Next you may wish to turn to the *Encyclopedia Americana* for a more specialized discussion of your topic. This reference provides extensive coverage of science and technology and excellent coverage of American history. And for a more journalistic approach, you may turn to *Collier's Encyclopedia,* where you will find useful discussions of contemporary issues related to your topic.

Once you have completed your review of general encyclopedias, you may wish to turn to special-subject encyclopedias. These references usually discuss one area of knowledge, such as philosophy, communication, art, criminology, or sociology. The *Encyclopedia of Philosophy* includes philosophical perspectives represented in Eastern and Western cultures. The *Encyclopedia of Education* covers educational interests, practices, philosophies, institutions, and educators. A third reference is the *International Encyclopedia of the Social Sciences,* which reflects the development of anthropology, economics, geography, history, law, political science, psychiatry, sociology, criminology, communication, statistics, and other social sciences. And the *McGraw-Hill Encyclopedia of Science and Technology* uses nontechnical language to cover topics related to the physical, natural, and applied sciences.

As you make regular use of the library, you will quickly discover that there are many different research strategies available to you. Researchers make best use of library resources by shaping their searches according to their individual needs. For example, one researcher may choose to start with a particular encyclopedia and work from there. Other researchers may not even need encyclopedias, because they already have enough knowledge about the topic and about relevant sources to be able to go directly to journals or books.

Journals   Researchers often prefer to begin with a review of journal articles relevant to their topic. Journals afford researchers the opportunity to read several short articles about specific dimensions of the topic before reading complete books about it.

If you decide to look for journal articles, you will want to review the periodical and newspaper indexes available in the reference section of the library. Here you will find journal article citations not necessarily listed in encyclopedia bibliographies. The *Reader's Guide to Periodical Literature* is especially useful. This reference covers general and popular journals. The index in this reference lists the author, subject, and article title.

You may also find valuable assistance in *The New York Times Index.* This source covers national and international news items, editorials, feature articles, and critical commentaries. This index also helps researchers find a number of official reports, documents, speeches, and other primary sources relevant to their topic.

As you continue your search for journal articles, you may find it necessary to turn to more specialized periodical and newspaper indexes. If your topic is of a scientific or technical nature, for example, the *Applied Science and Technology Index* may be of some value to you. Or perhaps your topic calls for use of the *Art Index,* which covers periodicals in the various arts. Or you might want to look at *The Education Index,* which covers journals, monographs, proceedings, and yearbooks in elementary, secondary, and higher education.

The three remaining indexes are also of value to many researchers. The *Public Affairs Information Service Bulletin,* for example, refers researchers to journals, books, pamphlets, and reports on economics, social conditions, public administration, international relations, political science, government laws, and legislation. The *Social Sciences and Humanities Index,* originally known as the *International Index,* has split into the *Humanities Index* and the *Social Sciences Index.* The *Humanities Index* provides lists of relevant philosophic works. The *Social Sciences Index* provides journal citations in anthropology, economics, geography, history, political science, law, criminology, communication, psychology, and other social sciences.

Card Catalogs   Once you have listed relevant journal articles, you will be ready to determine the availability and location of the journals. You will also be ready to search for additional sources. Libraries that are computerized provide on-line computer systems for these purposes. In libraries that are not computerized, researchers must rely upon the card catalog.

The two kinds of card catalogs you will encounter are "divided" catalogs and "dictionary" catalogs. The divided catalog is in two alphabetical sections: author/title and subject. The dictionary catalog combines all three—author, title, and subject—into a single alphabet.

If you know very little about your topic, you will probably rely heavily on the subject headings provided in the encyclopedias. After you have made a list of these headings, you must find out exactly how they appear in the card catalog. To do this, read the items in the *Library of Congress Subject Headings* listed under their general subject headings. This reference is a large, red two-volume set usually found near the card catalog. As well as listing headings as they appear in the card catalog, the LCSH helps the researcher find additional materials under related subjects.

Once you have found the correct listings in the LCSH, you will be ready to use the card catalogs. At first, you may find the listings on these cards confusing. But soon you will learn to identify and use each of these items. You will quickly discover, for example, that each book and journal has its own call number. Without knowing the complete call number, you will not be able to find the book or journal in the library. It could be argued that the most important item on each card in the catalog is the call number.

Card catalogs provide other important information as well. They list the author, title, place of publication, publisher, date of publication, information about illustrations, subjects under which the item is listed in the subject catalog, along with other notes on the book or journal. Most researchers quickly come to appreciate the importance of the card catalog in their library search.

Book Review Indexes   With only a limited amount of time, you cannot read every book related to your topic. Instead, for certain books, you may want to read only some reviews of them. The book review indexes will lead you to reviews that evaluate books, summarize a book's content, make observations about the author, and provide extracts from the book. You may wish to begin with general book review indexes, such as the *Book Review Digest,* the *Book Review Index,* the *Current Book Review Citations,* and the *Index to Book Reviews in the Humanities.* Once you have completed your review of these general resources, you may wish to turn to the *General Indexes with Reviews.* These indexes cover reviews in more specialized subjects or fields. They include the *Humanities Index,* the *Philosopher's Index,* the *Social Sciences Index,* and many others. *The New York Times Book Review Index* is particularly helpful. The five sections of this index provide access to book reviews by author, title, "byline" (that is, the name of the reviewer of the book), subject, and category.

Other Resources   For facts and statistical data about your topic, you may choose to rely on *Statistical Sources.* Among the many valuable statistical references available are the *Statistical Abstracts of the United States* (published by the U.S. Bureau of the Census) and the *World Almanac and Book of Facts.* Or, for information on a broad range of topics related to your topic, you may find assistance from *U.S. Government Documents.* Of special value are census reports, presidential papers, military reports, congressional documents, and vital statistics.[1]

Once you have gathered your resources, you will finally be ready to make use of them. At this point, you will need to rely on reading skills.

▼ ▼ ▼
READING SKILLS

As with listening, there are three types of reading skills. *Content* reading involves understanding the information in the written passage. *Empathic* reading involves understanding the spirit of the message. And *critical* reading combines the first two with an analysis and evaluation process.

---

1.   The foregoing discussion of library search strategies is based on Virginia Tiefel's "Tomorrow's Library Today," in *University Survey,* ed. Thomas L. Minnick (Columbus: Ohio State University, 1986), pp. 29–51. Used with permission of Virginia Tiefel.

Reading for content often requires that you write brief summaries of what you have read. Your summaries should answer such questions as:

▼ What were the author's conclusions?
▼ What reasons did the author give for arriving at those conclusions?
▼ What other relevant information did the author provide?

After completing a content summary of a written work, you will need to look more carefully at the author's purpose in writing it. In essence you will *interpret* each document to try to gain a better *understanding* of why the author wrote this piece. Questions appropriate for this phase of your reading include:

▼ What is the author's stated purpose in writing?
▼ What clues are available to determine the meaning behind the text?
▼ What is the author trying to communicate and why?

Empathic reading will prepare you for the most important stage of your reading—the evaluation stage. Critical reading raises many complex questions, such as:

▼ Who/what is the author/source?
▼ Is the author/source credible?
▼ What are the author's purposes?
▼ Has the author defined his or her key terms?
▼ Are the definitions adequate?
▼ Is the information relevant to this context?
▼ What help does this information give decision makers in this context?
▼ What are the author's conclusions?
▼ Has the author provided adequate support for these conclusions?
▼ What questions is the author trying to answer?
▼ What problems is the author trying to solve?
▼ Has the author chosen the most important question to answer or problems to solve?
▼ Has the author effectively answered those questions or solved those problems?
▼ What are the writer's underlying assumptions?
▼ Are the writer's assumptions warranted?
▼ What inferences has the writer made?
▼ Are these inferences justified?

The chapters to follow will guide you through the process required to answer these and related critical reading questions. For now it is important to realize that a careful search for relevant information is only a first step in thinking critically about your topic.

Information, once found, is useful only if it is understood and evaluated. And even then, information provides only one piece of the critical thinking puzzle. The discussion below will introduce two more pieces, *underlying assumptions* and *underlying values.*

▼ ▼ ▼
UNDERLYING ASSUMPTIONS

Human communication, whether written, oral, or visual, is complex. We seldom, if ever, explicitly state or present all that we intend to communicate. Communication can only work if readers and listeners either consciously or unconsciously fill in the blanks by providing the *missing assumptions.*

Political cartoons provide particularly good examples of this process. Picture, for example, a political cartoon that shows a young man armed with an assault rifle. Also shown are four people he has already gunned down and a fifth who is about to be shot. The assailant is carrying a flag and saying, "It's made in the USA." Beside him is a newspaper with the headline, "Ban on Imports of Assault Weapons."[2]

Readers of this cartoon were expected to share a number of factual assumptions. They were expected to know, for instance, that a tragic incident in which a gunman wounded some children and killed several others on a Stockton, California, schoolyard had helped motivate the country's leaders to support a ban on the import of assault rifles. Readers were also expected to share the factual assumption that opposition to a ban of any kind of weapon was strong. The National Rifle Association had launched an effective national campaign to block any such ban. Further, readers were expected to share the factual assumption that President Bush—an ardent opponent of gun control—had agreed to support a ban on the import of AK-14 assault rifles in an effort to satisfy people on both sides of the gun control debate.

The cartoonist hoped that readers who shared these factual assumptions would see an irony in the assailant's proud, "comforting" statement, "It's made in the USA." Readers who saw such an irony might then draw the cartoonist's intended inference and conclude that a ban on imported assault rifles fails to adequately protect the public's safety. These and other underlying assumptions, or "taken-for-granteds," provide the force of this political cartoon. Only readers who share this background perspective could "get" the political point of the cartoon.

Although the use of such underlying assumptions is less obvious in more formal communication contexts, it nonetheless plays a central role in *all*

---

2.   Herblock, *Columbus Dispatch,* April 16, 1989, p. B-3.

human communication. It is not possible to explicitly state all of our under-lying assumptions. Nor is it necessary.

Nor are all underlying assumptions unstated. In the political cartoon above, many of the underlying assumptions were *implicit,* that is, unstated. But underlying assumptions can also be *explicit,* or stated. Usually, authors and speakers rely on both explicit and implicit underlying assumptions, as the following paragraph illustrates. As you read the paragraph, see if you can uncover some of the author's more important underlying assumptions.

▼▼▼▼▼▼

AIDS is becoming an increasingly serious American problem. This dreaded disease has moved from drug users and homosexuals to promiscuous hetero-sexuals. Clearly, God is showing His wrath for those who violate His moral laws![3] ▼▼▼

The author has made several explicit and implicit assumptions in this para-graph. Two of the explicit factual assumptions are that AIDS is dreaded and that heterosexual persons who acquire it are promiscuous. That God exists is one of the paragraph's implicit factual assumptions.

Perhaps the most important assumptions in the paragraph, however, are both implicit and inferential. The author makes, and hopes the reader will accept, for example, the assumption that God determines who acquires AIDS. The author also assumes that whoever gets AIDS has violated God's moral laws. Yet another implicit inferential assumption made in the paragraph is the belief that God is using AIDS to demonstrate His discontent with certain portions of the American population.

Having uncovered these assumptions, it is now possible to meaningfully address the author's points. A critical response might read like the following:

▼▼▼▼▼▼

We have been told that AIDS is a sign of God's disapproval of homosexuality, drug use, and promiscuity among heterosexuals. At first glance, this seems a plausible view. However, this suggestion does not take into account the many nonpromiscuous heterosexuals who have acquired AIDS from blood transfu-sions. How are these "innocent" victims to be explained? More to the point, given that lesbians have the lowest incidence of AIDS (and every other sex-ually transmitted disease, for that matter), is God trying to tell all women that they should become homosexual? ▼▼▼

---

3. This paragraph, along with the companion paragraph to follow, were modeled after a number of arguments submitted by students in a basic argumentation and debate course from 1987–89.

This response, with its own implicit and explicit, factual and inferential assumptions, was made possible only by first uncovering central assumptions in the initial paragraph. As we will see in the chapters to follow, discovering underlying assumptions is a vital part of the overall critical thinking process.

▼ ▼ ▼
UNDERLYING VALUES

A communicator's values are among the many sources for his or her assumptions. It is important for critical thinkers to discover these values when reading, viewing, or listening to a message.

Sociologists, psychologists, communication scholars, philosophers, and others have worked hard to define the term *value*. Argumentation theorists Karyn Rybacki and Donald Rybacki provide a useful list of some of the more common definitions:

> ▼ Values are intangibles . . . things of the mind that have to do with the vision people have of "the good life" for themselves and their fellows.
> ▼ A value is a general conception of what is a good end-state or a good mode of behavior.
> ▼ A *value* is an enduring belief that a specific mode of conduct or end-state of existence is personally or socially preferable to an opposite or converse model of conduct or end-state of existence. A *value system* is an enduring organization of beliefs concerning preferable models of conduct or end-states of existence along a continuum of relative importance.
> ▼ Values may be defined as concepts that express what people believe is right or wrong, important or unimportant, wise or foolish, good or bad, just or unjust, great or mean, beautiful or ugly, and true or false, and that, therefore, underlie all choices.[4]

Values, then, are deeply held beliefs (or judgments) about what is right and wrong, good and bad, more or less important, and so on. Although each person has his or her own set of values, most people share certain fundamental values, such as a respect for life, an abhorrence of cold-blooded murder, the belief that lying is generally wrong, and so on. Usually, disagreements are based not upon competing values, but rather upon competing value hierarchies. A *value hierarchy* is an ordering of values. A person's value hierarchy determines which value or interest is more important to him or her in any given situation.

---

4. From Karyn C. Rybacki and Donald J. Rybacki, *Advocacy and Opposition: An Introduction to Argumentation* (Englewood Cliffs, N.J.: Prentice-Hall, 1986), pp. 150–151. The authors cited are Rescher; Rieke and Sillars; Rokeach; and Walter and Scott, respectively.

Value hierarchies play an important role in critical thinking and decision making. A particularly good example of this is when environmental policy makers accept the same scientific perspective and many of the same values, yet disagree about policy. Let's say that Senators Thompson and Jones find themselves in this situation.

Senators Thompson and Jones both believe that acid rain is caused by sulfur emissions. They also both believe that the elimination of acid rain will significantly reduce the loss of forest life in northern areas of the United States. Yet they strongly disagree about whether Congress should force companies to install the equipment needed to reduce sulfur emissions. Senator Thompson opposes such legislation because he places a higher priority on preventing serious economic problems than on preventing the environmental problems associated with acid rain. Senator Jones favors the legislation because she places a higher value on preventing the environmental damage created by acid rain than on preventing the economic problems associated with forced reduction of sulfur emissions.

Although Senators Jones and Thompson accept the same factual information and share many of the same values, they make opposing decisions because they place more or less value on each of the interests represented in this policy.

Vic and Leon's disagreement about whether Vic should expand his business further illustrates how much value hierarchies influence personal and professional decision making. Vic's company had been growing beyond his expectations for several years. He was making more money than he had ever dreamed he could make. His employees were earning excellent incomes, and his family was able to live in a safe, comfortable environment.

It was at this point that Vic had the opportunity to significantly expand his business. Expansion would mean even greater profits. Above all, expansion offered the promise of financial security for Vic, his wife, and their two children. But expansion would also mean that Vic would be unable to spend as much time with his family. And the time he would have with them would be threatened by the added stress he would likely bring home.

Vic's decision was a difficult one. On the one hand, he placed a high value on his family's financial security, because he associated it with a kind of freedom—a freedom he greatly valued. But he also valued the time he spent with his family. He wanted to play a major role in his young children's lives before they became more independent.

At this point, Vic consulted Leon. After hearing Vic's description of the options available to him, Leon strongly urged Vic to expand his business. Leon argued that the financial security which expansion would afford the family was more important at this time than the few experiences Vic would miss by spending less time with his children.

After listening to Leon's arguments, Vic decided not to expand. Through his dialogue with Leon, Vic came to realize that being with his children while they were still young was more important to him than the financial gains that expansion would likely afford him.

Of course, Vic might have been able to find a solution that would allow him to both expand his business and share in his children's development. Perhaps someday he will discover and adopt such a solution. But this is not the point of the example. The important point is that Vic and Leon's disagreement did not center on competing characterizations of fact. They agreed to the facts of the situation before them. Nor did their conflicting opinions center on competing values. Vic and Leon both place a high value on family life and financial security. Their difference in viewpoint rested on differing value hierarchies.

Often, decision makers are confronted with experts whose competing value hierarchies lead them to provide conflicting advice. Jan recently faced this situation.

Before last month, Jan had not spent much time thinking about euthanasia, or mercy killing. Her uninformed opinion was that it was always immoral to knowingly allow someone to die and hence it should not be allowed. In fact, when a neighbor came around recently with a petition favoring legislation to strongly punish those guilty of any form of euthanasia, Jan was happy to sign it.

But then Jan was faced with a painful personal dilemma. Her husband, Philip, was severely injured in a car accident. The accident left him in an irreversible coma. The doctors informed her that his brain waves were flat.

The attending physician, Dr. Smith, outlined a possible alternative to mechanically sustaining Philip's life. According to Dr. Smith, Philip could receive enough morphine to ensure his comfort. After administering morphine, Dr. Smith could then remove Philip from the respirator. Dr. Smith estimated that it would probably take Philip about an hour to die. She referred to this procedure as passive euthanasia, that is, allowing the patient to die without technological intervention.

Following her description of this option, Dr. Smith provided Jan two types of expert advice. Unlike most doctors, Dr. Smith had extensive training as both a physician and a medical ethicist. She was therefore able to offer a systematic and reflective account of the ethical dilemma Jan faced.

After discussing the case in detail, Dr. Smith concluded that the emotional and financial burdens imposed on Jan, and the possible suffering inflicted on Philip by artificially sustaining his life, greatly outweighed any moral misgivings Jan might have from not allowing doctors to prolong his life. Dr. Smith then strongly recommended that Jan give the hospital staff permission to perform passive euthanasia.

Jan was fortunate to have the additional advice of yet another practitioner with expertise in both medicine and medical ethics. This consulting physician, Dr. Johnson, disagreed with Dr. Smith's advice. Like Dr. Smith, Dr. Johnson had made an extensive study of medical ethics. And, like Dr. Smith, Dr.

Johnson had written extensively about the advantages and disadvantages of passive euthanasia. In his research, as in Dr. Smith's, Dr. Johnson had studied hundreds of relevant cases.

In his consultation with Jan, Dr. Johnson presented the same facts as Dr. Smith. He agreed with every aspect of the case, except Dr. Smith's conclusion. Dr. Johnson argued that Philip should be maintained on the respirator until he "chose to die." The risk of moral harm resulting from knowingly allowing Philip to die, he argued, outweighed the moral risk of possibly permitting Philip continued suffering and the emotional and economic costs to Jan resulting from Philip's prolonged life. Dr. Johnson urged Jan not to allow Dr. Smith to perform passive euthanasia.

Although the experts to whom Jan turned for help in making her painful decision presented her with the same facts, they also presented her with conflicting conclusions. This common phenomenon is a result of the two doctors' conflicting value hierarchies.

Faced with the doctors' shared facts but conflicting advice, Jan must use her own value hierarchy as she begins to think critically about her options. In this process, she realizes for the first time how complex the topic of euthanasia really is. She remembers signing the petition to punish "killers," as she contemplates becoming one of them. Should she leave Philip on the respirator? Should she give Dr. Smith permission to remove him from it? Jan's dilemma will face millions of other spouses and relatives as technological advances change the nature of modern medical practice.

As we have seen, facts alone do not provide adequate help to Jan and others like her. Nor does expert advice provide the solution. Medical practitioners armed with exactly the *same* information often support *opposing* decisions. The highly publicized Baby Fae case provides another example of this phenomenon.

Baby Fae was born with a serious heart defect. Doctors at Loma Linda University Medical Center, in California, concluded that without a great deal of medical intervention, Baby Fae would die within days after her birth. The options available to help her were corrective surgery, a human heart transplant, or an animal heart transplant.

The corrective surgery required to help Baby Fae is a sophisticated procedure known as the Norwood procedure. The mortality rate for infants receiving this procedure by anyone other than Dr. Norwood himself is approximately 60 percent. Dr. Leonard L. Bailey, Baby Fae's surgeon, had only tried the Norwood procedure once before, and that infant had died.

Loma Linda University Medical Center did not have immediate access to a human heart, though they might have been able to get one within a few days. Dr. Bailey had been experimenting with interspecies transplants, using goats and sheep, for seven years. Although he had made some progress with these studies, most experts agreed that a baboon heart would probably fail to keep Baby Fae alive. Additionally, most experts agreed that even if the baby did survive the transplant, no one could be sure what the quality of her life would be. Finally, all of the experts pointed out that the transplant would require killing a healthy young baboon.

Yet experts also agreed that Baby Fae would die without the transplant. Many experts also believed that the transplant surgery would provide some useful scientific information. The baby's ability to live with supports, the length of her life, her ability to tolerate an antirejection drug, and other information could be useful to scientists interested in determining the maximum period of time a person can wait for a heart donor.

Baby Fae's parents gave Dr. Bailey and his staff permission to perform the transplant. The heavy national media coverage included many photographs of her little body struggling to live with the aid of medical technology. Following the experts' predictions, however, she soon died.

This case stirred considerable debate in the medical and scientific communities. Many supported the Loma Linda procedure. Others argued against the decision to give Baby Fae the baboon heart.

What is most striking about this case is that these experts shared the *same* information. They did not dispute the facts in the case, yet they drew strongly opposing conclusions about it. Some of the experts, for example, believed that the potential scientific value of Dr. Bailey's experimental surgery outweighed Baby Fae's suffering. Others believed that the use of a nonconsenting human in an experimental procedure of this kind could not be justified by any amount of scientific progress. Still others believed that the amount of money required to do this and other highly experimental operations should be used instead to provide good preventive medical care for impoverished children. These opposing conclusions can be explained, in large part, as a result of the competing value hierarchies each of the experts brought to the case.

▼ ▼ ▼
SUMMARY

Questioning strategies form the foundation of critical thinking. Critical viewing, listening, and reading all depend on the development of a refined questioning habit. Many serious mistakes in judgment and practice can be avoided by asking the right questions about what we see, hear, read, and experience.

Critical viewing requires a sensitivity to the world of videality. As more of what we learn and experience comes to us from televised and film images, viewing skills will be increasingly important.

There are essentially three kinds of listening skills. Listening for content involves listening to what the speaker actually says and is used primarily to gather information. Empathic listening helps establish understanding between communicators. And critical listening combines content and empathic listening with tools of analysis and evaluation.

Listening is not the only tool available for acquiring information. Much valuable information can be found in written documents. Libraries provide storehouses of these resources.

To make effective use of a library, researchers may employ general and specific search strategies. These strategies guide the researcher to encyclopedias, journals, books, book reviews, and statistical sources.

Having found relevant resources, the critical thinker must read and evaluate them. Content, empathic, and critical reading skills are essential in effective evaluation of available resources.

But information, even when adequately understood and effectively evaluated, provides only one piece of the critical thinking puzzle. Discovering underlying assumptions and values is another fundamental element of critical thinking.

Values and value hierarchies play especially important roles in the critical thinking process. Many disagreements center not on competing information, or even values. They center instead on competing hierarchies of values.

▾ ▾ ▾
EXERCISES

1. Listen to a classmate's speech. First, record the content of the speech. Next, summarize your understanding of the speaker's remarks. And, finally, provide an overview of the speech's strengths and weaknesses.

2. Select a controversial topic. Next, plan general and specific search strategies to find information about the topic. Finally, go to the library and use these search strategies.

3. Read the following passages from an editorial by George F. Will[5] in favor of the Health and Human Services rule requiring federally funded birth-control clinics to notify parents whose daughters aged seventeen and under are receiving prescription contraceptive drugs or devices.

▾▾▾▾▾▾

Teenagers and Birth Control

It is devilishly difficult to prove cause-and-effect relationships between social policies and social changes. But this is clear: the problem of teen-age pregnancy has grown as contraceptives and sex education have become increasingly available. I am not saying the availability caused the growth. But it would be rash to say the availability is irrelevant. And many of those who today are predicting with such certitude awful results from the HHS rule predicted that teen-age pregnancies would decline as contraception and sex education became more available.

---

5. *Newsweek,* February 28, 1983, p. 80. Used with permission of George F. Will.

Law should express society's core values, such as parental responsibility. If HHS's mild rule is declared incompatible with public policy, what, for good-ness' sake is that policy? What values does it affirm, or subvert by neglect? HHS's rule at least does not express complacent acceptance of the inevitabil-ity of today's rate of teen-age sexual activity. Obviously the trend is against sexual restraint. But as has been said, a trend is not destiny. ▼▼▼

a. State the conclusion(s) you believe Will wants the audience to draw from these passages.

b. List some of the assumptions underlying Will's stated position(s).

c. List some of the values reflected in these passages.

d. List some of the value hierarchies implicit in these passages.

4. Read the following excerpts from an editorial by CBS News Correspon-dent Bernard R. Goldberg.[6] First, read the passages for content. Next, try to read the piece empathically. Finally, read the passages critically.

▼▼▼▼▼

Ads That Sell Men Short

Miami—it was front-page news and it made the TV networks. A mother from Michigan single-handedly convinces some of America's biggest advertisers to cancel their sponsorship of the Fox Broadcasting Company's "Married . . . With Children" because, as she put it, the show blatantly exploits women and the family.

The program is about a blue-collar family in which the husband is a chauvin-ist pig and his wife is—excuse the expression—a bimbo.

These are the late 1980s, and making fun of people because of their gen-der—on TV no less, in front of millions of people—is declasse. Unless, of course, the gender we're ridiculing is the male gender. Then it's OK.

In matters of gender discrimination, it has become part of the accepted or-thodoxy—of many feminists and a lot of the media anyway—that only women have the right to complain. Men have no such right. Which helps explain why there have been so many commercials ridiculing men—and getting away with it.

In the past year or so, I have seen a breakfast-cereal commercial showing a husband and wife playing tennis. She is perky and he is jerky. She is a regular Martina Navratilova of the suburbs and he is virtually dead (because he wasn't smart enough to eat the right cereal). He lets the ball hit him in the head.

I have seen an airline commercial showing two reporters from competing newspapers. She's strong and smart. He's a nerd. He says to her: I read your

---

6. *New York Times,* March 14, 1989, p. 29. Copyright © 1989 by The New York Times Company. Reprinted with permission.

story this morning; you scooped me again. She replies to him: I didn't know you could read.

In 1987, Fred Hayward, who is one of the pioneers of the men's rights movement (yes, there is a men's rights movement), studied thousands of TV and print ads, and concluded: "If there's a sleazy character in an ad, 100 percent of the ones that we found were male. If there's an incompetent character, 100 percent of them in the ads are male."

I once interviewed Garrett Epps, a scholar who has written on these matters, who told me: "The female executive who is driven, who is strong, who lives for her work, that's a very positive symbol in our culture now. The male who has the same traits—that guy is a disaster: He harms everybody around him; he's cold; he's unfeeling; he's hurtful."

The mother from Michigan hit on a legitimate issue. No more cheap shots, she seems to have said. And the advertisers listened. No more cheap shots is what a lot of men are saying also. Too bad nobody is listening to them. ▾ ▾ ▾

a. Write a brief content summary of these excerpts from Goldberg's editorial.

b. Write a brief response to the passages based upon your empathic reading.

c. Write a comprehensive response based upon your critical reading of the passages. What is Goldberg's central point? What support does he provide? Are his arguments persuasive? Why? Why not? What are the strengths of the passages? What are the weaknesses? How so? How would someone who disagrees with Goldberg be likely to respond to him? Whose views would you find more persuasive? Why?

ARGUMENTATION
SKILLS

CHAPTER

3

An Introduction to Argumentation

This chapter introduces a process of importance to anyone interested in thinking critically about controversial topics. Known as argumentation, this exciting type of communication interaction significantly contributes to effective group and personal decision making. By the time you finish reading this chapter, you should have a clear understanding of the nature and value of argumentation.

WHAT IS ARGUMENTATION?

Many people think of arguing in negative terms. They learned at an early age that it is impolite to argue. For them, the word *argue* connotes irrational conflict between individuals. They work hard to avoid "having arguments" of this kind. The type of exchange these people are trying to avoid is not, however, argumentation. It is instead *combative interaction*. Judith and Jesse's exchange illustrates some of the problems associated with combative interaction.

Judith read an article suggesting that aspartame—an artificial sweetener—may cause the brain to believe that more sugar (or carbohydrate) is needed by the body. She read further that the brain chemical serotonin, stimulated by sugar, carries a message that enough sugar has been taken in. From the same article she learned that sugar contains only sixteen calories a teaspoon. She concluded from her reading that Jesse's attempts to lose weight would be poorly served by his practice of substituting sugar with aspartame. Based upon her conclusion, Judith opened a dialogue with Jesse on the topic:

Judith: I read an article today about the artificial sweetener, aspartame. Based upon what I read, I think you should go back to using sugar instead of consuming so many artificially sweetened foods.

Jesse: There you go again, Judith, butting into my business. For once would you try to remember that what I eat is none of your business!

Judith: How typical of you, Jesse. I've read an important article that could give you so many health benefits. But do you listen to me? No, of course not! You're always ignoring what I have to say, showing no sensitivity to my feelings. You did the same thing yesterday, when you ignored what I had to say about car repairs.

Jesse: Oh right, I know, you're an expert on everything and everyone is always supposed to listen attentively to your every word. The fact is, you know very little about most of the things you talk about. Besides, you're always telling everybody what to think and how to behave. I'm tired of your "know it all" attitude, Judith, so just give me a break.

During the course of this short exchange, neither Jesse nor Judith gained the benefits we've attributed to critical thinking. Jesse learned little about the possible problems associated with consuming foods containing aspartame. And Judith learned little about Jesse's reasons for favoring artificially sweetened foods. For Jesse and Judith, this combative interaction was an unpleasant, unconstructive experience.

It is obvious why people try to avoid combative interaction. Such encounters are not, however, examples of argumentation. Argumentation is a *process of reasoned interaction about controversial topics*. Although Jesse and Judith's exchange was interaction about a controversial topic, it was not *reasoned* interaction.

Reasonableness—the essence of reasoned interaction—is a difficult concept to define. In some cases, reasonableness is much like what former Supreme Court Justice Potter Stewart once said about obscenity: "I know it when I see it." As with recognizing obscenity, however, finding general agreement about what constitutes reasonableness in any given situation is often difficult.

One important aspect of reasonableness is *logic*. Logic establishes connections between the different parts of every *argument*. Arguments are *units of argumentation*. They are made up of *conclusions* and *supporting reasons*. Usually, arguments are strung together in a kind of web, leading to a single overall conclusion or thesis. Intermediate conclusions, supported with reasons, form an argumentative web leading to the central argument's conclusion. In the following example, the speaker presents three related arguments:

▼ ▼ ▼ ▼ ▼ ▼

We should move out of Los Angeles because living here is bad for our health. Living here prevents us from having access to nature's blessings. Therefore, it causes us anxiety and needless stress. ▼ ▼ ▼

These sentences contain at least the following three arguments:

Argument 1:	conclusion:	We should move out of Los Angeles.
	reason:	Living in Los Angeles is bad for our health.
Argument 2:	conclusion:	Living in Los Angeles is bad for our health.
	reason:	Living in Los Angeles causes us anxiety and needless stress.
Argument 3:	conclusion:	Living in Los Angeles causes us anxiety and needless stress.
	reason:	Living in Los Angeles prevents us from having access to nature's blessings.

Notice how the conclusion of one argument serves as the primary supporting reason for another. Each of these arguments is connected to the other. Notice too that these arguments will work only if the reader or listener fills in the missing reasons. In the second argument, for example, the reader or listener is expected to fill in the assumption that whatever causes anxiety and needless stress is bad for people's health. As we learned in Chapter 2, the success of nearly every argument depends on the audience's contribution of missing parts.

Logic connects an argument's various parts. These connections are known as *inferences*. Accepting an inference means accepting one statement because you believe at least one other statement provides adequate support for it. Logical analysis is the *determination of whether inferences are correct, reliable, adequate, or acceptable.* Making this determination requires the tools discussed in Chapter 2, as well as those to be discussed in the chapters that follow. For now it is important to understand that every argument involves at least one, and usually many, inference(s), or moves between supporting reasons and a conclusion. Logic helps make these moves reasonable.

Logic is not enough for reasoned interaction. Emotions also play an important role. *Good argumentation involves a balance between logic and emotion.* Unlike machines, humans have the capacity to experience a rich variety of emotions, from love to hate, joy to despair, anger to compassion. These emotions often significantly contribute to effective decision making.

Consider, for example, the recent debate about the appropriate role of computers in social policy making. We now have the capacity to program computers for logical analysis and inference making. These capabilities have led some technocrats to argue that social policies should be determined by computers.

Opponents of computer-based decisions point to the fact that technologists have not yet been able to create machines capable of directly experiencing human emotions. Computers cannot, for example, feel compassion for homeless or handicapped persons. Nor can computers experience the joy of spotting a newborn fawn or the enchantment of watching an exquisite performance in a ballet.

Consider the tragic consequences if legislators no longer brought compassion, joy, or enchantment into their discussions about social policy. Without compassion, legislators might determine that society's homeless and handicapped are not worth caring for. Without the experience of joy, legislators would likely stop protecting precious forests and wildlife. And without the experience of enchantment, policy makers might diminish support for the development of people's artistic potential.

Even more troubling is the prospect of foreign policy decisions made without emotional considerations. The emotional concerns of families whose relatives have been taken hostage would no longer play a role in governmental dealings with terrorists. Concerns for human suffering would no longer be factored into decisions about economic aid to foreign nations. And major military decisions would focus only on strategic advantage, without consideration of human dignity.

Some have suggested that Hitler's Final Solution offers an example of inadequate emotional considerations. These people contend that Hitler's plans for the revival of the German economy were logically sound. They note, for example, that the extremely high unemployment rate in pre–World War II Germany was significantly lowered after Hitler put his policies into effect. Further, Hitler's scientific community learned much from its experimentation on humans. Recent investigations have shown that major American scientific advances in the space industry were based upon information forwarded by Hitler's scientists.

Few would deny these accomplishments of Hitler's regime. Yet many would challenge the view that his methods of achieving these ends were logically sound. The more popular interpretation of Hitler's decision making is that his nation's great tragedies resulted from his maniacal commitment to Aryan supremacy and passion for German domination. On this interpretation, Hitler's reasoning was purely emotional, without the benefit of logic.

On either interpretation of this episode in German history, we see a clear imbalance between logic and emotion. Hitler's decision making may have been purely logical, or perhaps it was obsessively emotional. Few would suggest, however, that his Final Solution was reasonable.

Today most of the world recognizes that Hitler's ends did not justify his means. His perverted logic and abhorrent behavior serve as an extreme example of what tragedies can occur when decisions fail to reflect an adequate balance between logic and emotion. Hitler's decisions were not guided by reasoned interaction. They were forged by prejudice, a misplaced worship of efficiency, and a failure to value human life and dignity.

Unchecked scientific inquiry provides further illustration of the importance of balancing emotion and logic. Scientists dedicated to their pursuit of knowledge sometimes make discoveries that, if utilized outside the laboratory, could have destructive potential. Without checks, for example, technological development of discoveries made by geneticists could endanger much of the world. On a smaller scale, scientific experimentation on human embryos has the potential to violate basic human rights. And the recently publicized implantation by scientists of human sperm into female chimpanzees has the potential to violate human dignity.

Fortunately, most bioethicists, and the policy makers they influence, understand these and related dangers. They recognize that policies governing medical and scientific practices require careful balancing of emotion and logic. They understand that neither unchecked emotion nor pure scientific reason provides an adequate basis for laws regulating scientific practices. Here, as in every other human domain, reasonableness is achieved by the delicate combination of logic and emotion.

Reasoned interaction is not the only component of argumentation. A second ingredient is *controversy*. Without controversy, there would be no need for argumentation. We would simply turn to an authority for answers to our question or solutions to our problem. Controversy sparks the need to investigate, question, and arrive at the most reasonable answer. It is the lifeblood of argumentation, as it is the driving force of critical thinking.

Because argumentation is motivated by controversy, it is often aimed at gaining or increasing the adherence of minds to a thesis.[1] In this sense, argumentation encompasses the art of *persuasion*. When a person has formulated his or her views on a topic, he or she is ready to use argumentation to persuade others to accept those views.

But before argumentation is directed at persuasion, it is a primary tool of *deliberation*. United States Supreme Court procedures illustrate this process. Once the nine justices decide to take a case, they are presented with numerous arguments reflecting a variety of perspectives. To assist their deci-

---

1.   Chaim Perelman and L. Olbrechts-Tyteca, *The New Rhetoric* (Notre Dame, Ind.: University of Notre Dame Press, 1969), p. 45.

sion making, justices read and listen to arguments made by the legal advocates on both sides of the case and they read precedents (previous cases). The justices also draw on their own experiences and values in forming a judgment.

Once the justices have made their initial decisions, they meet to discuss the case. During these sessions, justices often use arguments of their own to try to persuade each other of their points of view. This use of argumentation is said to significantly influence the justices' deliberation process. Justices say, for example, that arguments presented during these sessions have often led them to change their decisions. Justices also frequently comment upon the value of these persuasive exchanges to the quality of their deliberation.

Upon reaching their final decisions, the justices write opinions attempting to *justify* them. This use of argumentation is intended to demonstrate to the public that the justices made reasoned decisions given the information available to them. The arguments presented in judicial opinions are also intended to persuade future Supreme Court, as well as lower court, justices to maintain the precedents established in the case.

Supreme Court justices use argumentation, then, for three distinct but related purposes: to improve the quality of their deliberation, to justify their decisions, and to persuade each other and a broader audience. These three uses of argument service decision makers and advocates in a wide variety of situations.

Whether used in persuasion, deliberation, or justification, argumentation helps participants make good decisions. Reike and Sillars reflect this view of the argumentation process in their definition of the term: *Argumentation is the process of advancing, supporting, modifying, and criticizing claims so that appropriate decision makers may grant or deny adherence.*[2]

▾ ▾ ▾
COMPETITIVE VERSUS COOPERATIVE ARGUMENTATION

There are at least two approaches to argumentation. *Competitive* argumentation focuses on winning something, from an audience's vote to a debate prize. *Cooperative* argumentation focuses on the shared goal of finding the best answer or making the best decision.

In public domains, competitive argumentation often takes precedence over cooperative argumentation. Public pro and con forums provide good examples of this type of interaction. Participants in pro and con forums generally seek to win the audience's vote. Each side presents the best argu-

---

2.   Richard D. Reike and Malcolm O. Sillars, *Argumentation and the Decision-Making Process,* 2nd ed. (Glenview, Ill.: Scott, Foresman, 1984).

ments available in the hope that the audience will ultimately recognize that side's position as the true or correct perspective.

Our adversarial system of justice similarly depends on the successful use of competitive argumentation. The prosecutor and defense attorney in a criminal trial, for example, each do his or her best to persuade the jury of the client's guilt or innocence. Each wants to win the jury's verdict. In an ideal trial, the two sides are equally well represented and the jury is competent to make a reasoned judgment. Ideally, competitive courtroom argumentation leads to a just decision.

But competition in these settings sometimes discourages, rather than fosters, reasoned decision making. Often the competitors' desire to win overshadows their desire to contribute to a just outcome. Sometimes, for example, a legal advocate seeks biased jurors, easily manipulated into voting for his or her client's perspective. Attorneys sometimes present evidence in a way that is intended to mislead jurors. And when confronted with unskilled opponents, legal advocates sometimes avoid raising the competing arguments needed for full representation of the opposing case. In these situations, jurors are provided inadequate information on which to base their decisions.

Competitive argumentation also often leads attorneys and clients to hide possibly damaging evidence and arguments from the opposition, thereby limiting jurors' abilities to make reasoned assessments. Often, competitive argumentation leads legal advocates to seek only evidence that advances a preconceived, narrow perspective, rather than searching for a more comprehensive understanding of the relevant topic.

Secretary of State George Schultz recognized the shortcomings of competitive argumentation during his testimony before the congressional committee investigating the Iran-Contra affair in 1987. He noted that CIA Director William Casey presented arguments to President Reagan for particular policies without adequately representing alternative perspectives. According to Secretary Schultz, this competitive approach to foreign policy development prevented the president from making a reasoned assessment of the situation. Cooperative argumentation between all of the president's advisers would have provided the president a much clearer, more accurate, and constructive picture on which to base his vital foreign policy decisions.

Cooperative argumentation, in contrast, is a *process of reasoned interaction on a controversial topic intended to help participants and audiences make the best assessments or decisions in any given situation.* Advocates participating in cooperative argumentation share evidence and ideas with one another. They recognize that their views can only be enlightened by as comprehensive and open an exchange as is possible. They view opposing advocates as colleagues potentially capable of enlightening them.

At this point, our attention will turn primarily to cooperative argumentation, which we will view as a process used in making effective personal and professional decisions.

▼ ▼ ▼

THE VALUE OF COOPERATIVE ARGUMENTATION

Cooperative argumentation provides opportunities to exchange and test our ideas, to consider alternative perspectives, to learn new information, and to evaluate available information. This sharing of information and perspectives enriches the quality of our thinking and enhances our ability to make informed, reasoned personal and professional decisions.

Argumentation as Fundamental to Democracy

We learned in Chapter 1 that critical thinking helps preserve freedoms essential to democracy. As a primary tool of critical thinking, argumentation is of special importance to democracy for a number of reasons.

During the twentieth century, the United States has given all of its adult citizens the right to vote, regardless of their sex, race, or ethnic origin. During the same period, this country has attempted to provide all of its children a minimum of twelve years of schooling. Philosopher Mortimer Adler points out that these two gifts—universal suffrage and universal schooling—"are inextricably bound together."[3] Without adequate schooling, he argues, citizens will not be adequately equipped to exercise their right to vote.

Adler's observation is based on the recognition that schooling provides citizens the basic skills, knowledge, and understanding they need for participation in democracy. Without the ability to read, write, and think critically, they would be unable to acquire the clear understanding of political issues needed to vote responsibly. Nor would they have access to the information they need to assess the competencies and personalities of competing political candidates.

Adler's views on the relationship of education to voting rights are of considerable importance. For example, we've all come across people who have regretted their vote for a particular candidate. At the time that they cast their votes, these citizens assumed that the candidate would represent their best interests. But later they discover that their assumption was ill founded. Similarly, given the complex nature of many election issues, how often have we cast votes on an issue without adequately considering the consequences of our position? No doubt most people have had to deal with negative consequences of such uncritical voting behavior.

At the heart of Adler's concern, then, is the ability to responsibly participate in democratic institutions. Argumentation provides the tools needed for such participation. Through reasoned interaction with other members of the

---

3. Mortimer J. Adler, *Paideia Proposal* (New York: Macmillan, 1982), p. 3.

community, voters become aware of alternative perspectives and gain insights into their own. Argumentation by its very nature requires careful thought and energetic dialogue. This reasoned interaction on controversial topics helps participants learn what the relevant issues are, gain understanding of them, and ultimately make responsible decisions.

Freedom of expression is designed precisely for these purposes. The freedom to express our competing views on controversial topics enables us to prepare for participation in the community. Exercising this freedom through public and private argumentation protects not only this freedom, but the many others we associate with our cherished way of life.

Just as argumentation prepares people for full and responsible participation in democratic institutions, this form of communication also prepares members of groups for participation in group decision making. The discussion that follows will highlight some of the contributions cooperative argumentation makes to effective group decision making.

Argumentation as Valuable to Group Decision Making

Psychology professors Irving Janis and Leon Mann have carefully studied effective decision making. Through their research, they have "extracted seven major criteria that can be used to determine whether decision-making procedures are of high quality." Janis and Mann believe that decisions satisfying these seven ideal procedural criteria have a better chance than others of attaining the decision maker's objectives and of being adhered to in the long run.[4] As you look over Janis and Mann's seven criteria for good decision making, see how closely they match the constituents of critical thinking:

1. Canvas alternative courses of action
2. Survey the full range of objectives and the values implicated by the choice
3. Examine consequences of each alternative
4. Search for new relevant information
5. Assimilate new information
6. Reexamine consequences of each alternative
7. Make detailed provisions for implementing or executing the chosen course of action

Janis and Mann note that failure to meet any of these seven criteria when making a fundamental decision "constitutes a defect in the decision-making

---

4.   Irving L. Janis and Leon Mann, *Decision Making* (New York: Free Press, 1979), p. 11.

process. The more defects, the more likely the decision maker will undergo unanticipated setbacks and experience postdecisional regret." They add that "the more adequately each criterion is met, the lower the probability that the decision maker will make serious miscalculations that jeopardize his [or her] immediate objectives and long-term values."[5]

Cooperative argumentation plays a significant role in helping group decision makers meet these seven criteria. From identifying and evaluating alternative courses of action, to anticipating consequences of employing each alternative, the seven procedures adopted by good decision makers are considerably enhanced through reasoned interaction.

An official investigation into causes of the most disturbing problems experienced by the Reagan administration illustrates how cooperative argumentation helps satisfy these group decision-making procedures. Upon learning details of the Iran-Contra affair, President Reagan asked then Senator John Tower, a conservative with special expertise in national security, to head a commission to investigate the affair. Joining Senator Tower on the Tower Commission were then Senator and Secretary of State Edmund Muskie, known for his levelheadedness; and Brent Scowcroft, a retired Air Force general who served several Republican presidents as a key foreign-policy adviser. Their task was to identify what led to the illegal selling of arms to Iran.

In its published report, the Tower Commission cited a flawed decision-making process as the primary culprit. They found, among other things, that "the opportunity for a full hearing before the President was inadequate." "Rigorous review" of proposed initiatives was not provided. In general, the commission found that there had been inadequate discussion of competing alternatives.

The Tower Report clearly indicated that cooperative argumentation between cabinet members, National Security Council members, members of Congress, and the president would have significantly improved the quality of the Reagan administration's decision-making process. Such interaction would have, in the words of the Tower Commission, helped the "nation's history bear one less scar, one less embarrassment, one less opportunity for opponents to reverse the principles this nation seeks to preserve and advance in the world."[6]

Investigations of decision-making procedures used by other presidential administrations indicate that they too were sometimes flawed. One of the most disturbing examples of such poor decision making, the Bay of Pigs fiasco, reveals a serious breakdown of effective decision making during John Kennedy's presidency.

---

5. Janis and Mann, p. 13.

6. John Tower, Edmund Muskie, Brent Scowcroft, *The Tower Commission Report* (New York: Bantam Books, 1987), pp. 63–99.

According to Irving Janis, for example, President Kennedy's ill-fated decision to go forward with a CIA plan to overthrow the Castro government in Cuba was based upon acceptance of at least six false assumptions. Most of Kennedy's advisers were well qualified for their positions, and under better circumstances they would likely have recognized serious problems with the CIA plan. Yet they were encouraged to suppress their personal doubts and discouraged from questioning the administration's plan. In an effort to enhance "group solidarity," members fostered a false sense of unanimity, seriously jeopardizing the quality of the president's decision making.[7]

This dangerous episode in our country's history underscores the importance of avoiding *Groupthink*—a particularly disturbing flaw in group decision making. As the following discussion will illustrate, cooperative argumentation protects against Groupthink.

Argumentation as Protection Against Groupthink

Janis defines Groupthink as "a collective pattern of defensive avoidance" and gives eight symptoms of this problem.[8] As you read Janis's list of Groupthink symptoms, consider how reasoned interaction about the controversial topics facing a group would prevent each symptom:

1. An illusion of invulnerability, shared by most or all the members, which creates excessive optimism and encourages taking extreme risks

2. An unquestioned belief in the group's inherent morality, inclining the members to ignore the ethical or moral consequences of their decisions

3. Collective efforts to rationalize in order to discount warnings or other information that might lead the members to reconsider their assumptions before they recommit themselves to their past policy decisions

4. Stereotyped views of enemy leaders as too evil to warrant genuine attempts to negotiate, or as too weak and stupid to counter whatever risky attempts are made to defeat their purposes

5. Self-censorship of deviations from the apparent group consensus, reflecting each member's inclination to minimize to himself or herself the importance of his or her doubts and counterarguments

6. A shared illusion of unanimity concerning judgments conforming to the majority view (partly resulting from self-censorship of deviations, augmented by the false assumption that silence means consent)

7. Direct pressure on any member who expresses strong arguments against any of the group's stereotypes, illusions, or commitments, making clear

---

7. Irving L. Janis, *Groupthink*, 2nd ed. (Boston: Houghton Mifflin, 1982), pp. 14–47.
8. Janis, pp. 174–175.

that this type of dissent is contrary to what is expected of all loyal members

8.   The emergence of self-appointed mindguards—members who protect the group from adverse information that might shatter their shared complacency about the effectiveness and morality of their decisions

One of the primary factors motivating these eight symptoms of Groupthink is the group's desire to gain and maintain group cohesiveness. As groups form, members naturally want to develop a sense of community. Unfortunately, group members often confuse argumentation between group members (particularly if it involves challenging a leader's views) with disloyalty toward the group. Janis points out that if "group members had been less intent upon seeking for concurrence within the group they would have been able to correct their initial errors of judgment, curtail collective wishful thinking, and arrive at a much sounder decision."[9] Similarly, group members who understand that engaging in cooperative argumentation ultimately benefits the group quickly abandon the false perception that this type of interaction somehow reflects disloyalty toward the group.

Unlike groups that engage in Groupthink, groups trained to employ cooperative argumentation are able to form *constructive* forms of cohesion. Their cohesiveness stems from their unity of purpose. Members in these groups share the goal of reaching the best decision possible given their circumstances. They understand that good group decision making requires questioning assumptions, inferences, and information. They encourage disagreement and the expression of opposing views. They seek just and reasonable decisions, rather than a false sense of cohesion. They reward members who introduce relevant new information and encourage open sharing of alternative perspectives among members. They deplore censorship in any form, even if it is self-imposed. They value deviations from apparent group consensus because they understand that such discussion protects them from judgment errors and premature confidence in the group's decision. In short, groups that employ cooperative argumentation protect themselves from Groupthink, as well as from other forms of flawed decision making.

Argumentation as Valuable to Personal Decision Making

Just as cooperative argumentation enhances the quality of group decision making, it significantly contributes to good personal decision making. Tim and Eve's exchange illustrates some of these contributions.

---

9.   Janis, p. 197.

Tim and Eve find themselves disagreeing about whether preschool children should be kept on rigorous bedtime schedules. Tim believes young children should be put to bed at the same time each night. Eve believes preschool children should be allowed to determine their own sleeping schedules. Both Tim and Eve have a stake in resolving this controversy. Tim's child, Laura, is Eve's grandchild. Eve would like Laura to spend the night at her house. Tim would like Laura to stay with her grandmother as well, but he is concerned that Laura be put to bed at her usual bedtime. Tim and Eve begin their discussion by recognizing that, above all else, they both want what is best for Laura.

Through cooperative argumentation, Tim and Eve exchange their reasons for believing as they do. Eve points to an article she read regarding children's natural biological clocks. According to some researchers, these internal clocks let children know when they need to go to sleep. Eve notes further that children need to have as much autonomy as possible at an early age. This ability to determine their own destinies gives children a sense of independence and helps prepare them for future decision making. Further, argues Eve, allowing children to select their own bedtimes helps them adapt to the many types of situations they are likely to encounter during their lives.

Tim listens carefully to Eve's reasoning. He shares Eve's beliefs regarding children's early need for autonomy. However, his research into child development has led him to conclude that preschool children are not yet capable of making decisions involving their schedules. Tim also agrees that children have natural biological clocks, but he believes that the force of these clocks is often overridden by children's compelling desire not to miss out on something while they sleep. Finally, Tim cites the testimony of many child psychologists who believe that maintaining a rigorous bedtime schedule helps children feel secure in an otherwise chaotic world. Security at an early age, argues Tim, helps children gain the foundation they need to adapt to the many difficult situations they will encounter in their later years.

This cooperative exchange of arguments has made at least the following contributions to Eve and Tim's decision making: Their argumentation has (1) exposed points of agreement and disagreement; (2) introduced each of the participants to alternative perspectives; and (3) exposed underlying assumptions. As a result of this process, both Eve and Tim are now more able to evaluate their personal views about the topic.

As each probes more deeply into the reasons behind their differing points of view, Tim and Eve determine that their stated reasons do not account for the intensity of their disagreement. Through more discussion, they learn that their respective parents have influenced their thinking. This discovery affords Eve and Tim the opportunity to probe the origins of their beliefs.

Eve recalls, for example, that her mother lived in a closely knit extended family atmosphere where nearly every decision other than bedtime was imposed upon children. In this environment, the little autonomy given children in determining their bedtime could be of considerable value to them.

Tim recalls that his father's career as a traveling comic forced the children to experience chaos and irregularity. Tim's father did what he could to help Tim and his sisters suffer minimally from the family's frequent moves. Given the life style these children experienced, a rigorously maintained bedtime schedule was probably important to them.

Through a discussion of the circumstances influencing their parents' views, Eve and Tim are able to decide whether they apply to Laura's situation. Through further discussion, they argue that Laura generally experiences more overall autonomy than did Eve's generation, but she experiences less chaos than did Tim's generation. They concur that a moderate adherence to a bedtime schedule would probably best meet Laura's needs.

Tim and Eve's cooperative argumentation enabled them to carefully evaluate the best reasons for and against their respective views. As a result of their exchange, they were able to make the best decision possible regarding Laura's schedule, thereby achieving their ultimate shared goal.

Cooperative argumentation is naturally designed to make these and other valuable contributions to personal decision making. Often, our most passionate beliefs are founded on reasons given to us by other people in circumstances no longer appropriate to us. Argumentation helps uncover these reasons so that we may carefully evaluate them in light of our own special situation.

Just as often, our limited exposure to alternative perspectives needlessly limits our thinking. Consider Harvey. He has spent weeks trying to prevent his kitchen from being overrun by mice. He has set up several mousetraps, with no success. Somehow the mice consistently outsmart him and avoid the trap. Each day, Harvey puts down a more sophisticated mousetrap. Yet he continues to fail in his purpose.

Along comes a friend who points out that mousetraps are not the only way to alleviate Harvey's problem. Many alternatives have been successfully used. According to Harvey's friend, acquiring a cat is a particularly effective solution to the problem. The next day, Harvey acquires a cat who happily serves his guardian's purpose. Within a week, Harvey's kitchen is free of mice.

Like Harvey, most of us occasionally fail to consider the many alternatives open to us regarding a given situation. Cooperative argumentation with friends, family members, colleagues, and even adversaries helps us discover and evaluate these alternatives. This is but one of the many ways in which cooperative argumentation enriches the quality of our personal decision making.

▾ ▾ ▾
SUMMARY

Argumentation is a process of reasoned interaction about controversial topics. Reasonableness—the essence of this process—is difficult to define.

An important aspect of reasonableness is logic. Logic connects supporting reasons to conclusions in arguments. These logical connections are known as inferences. Generally, arguments join together to form a web of intermediate inferences that lead to a central conclusion or thesis. Logical analysis is the determination of whether these inferences are correct, reliable, or acceptable.

Logic is not enough for reasoned interaction. Emotions also play an important role. Good argumentation involves a balance between logic and emotion. Reasonableness combines both of these basic ingredients of reasoned interaction.

Controversy is another basic component of argumentation. Without controversy there would be no need for argumentation. Because argumentation is motivated by controversy, it encompasses the art of persuasion. People use argumentation to persuade others of their points of view.

But before argumentation is directed at persuasion, it is a tool of deliberation. Supreme Court procedures illustrate this process. Justices listen to persuasive arguments in an effort to reach a just decision. After they make their initial decisions, they attempt to persuade one another of their points of view. These exchanges often lead justices to change their initial decisions. Once they have made their final decisions, justices write persuasive arguments intended to justify them.

Whether used in the service of persuasion, deliberation, or justification, argumentation helps participants make good decisions. For the purposes of this text, then, argumentation is defined as the process of advancing, supporting, modifying, and criticizing claims so that appropriate decision makers may grant or deny adherence.

There are at least two approaches to argumentation. Competitive argumentation aims at winning something. Cooperative argumentation focuses on the shared goal of finding the best answer or making the best decision in any given situation.

Cooperative argumentation—reasoned interaction on controversial topics intended to help participants and audiences make the best assessments or decisions possible—is a basic tool of critical thinking. As such, it is fundamental to the preservation of democratic principles and institutions.

Cooperative argumentation is also valuable to group decision making. Through reasoned interaction on controversial topics, group members are able to satisfy the seven criteria for good decision making. Similarly, cooperative argumentation helps prevent groups from falling prey to Groupthink.

Finally, argumentation is valuable to personal decision making. Cooperative argumentation with friends, family members, colleagues, and even adversaries helps us discover and evaluate the many alternatives open to us. Here, as elsewhere, argumentation used in the service of critical thinking helps us fully develop our personal and professional potential.

▾ ▾ ▾

EXERCISES

1. Find three arguments in this chapter. In each case, find the conclusion and the supporting reason(s) for that conclusion. Label each argument as primarily directed at deliberation, persuasion, or justification.
2. Carefully read the following excerpts from a newspaper editorial by George F. Will.[10] Identify Will's primary conclusion. Next, identify at least two reasons given in support of that conclusion.

▾▾▾▾▾▾

Playing with Guns

Our leaders are talking a lot about hunters. They have to talk loudly to be heard over the Washington gunfire that this year, through last Friday, had killed 113. People, not deer . . .

Why are we talking about hunting when the issue is urban mayhem? Law must not diverge far from culture so, although the culture is becoming more grown-up about guns, the law will for a long time be too permissive. But must we talk about hunting when the issue is the importation, domestic manufacture and sale of weapons no sensible society should permit in circulation? The reason we do is political fear of a lobby. It is an old story. So is this. In a bourgeois city, violence by the underclass against itself is a "concern" to correct thinkers. But when bullets come near the bourgeoisie, that's a *crisis*. However, bullets rarely do.

Our leaders are talking about hunters' rights. Most hunters, like most lawmakers, are white and middle class. While terrified poor black families live and die amid gunfire, white politicians who live and work in tranquil neighborhoods weigh, with Solomonic judiciousness, the right of sportsmen to have military arsenals against the right of poor people not to have neighborhoods sounding at night like the third afternoon at Gettysburg.

A ban will not disarm criminal users, at least not soon. But neither is the ban on cocaine now effective. That is not a reason for surrendering. Law's expressive function matters. It is time to express disgust with levels and kinds of violence known in no other developed democracy. And a law banning assault rifles would at least say to the suffering minority that the safe majority cares. ▾▾▾

---

3. Identify three public or private contexts in which competitive argumentation is the most appropriate and effective form of interaction for achieving the participants' goals. Next, identify three public or private contexts in which cooperative argumentation provides the best tools for achieving the participants' goals.

4. As you read the following excerpts from a newspaper editorial,[11] identify statements serving as conclusions and statements serving as supporting reasons.

▼▼▼▼▼▼

Wanted: Liberal Artists

The results of a recent survey of job-hiring practices provide welcome encouragement for everyone who followed the advice, "Get a liberal education." Corporate America wants to hire generalists, not just specialists.

About one-fourth of 535 chief executives surveyed by Boston University specifically encouraged the hiring of liberal arts graduates and nearly half of their companies reported seeking humanities majors by recruiting on campus.

The study, completed last month, included written surveys of chief executives of the nation's 1,000 largest corporations and 200 midsize companies. Forty-five percent responded, including more than half the nation's top 100 companies. In addition, 505 middle and senior managers at large companies were interviewed about their experiences in working with other managers with various types of schooling.

College students and recent graduates who steered a liberal arts course have heard plenty of discouraging news about industry's increasing demands for engineers, computer scientists and others in highly specialized fields. It's heartening to know that many company leaders still appreciate the importance of pursuing a well-rounded education.

"Top corporate executives are more concerned than before, certainly than in the 1970s, about the overly narrow education of some of those who are applying for white-collar jobs in the corporation," said Michael Useem, director of the university's Center for Applied Social Science, who conducted the survey.

Many times it takes the family doctor to discover a patient's particular illness and point the way to just the right specialist. The right complement of generalists and specialists will keep the country's businesses healthy, too. ▼▼▼

---

11. Editor's Commentary, *Columbus Dispatch,* June 8, 1988, p. A-12. Reprinted with permission.

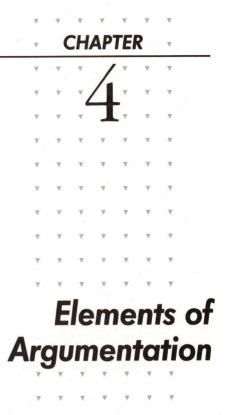

CHAPTER

4

Elements of
Argumentation

Chapter 3 highlighted some of the ways argumentation can serve personal and professional decision making. This chapter introduces tools needed to make effective use of argumentation.

In particular, the chapter introduces three types of *claims: empirical* or *factual, value,* and *policy.* Discussion turns next to the process of discovering *central issues* and to the need to distinguish these from *nonessential issues.* Attention then turns to *commonplaces* and to the relationship between *presumptions* and *burden of proof.* Finally, the chapter introduces *types of evidence* and *forms of inference.*

After reading this chapter, you should have enough familiarity with these basic elements of argumentation to be able to begin effectively using argumentation in a variety of contexts.

▼ ▼ ▼

CLAIMS

Claims are the most basic elements of argumentation. Some people use the term *claim* to refer to the conclusion of an argument. In this text, we will use the term more broadly: A claim is *any statement, either implied or openly stated, within an argument.* We will refer to the *concluding claim* of an argument as the *conclusion.* And we will use the term *premise* to refer to *any claim used to defend the conclusion or to lead the audience toward accept- ance of the conclusion.*

We will distinguish three types of claims: empirical or factual, value, and policy.[1] *Empirical* or *factual claims* are usually statements that may be veri- fied with reference to so-called objective data. The word *empirical* refers to experience. Through scientific and other methods, we are usually able to determine whether empirical claims are indeed factually correct. Each of the following statements, whether true or false, is an example of an empirical or factual claim:

> ▼ **Claim 1:** There are forty-five students in Dr. Kim's class.
> ▼ **Claim 2:** Manufacturers released or disposed of at least 22.5 billion pounds of hazardous substances in the United States in 1987.
> ▼ **Claim 3:** Pregnant sows on more than 40 percent of America's factory farms wear collars chained to the floor in pens eight feet by two and one-half feet.

Claim 1 is a factual claim about an imaginary character named Dr. Kim. Claim 2 is an empirical claim open to debate by experts. Claim 3 is a factual claim easily verifiable by use of the senses.

A second type of claim—the *value claim*— is usually not empirically verifiable. Value claims are subject to a different type of inquiry from the type employed in assessing the truth of a factual claim. Chapter 2 reviewed many of the different ways that experts have defined the term *value.* For now, it may be helpful to recall sociologist Milton Rokeach's definition: Values are types of beliefs "centrally located within one's total belief system, about how one ought or ought not to behave, or about some end-state of existence worth or not worth attaining."[2]

Value claims express these types of beliefs. However, they also express other types of judgment. For example, aesthetic judgments are expressed

---

1. Philosophers have traditionally discussed a fourth type, usually known as an analytic claim. Because this type of claim is dependent on conceptual validation, it is formally distin- guishable from empirical, value, and policy claims. This type of claim does not, however, generally play a central role in decision-making practice. Thus, our focus will be on the three types of claims discussed above.

2. Milton Rokeach, *Beliefs, Attitudes and Values* (San Francisco: Jossey-Bass, 1973), p. 112.

with value claims. The following examples illustrate the wide variety of value claims:

> ▾ **Claim 4:** Ripened bananas taste delicious.
> ▾ **Claim 5:** Two wrongs do not make a right.
> ▾ **Claim 6:** Art songs are beautiful.

Claim 4 expresses an aesthetic judgment about the taste of ripened bananas. Claim 5 expresses an ethical judgment, and Claim 6 makes an aesthetic judgment about art songs. Each of these claims makes some kind of aesthetic or ethical judgment about a person, place, or thing.

A related type of claim is the *policy claim*. Like value claims, policy claims are not empirically verifiable. Unlike the aesthetic or ethical judgments characteristic of value claims, however, policy claims explicitly prescribe behavior. The following examples illustrate the prescriptive nature of policy claims:

> ▾ **Claim 7:** Congress should repeal the Baby Doe law.
> ▾ **Claim 8:** People should not deceive their friends.
> ▾ **Claim 9:** Abortions should be permitted only up to the twelfth week of pregnancy.

Each of these claims prescribes specific behavior. Claim 7 urges Congress to repeal an existing law. Claim 8 proposes a rule for ethical behavior. And Claim 9 supports a law that sets limits on legal abortions. Note that each of these examples employs the word *should*.

As you begin to develop and evaluate arguments, you will quickly see the valuable role that impassioned debate involving the acceptance or rejection of a variety of value and policy claims has in the argumentation process.

You will also see, however, how difficult it often is to distinguish between factual, value, and policy claims. For example, the following factual claim could easily be confused as a value claim:

> ▾ **Claim 10:** Doctors have a legal duty to prevent suffering in humans.

Claim 10 appears to be a value claim because it appears to make reference to a doctor's duty. However, the word *legal* in Claim 10 changes the nature of the claim. The claim makes no judgment about a doctor's moral or ethical duty to prevent suffering in humans. Instead, it simply makes reference to the *fact* that doctors have a legal duty to prevent suffering in humans. Without the word *legal,* Claim 10 would be a value claim.

As with every aspect of argumentation, careful attention is required to ascertain whether any given claim may be verified as a fact or assessed as a judgment of value.

Identifying types of claims helps arguers evaluate the acceptability of various claims. But successful argumentation relies on more than this fundamental ability. Arguers must also learn to identify issues.

▼ ▼ ▼

ISSUES

An *issue* arises whenever there is *a clash between two or more claims.* For example, Michael and Maria are discussing whether animals should be used in medical, military, and industrial experiments. They agree that experiments which make use of animal models sometimes offer results that improve the quality of human life. They also agree that some animal experimentation has proven to be useless, whereas other experiments with animals have proven to be counterproductive. They agree too that because results of animal experimentation do not always apply well to humans, animal experiments sometimes mislead scientists. And they both recognize that these improper applications have sometimes caused harm to humans.

Additionally, Michael and Maria agree that American taxpayers spend approximately 4 billion dollars annually to fund animal experimentation. Both agree that between 20 and 40 million animals are used for medical, military, and industrial experiments in American laboratories every year, two hundred thousand of which are provided by pounds and shelters. And neither disputes the fact that many of these animals suffer varying degrees of emotional stress or physical pain during experimentation. As points of agreement, these claims do not generate issues for Michael and Maria.

But Michael believes that alternative methods of experimentation would provide more useful results than does animal experimentation. Maria disagrees. She believes that animal models provide the most effective means of acquiring scientific knowledge. For Michael and Maria, the question of which methods would render the most useful results is an issue. It is an issue of fact.

Michael and Maria also disagree on issues of value and on related issues of policy. Michael believes, for example, that the emotional and physical suffering of as many as 40 million animals overrides the achievements that scientists attribute to animal experimentation. Maria does not share Michael's value hierarchy. She believes that the medical, military, and industrial advances associated with animal experimentation justify the suffering that animals experience in laboratories. For Michael and Maria the question of which interests—scientific, industrial, military, or humanitarian—should take precedence is an issue of policy.

They also disagree about the value of the money spent on animal experimentation. Michael believes that the taxpayers' 4 billion dollar annual outlay for animal experimentation would be better spent on finding scientifically reliable alternatives to animal research. He also proposes spending money on computer networks that would provide information to scientists about previous research on the problems they plan to investigate, thereby helping to minimize needless duplication in labs. He believes too that expenditures on alternatives to the use of animals in labs would help scientists work more efficiently toward cures for many diseases that plague humans, but which are foreign to other species. Finally, Michael believes that tax dollars would be more effectively spent on preventive health care for those unable to pay for such care.

Maria disagrees with Michael's assessment of the best use of tax dollars. She believes that the scientific, military, and industrial progress associated with animal experimentation justifies the 4 billion dollar annual expenditure on these experiments. In Maria's estimation, spending more on alternatives to these experiments and on preventive health care for the poor would not be as prudent as continuing to invest in experiments using animals.

The quality of Michael and Maria's discussion about animal experimentation depends, at least in part, on what issues they discover. Equally important will be their assessment of the role each issue should play in their discussion. For example, as Michael and Maria continue their discussions, they find that they disagree about whether the cages used to house primates at the University of California at Davis Cancer Research Center are adequately supervised. Michael believes they are adequately supervised, whereas Maria believes they are not. Resolving this issue is not essential to resolving the overall question of whether animals should be used so extensively in scientific and industrial research. This is a *nonessential* issue.

If Michael and Maria were called on by the University of California at Davis to determine whether animals in the university's labs were adequately supervised, this would become a *central* issue for discussion. As this example illustrates, the determination of which issues are central and which are nonessential depends on the nature of the topic, the occasion and purpose of discussion, and so on. Incorrectly defining the centrality of issues can lead arguers to waste precious time and energy discussing tangents. Good argumentation requires rigorous attention to the nature and scope of issues surrounding a topic.

▼ ▼ ▼

COMMONPLACES

Just as good argumentation requires arguers to recognize points of clash, effective argumentation also depends on the ability to identify and exploit points of agreement. In this text, these *points of agreement* will be called *commonplaces.*[3] Effective argumentation depends as much on finding such commonality as on discovering issues. Without commonality, there can be no starting point for argument.

---

3. In classical times, the term *commonplaces* referred to "setpieces" that rhetors used in different speeches. Some writers continue to employ this classical use of the term. Perelman and Olbrechts-Tyteca, for example, provide a useful discussion of specific types of such commonplaces, or *loci.* See Chaim Perelman and L. Olbrechts-Tyteca, *The New Rhetoric* (Notre Dame, Ind.: University of Notre Dame Press, 1969), pp. 84–110.

In our example, Michael and Maria were able to meaningfully discuss the topic of animal experimentation because they were able to find much commonality. Recall, for instance, that they share a number of important *factual* commonplaces. They agree that taxpayers spend 4 billion dollars annually to fund animal experimentation and that between 20 and 40 million animals are used by medical, industrial, and military researchers in American laboratories each year. And they share a recognition that many of these animals suffer emotional stress or physical pain in the course of these experiments.

Michael and Maria also share a number of *value* commonplaces. Both would like scientists to use experimental methods that will improve the chances of finding useful scientific information. Similarly, both Michael and Maria place a high value on the quality of human life, and both would like to see scientific, military, and industrial research used for the improvement of human life. These are but a few of the value commonplaces that Michael and Maria share.

Without these and other commonalities, Michael and Maria would have no starting point for their discussion. All of their time would be spent disputing every possible fact and every relevant value. The more commonplaces they are able to find, the more likely they will be able to discover and address issues that are central to the topic.

Cross-cultural argumentation sometimes fails because participants have difficulty discovering commonplaces. Television host Phil Donahue's efforts to engage Soviet and American citizens in argumentation illustrate this difficulty. During a discussion about America's First Amendment rights, one of the American participants in this televised exchange expressed the widely held American belief that the Soviet people are deprived of the basic freedoms of press and expression that Americans cherish. To illustrate her point, the participant noted that the Soviet Union censors its citizens' free speech.

Several Soviet participants in the exchange responded to the American's remarks with amazement. They expressed astonishment at the American belief that Soviet citizens are less free than are their American counterparts. To illustrate the foolishness of this American belief, one of the Soviet participants pointed out that in America journalists are allowed to say and write extremely critical things about the World Revolution. This, he argued, clearly illustrates that Americans lack certain freedoms.

The Americans listening to this response became confused. They saw this example as further proof that Americans have more, not fewer, rights and freedoms than do their Soviet counterparts. After all, they argued, in the United States journalists can freely express whatever they like about the World Revolution or anything else.

The confusion reflected in this exchange was based on competing conceptions of freedom. The American participants came to the exchange with the belief that freedom means being free *from* the state. According to this view, journalists help protect people from the government. They serve as watchdogs of governmental behavior.

The Soviet participants came to the exchange with a competing view of freedom. For them, people are most free if they are free *within* the state. For the Soviets, the people *are* the government. According to this view, journalists best protect people when they work on behalf of the government.

Without a commonplace understanding of freedom, and of the ideal relationship between citizens and their government, participants in Donahue's attempted "summit" had difficulty effectively communicating with one another. Without fundamental commonplaces, they were unable to take full advantage of their opportunity to engage in cooperative argumentation.

In this example, successful argumentation depended on the participants moving up one level of abstraction to find their commonplaces. This move would have helped them discover that they all share a deep love of freedom. They all share a sense that protecting citizens' rights of free expression is of great importance. Had they begun their exchange with a recognition of these commonplaces, the participants could have meaningfully addressed their real issues: How can we best achieve freedom of expression? Are citizens more free within the American model of freedom-from-the-state or within the Soviet model of freedom-within-the-state?

Often, sets of issues and commonplaces change as a result of interaction. For example, Soviet and American participants came to their exchange with competing concepts of freedom. For them, these concepts were themselves issues. It is possible that argumentation on these issues would later have led to a shared concept of freedom. In this case, what was once an issue would then have become a commonplace.

Identifying a claim as generally accepted by a group of decision makers does not, however, necessarily provide clarity about the degree or type of agreement surrounding it. Some commonplaces are shared more strongly than others. Some have a kind of societal privilege earned over time. Others result from careful discussion. In some instances, commonplaces are held so strongly that they serve as *presumptions,* creating a *burden of proof* for those who wish to challenge them.

▾ ▾ ▾
PRESUMPTIONS AND BURDEN OF PROOF

The concept of presumption has played a central role in discussions about practical reasoning for many years. The concept is difficult to define and has often been the source of much controversy. Yet most argumentation theorists recognize that presumption is an important element of reasoning, especially in practical contexts.

In this textbook, the term *presumption* will refer to *a statement or belief that is granted without argument* by decision makers in a given context. There are essentially two different types of presumption: *technical* and *conventional.*

Technical presumptions are imposed upon participants in an argumentation context. Usually, this type of presumption appears in the form of a rule regarding the acceptance of fundamental commonplaces in a decision-making setting. Imposing a technical presumption on decision makers requires them to accept given claims without argument. Someone arguing against the predetermined commonplaces must overcome the *burden to prove* that the commonplaces are false. Technical presumptions play an important role in influencing the outcome of argumentation or debate in a number of practical contexts.

Conventional presumptions, which also significantly affect decision making, are the *beliefs accepted without argument by a group of decision makers.* Anyone who wishes to argue against one of these beliefs has the *burden to prove* that the claim is false (or that the relevant counterclaim is true). In the following citation, Rieke and Sillars are referring to conventional presumptions:

▼▼▼▼▼▼

The concept of presumption suggests the momentum of the decision makers. Which way are they leaning? Where do they seem inclined to go if no counterargument intervenes?[4] ▼▼▼

Not all presumptions carry the same weight in decision making. Some presumptions are *ideal,* but not *real.* Philosopher Robert C. Pinto has ideal presumptions in mind when he writes that "good arguments are those which confer upon their conclusions the status of presumptions."[5]

Ideal presumptions have the weight of relevant authority or some other basis to *justify* their role in determining the outcome of argumentation, debate, or decision making. A presumption is *real* when it is *accepted by the relevant decision makers.* Only some presumptions are both ideal and real. Some presumptions are only ideal, whereas others are real, but not ideal.

As the following discussion will illustrate, technical presumptions are often imposed on a group of decision makers to protect the argumentation, debate, and decision-making *processes,* even when they are not necessarily accepted by the decision makers.

---

4.   Richard D. Reike and Malcolm O. Sillars, *Argumentation and the Decision Making Process,* 2nd ed. (Glenview, Ill.: Scott, Foresman, 1984), p. 153.

5.   Robert C. Pinto, "Dialectic and the Structure of Argument," *Informal Logic* vi: (January 1984): 17.

Technical Presumptions

In this section we will focus on the role of technical presumptions in two different contexts: intercollegiate debate on policy resolutions and criminal law proceedings. This discussion will show the significant role that technical presumptions—whether ideal, real, or both—play in shaping argumentation and decision making in diverse contexts.

Technical presumption plays a major role in competitive formal policy debate. In this type of argumentation context, opponents are instructed to argue about whether or not to adopt a policy that deviates significantly from the status quo, or the way things are. "Affirmative" teams have the *burden to prove* that such a change is needed. They must establish that there are significant, inherent problems with the status quo that call for adoption of the "affirmative" plan of action.

In the traditional debate format, the "negative" team has presumption in its favor. The status quo is *presumed* adequate; the negative team therefore focuses much of its attention on showing that the affirmative side has not adequately fulfilled its burden to establish significance, inherency, and solvency.

Technical presumption in competitive debate is designed in part to reflect the traditional view of presumption. On this view—usually associated with the eighteenth-century theorist Richard Whately—whatever exists carries presumption. Technical presumption in formal competitive policy debate has institutionalized this long-standing, conservative view of presumption.

In preserving this traditional view, technical presumption in competitive debate helps to maintain the social order. At the same time, this use of presumption is intended to ensure fairness in the debate process. Preassigning presumption and burden of proof helps create a conformity of argument designed, in part, to help participants anticipate outcomes. But, more importantly, technical presumption in competitive debate is designed to help judges make fair decisions.

This country's legal system makes similar use of technical presumption. Technical presumptions are imposed on legal advocates, judges, and juries in criminal proceedings in an effort to ensure fairness in the system's decision-making process.

According to the rules of the system, for example, a defendant in a criminal trial must be presumed innocent. This ideal technical presumption requires the prosecution to prove beyond a reasonable doubt that the defendant is guilty of the crime in question.

In reality, of course, some jurors do not actually presume the defendant's innocence at the beginning of a trial. Media coverage of cases, for example, sometimes encourages whole groups of potential jurors to doubt the defendant's innocence before the trial begins. Yet the imposition of an ideal technical presumption of innocence is intended to help ensure that the jurors will insist on proof of the defendant's guilt, beyond a reasonable doubt, before rendering a guilty verdict. If there is evidence that the jurors have not used the presumption of innocence in their decision making, this finding would give an appellate court cause to override the jury's decision.

Despite their differences, then, technical presumptions in the invented world of competitive debate and the real world of criminal law share an important feature in common: They are imposed on decision makers in an effort to preserve the integrity of the decision-making process.

Conventional Presumptions

Conventional presumptions also influence decision making. But they are usually not imposed on decision makers. Nor are they necessarily designed to protect the integrity of the decision-making process. Instead, conventional presumptions are beliefs that a specific set of decision makers choose to take for granted as they approach their topic.

Some conventional presumptions are more ideal than real. For example, in the field of applied ethics, truth-telling has ideal presumption. Someone who wants to mislead always has the burden to prove that deception is justified in that context. One commonplace in applied ethics is that physicians must sometimes conceal or withhold information from their patients. However, this commonplace does not override the presumption against deception: A doctor who contemplates misleading a patient through the concealment of information still has the burden to prove that such concealment is in fact necessary.[6]

In reality, this ideal presumption is not always accepted by medical practitioners. Some physicians regularly withhold information, viewing this practice as either harmless or even beneficial to their patients. These physicians do not feel the need to justify their behavior, because the ideal presumption in favor of truth-telling is not real for them.

Other ideal conventional presumptions are more widely accepted by decision makers. Consider, for instance, the scientific presumption that the earth is not flat. This presumption is ideal because it has been established through years of testing by the most rigorous standards available to the scientific community.

Interestingly, this now widely accepted ideal presumption was once widely rejected by the scientific community. In the past, the earth was presumed to be flat. Anyone wanting to argue that the earth was not flat had the

---

6. This is one of many examples that Sissela Bok provides for illustrating the role that the presumption in favor of truth-telling plays in applied ethics. See Sissela Bok, *Lying: Moral Choice in Public and Private Life* (New York: Vintage Books, 1978), p. 252. For more discussion of this presumption, see the discussion of the veracity principle in Chapter 6 of this textbook.

burden to prove it. In this instance, what is now a widely accepted ideal conventional presumption was once not a presumption at all.

Some ideal conventional presumptions cross disciplines and even cultures. Consider, for example, the presumption that intimate friends may and should be trusted. This widely held conventional presumption significantly affects people's perceptions about the quality of their relationships. In most cultures people know the difficult burden of proof that comes with trying to persuade someone that his or her friend is not trustworthy. Most people know too that satisfying this burden often leads to a painful shift of presumption. If the friend is shown to be untrustworthy, he or she is likely to lose the presumption of trust. This shift usually undermines and often destroys the quality of the relationship.

A different type of conventional presumption is associated with acceptance of a given philosophical perspective. Most Western philosophers believe, for example, that "moral judgments must be universalizable: whatever is right (or wrong) in one situation is right (or wrong) in any relevantly similar situation."[7] For these philosophers, this presumption plays a major role in the assessment of moral justification.

The importance of conventional presumptions is especially evident in group decision making. Consider, for example, situations in which members of a group are deadlocked on an issue. This situation occurs often in bioethics committees forced to consider the fate of a patient whose life is sustained by a mechanical support system. A kind of "double" presumption functions in these cases. Bioethics committees continue to accept the long-standing presumption that the medical practitioner's first responsibility is to "do no harm." They further accept the presumption that "not prolonging life does harm." Taken together, these presumptions often lead an otherwise deadlocked committee to lean in favor of maintaining the patient's life support system. Someone wishing to move the committee in the opposite direction has the burden to overcome this double presumption.

The Interplay Between Different Types of Presumptions

Sometimes, conventional presumptions influence the evolution of technical presumptions. This is especially evident in noncriminal legal contexts. For example, unlike the rigid technical presumptions associated with criminal law, technical presumptions in American constitutional law are often influenced by society's conventional presumptions. Cases involving the government's right to regulate businesses illustrate this evolutionary process.

---

7.   James A. Jaksa and Michael S. Pritchard, *Communication Ethics* (Belmont, Calif.: Wadsworth, 1988), p. 68.

At one time, if the government wished to regulate a business, it faced an almost impossible burden to establish its need to do so. Governmental efforts to protect laborers from abuses were almost invariably frustrated by the Supreme Court's presumption in favor of a doctrine known as "laissez faire." This doctrine held that our government must not intervene in the everyday affairs of business. According to its adherents, the laissez-faire doctrine best served the long-term public interest.

Given its presumption in favor of laissez faire, the Supreme Court almost invariably ruled in favor of businesses' right to be left unregulated. During the New Deal era under President Franklin Roosevelt, however, new conventional presumptions about the government's regulatory function took the place of the once widely held laissez faire doctrine. This new view held that the government should intervene in the public interest whenever individual rights were either actually or potentially violated by businesses.

This newly evolving conventional presumption significantly influenced Supreme Court decision making. Today, the technical presumption in favor of the government's right (and even responsibility) to regulate business is almost inviolate. In most economic regulation cases, today's Court "defers" to the government's claim that its regulations are necessary and within constitutional limits.

In the spring of 1989, supporters of legalized abortion attempted to take advantage of the interplay between conventional and technical presumption. On April 10, 1989, several hundred thousand men and women marched in Washington, D.C., in support of women's right to choose abortion. According to a report in the *New York Times,*

▼▼▼▼▼▼

this march was intended to bring public opinion to bear on the nine Justices of the Supreme Court who will begin on April 26 the consideration of a Missouri case that could be used to limit, or even to reverse, Roe v. Wade, the Court's still blazingly controversial 1973 decision giving pregnant women the right to choose abortion.[8] ▼▼▼

The report's headline speaks graphically to the effect that conventional presumption can have on technical presumption in American constitutional law: "The Justices Are People: Climate of the Era May Have an Effect."

Technical presumptions in domestic law cases involving child-custody disputes may be even more dramatically and directly affected by conventional presumptions. For example, child-custody hearings in many parts of the country have recently been influenced by strong challenges to the long-standing conventional presumption that women are more competent than

---

8.   Robin Toner, "Right to Abortion Draws Thousands to Capital Rally," *New York Times,* April 10, 1989, pp. 1, 8.

men in caring for young children. For years, this belief served as both a technical and a conventional presumption in favor of the mother during child-custody hearings. A father who wished to gain custody of his children had the burden to establish that the children's mother was either morally corrupt or otherwise woefully incompetent to raise the children. Today, as men's and women's roles evolve, the legal system's technical presumption is giving way to changes within the society.

Notably, just as presumptions regarding parenting skills find varied acceptability among specific sets of decision makers, these changing presumptions influence domestic law judges to varying degrees. In some parts of the country, women are still presumed to be more competent caregivers. In other parts of the country, this presumption has given way to a less traditional view of parenting skills.

Problems with Presumptions

Because presumption in this and other decision-making contexts is associated either with decision makers' prevailing beliefs or with long-standing rules of a system, both technical and conventional presumption may be said to have a conservative bias. After all, that which exists is likely to be widely shared and hence to carry presumption.

History reveals many instances in which such a bias has prevented society from recognizing the wisdom of enlightened calls for change. Consider, for example, the once widely held conventional presumption in favor of slavery. Consider too the long-standing technical and conventional presumption that rape victims were somehow responsible for their assailants' brutal attacks.

Today we recognize the serious flaws in the reasoning that led to widespread acceptance of these presumptions. Yet it is not so easy for us to see whether currently accepted presumptions are equally vulnerable to attack. We may one day decide, for example, that the presumptions which now favor maintaining life support for the terminally ill fail to serve the interests they were designed to serve. Perhaps one day bioethics committees will require that someone who wishes to maintain life support in such a case must satisfy a burden to prove the wisdom of this practice.

Animal welfare activists believe that the widely held technical and conventional presumptions favoring factory-farming methods, hunting, animal experimentation, and other common uses of animals will one day be replaced with presumptions favoring stronger consideration of animal, as well as human, welfare. Many people regard these views as radical and without substance. It will be fascinating to see which of these perspectives prevails in the years ahead.

Although presumption often does place an advantage on those who support the status quo, recognizing the role that presumption plays in decision making can only help improve the quality of the overall decision-making process. As long as decision makers consider alternative perspectives, and adopt the decision-making strategies discussed throughout this text, their acknowledgment of presumption in any given situation is only likely to enhance their critical reasoning about the issues.

The Relationship Between Presumption and Critical Thinking

As demonstrated throughout this text, cooperative argumentation is intended to help decision makers recognize and question prevailing systems of belief. In this sense, cooperative argumentation helps decision makers continually assess the validity and wisdom of their technical and conventional presumptions. To a degree, then, critical thinking is a process of evaluating and re-evaluating the status of claims. Should a claim have presumption in its favor? Should someone who wants to defend the claim have a burden to prove its acceptability? To what degree? In what contexts? Why?

Robert Pinto goes so far as to suggest that it would be "enormously fruitful" to view arguments as "attempts to confer on their conclusions the status of a presumption—or, what is to say the same thing, to shift the burden of proof to those who would dispute them."[9]

Even if we do not go so far as to view all arguments in these terms, we can share Pinto's belief that presumption is an important element of argumentation. As we begin applying the elements of argumentation in real situations, we should not underestimate the importance of understanding, recognizing, and acknowledging the role that presumption plays in decision making.

▼ ▼ ▼

DEFINITIONS

Now that we have discussed the importance of identifying types of claims, discovering issues and commonplaces, and determining degrees of controversy and agreement, we are ready to address another basic element of effective argumentation. *Definitions* of key terms serve important functions that make possible the discovery of issues and commonplaces, presumptions, and burdens of proof.

In order to discover issues and commonplaces, presumptions, and burdens of proof, participants in argumentation must first have a sense of how terms of the dispute are being used. Definitions help fulfill this need. In

---

9. Pinto, p. 17.

some instances, definitions are either obvious or quickly shared. However, often definitions of terms can themselves become issues. In either case, it is important that participants in argumentation find definitions acceptable to all of them. Only with a common language can arguers and their audiences make the most effective use of argumentation.

One type of definition is *formal* in nature. Dictionaries provide formal definitions, which characterize the essential qualities associated with a term. For example, the term *definition* is defined in *Webster's Dictionary* as: "description of a thing by its properties; explanation of the exact meaning of a word or term."

Words can also be defined by *example.* In the paragraph above, we used an example of a definition to define the term.

Some of the most useful definitions come from *common usage.* Defining by common usage is often helpful in argumentation because it takes advantage of the audience's common understanding of the term. For example, the term *pathetic* in common usage means "pitiful." In more specialized contexts, this same term has a different meaning.

Another type of definition is *operational* in nature. Operational definitions require the advocate to explain "the function or special purpose represented by the terms in a specific context."[10] Operational definitions are especially useful for people arguing about whether to adopt a proposed policy. When discussing whether the government should regulate prime-time television programming, for example, discussants need to define the terms *regulate* and *prime-time television programming.* An operational definition of the latter set of terms might be presented as follows:

Ian: We propose to impose careful restrictions on prime-time television programming. In particular, we plan to carefully regulate what is shown on network television every evening from 7:00 P.M. through 10:00 P.M.

Here, Ian is presenting his group's operational definition of prime-time television programming by providing details of his group's specific plan for network television regulation. In this example, Ian still has to provide a definition for the term *regulate.*

Terms may also be defined by *negation.* To use this method, advocates clarify what they do not mean by the term. For example, suppose the topic under discussion is argumentation. In defining the term *argument,* it would be useful to explain that you are not applying the common usage of the term. For many people, argument refers to the type of combative interaction that sometimes leads husbands and wives to divorce court. Negating this meaning helps clarify your use of the term.

---

10. Austin J. Freeley, *Argumentation and Debate* (Belmont, Calif.: Wadsworth, 1981), p. 44.

Another type of definition is by *comparison or contrast*. Comparing the term to something familiar to all participants in the argument will often help everyone understand your use of the term.

But perhaps the most effective way to ensure common understanding and usage of key terms is to use a combination of types of definitions. Providing formal and operational definitions, examples, common usage, negation, *and* comparison helps avoid needless misunderstandings between advocates and their audiences.

▾ ▾ ▾

TYPES OF EVIDENCE

Once usage of terms has been established, issues have been identified, and commonplaces have been discovered, argumentation can begin. We learned in Chapters 1 and 2 that thinking critically about a topic requires extensive knowledge about it. Similarly, argumentation requires extensive research and preparation. Without adequate research, an advocate will not be able to provide *support* for his or her controversial claims.

Evidence is the most common source of support for a controversial claim. Usually, when you are asked to prove or establish the truth of a controversial claim, you are being asked to provide evidence. For example, Halle has told Linda that travel agencies in Boston work more efficiently than travel agencies in other major American cities. Linda does not accept this claim on face value. She asks Halle what support she can offer on its behalf. She might ask, "How do you know that Boston travel agencies are more efficient than others around the county?" Or perhaps she will say, "Why should I accept your claim . . . can you prove it?"

What Linda wants from Halle is evidence to support her claim. Halle may use several types of evidence. *Specific instances* are particularly useful. *Examples* and *illustrations* are specific instances. Whenever they are used as support for a claim, examples and illustrations serve as evidence for it.

Halle may support her claim by citing several highly efficient travel agencies in Boston and several inefficient operations in New York, Chicago, and other representative cities. These examples provide evidence for her claim that Boston firms are more efficient than their counterparts elsewhere.

Sometimes, examples do not serve merely as evidence. They may also be used to illustrate a point or to reinforce one. Illustrations can be powerful in helping lend presence to a problem or point of view. Many films and books make effective use of this strategy. The film *Coming Home* provides an example of the role that illustration can play in helping audiences carefully attend to a problem or perspective.

Coming Home portrayed the plight of a soldier seriously wounded during the Vietnam War. Through a sensitive depiction of this character's homecoming, painful rehabilitation, and emotional healing, this film helped viewers identify with the character and with his suffering. Through its powerful illustration of one man's suffering, this film helped make present in the public's mind an otherwise hidden aspect of the Vietnam War.

Perhaps the best demonstration of the power of "making present," however, is the story that unfolds in the *Diary of Anne Frank*. People listening to lists of examples of World War II tragedies have been known to become immune to these instances. But there are few people who are not moved by the story of Anne Frank, a young girl hiding with her family in an Amsterdam basement during the German occupation of Holland. Against all odds, she survived weeks and months of the occupation. Her diary shows strength and sensitivity, charm and innocence. What reader is not moved when, in the end, Anne Frank is killed because she is Jewish?

Although examples may effectively illustrate important points, heavy reliance on them can defeat the purposes of argument. Examples and illustrations can be overcome by *counterexamples* and illustrations. In Halle and Linda's argument, for example, Halle's use of examples is vulnerable to numerous counterexamples. Linda might think of several inefficient Boston agencies and several highly efficient agencies in New York and San Francisco. Even carefully developed illustrations such as those provided in *Coming Home* and the *Diary of Anne Frank* are vulnerable to refutation. The story in *Coming Home,* for instance, may be overshadowed by the personal story of a wounded Vietnam veteran who is given a warm homecoming and generous support from his community. This veteran might be portrayed as proud to have served his country in Vietnam. Perhaps today he holds an outstanding position in government and has the respect of thousands. Such a portrayal could seriously undermine the point *Coming Home* was intended to illustrate.

To effectively serve as support, examples need to be *representative and sufficient in number*. Future chapters will provide more discussion of these criteria for effective use and evaluation of specific instances.

The examples Halle used were real. Anne Frank's experience was also real. The story in *Coming Home,* though fictitious in development, was based on fact. When real examples are not available, advocates can create *hypothetical* examples to support their controversial claims. In her book *A Room of One's Own,* Virginia Woolf makes effective use of a hypothetical example.

Woolf uses her example to support her claim that sexual discrimination prevented generations of great women from fully developing their human potential. In particular, her example addresses her opposition's claim that the historical dearth of great women in literature proves that women are less capable of literary excellence than are men.

As she begins developing her hypothetical example, Woolf asks her audience to imagine that Shakespeare had a sister who was born with a great literary talent. Judith was as

▼▼▼▼▼▼

adventurous, as imaginative, as agog to see the world as her brother. But she was not sent to school. She had no chance of learning grammar and logic, let alone of reading Horace and Virgil. She picked up a book now and then, one of her brother's perhaps, and read a few pages. But then her parents came in and told her to mend the stockings or mind the stew and not moon about with books and papers. They would have spoken sharply but kindly, for they were substantial people who knew the conditions of life for a woman and loved their daughter—indeed more likely than not she was the apple of her father's eye. Perhaps she scribbled some pages up in an apple loft on the sly, but was careful to hide them or set fire to them. Soon, however, before she was out of her teens, she was to be betrothed to the son of a neighbouring wool-stapler. She cried out that marriage was hateful to her, and for that she was severely beaten by her father. Then he ceased to scold her. He begged her instead not to hurt him, not to shame him in this matter of her marriage. He would give her a chain of beads or a fine petticoat, he said; and there were tears in his eyes. How could she disobey him? How could she break his heart? The force of her own gift alone drove her to it. She made up a small parcel of her belongings, let herself down by a rope one summer's night and took the road to London. She was not seventeen. The birds that sang in the hedge were not more musical than was she. She had the quickest fancy, a gift like her brother's, for the tune of words. Like him, she had a taste for the theatre. She stood at the stage door; she wanted to act, she said. Men laughed in her face. The manager—a fat, loose-lipped man—guffawed. He bellowed something about poodles dancing and women acting—no woman, he said, could possibly be an actress. He hinted—you can imagine what. She could get no training in her craft. Could she even seek her dinner in a tavern or roam the streets at midnight? Yet her genius was for fiction and lusted to feed abundantly upon the lives of men and women and the study of their ways. At last—for she was very young, oddly like Shakespeare the poet in her face, with the same grey eyes and rounded brows—at last Nick Greene the actor-manager took pity on her; she found herself with child by that gentleman and so—who shall measure the heat and violence of the poet's heart when caught and tangled in a woman's body?—killed herself one winter's night and lies buried at some cross-roads where the omnibuses now stop outside the Elephant and Castle.

That, more or less, is how the story would run, I think, if a woman in Shakespeare's day had had Shakespeare's genius.[11] ▼▼▼

This powerful hypothetical example provides strong support for Woolf's claim. Based on details found through historical research, Woolf's hypothetical example aligns well with historical fact. A reader familiar with the Shakespearean era recognizes the realism of Woolf's example. This close match

---

11. Virginia Woolf, *A Room of One's Own* (New York: Harcourt, Brace and World, 1929), pp. 49–50. Copyright 1929 by Harcourt Brace Jovanovich, Inc., and renewed 1957 by Leonard Woolf. Reprinted with permission of the publisher.

between the hypothetical example and reality helps give the example its strength.

The example's power also comes from Woolf's ability to control all of its details. When the details match the audience's conception of reality, the example can serve the advocate and the audience. When the hypothetical example does not reliably match the audience's conception of the world, its value is diminished. In such a situation, what was once a source of its power becomes a hypothetical example's weakness. Because advocates control the details of their hypothetical examples, they may easily reshape these details.

For example, Kip and Scott have been arguing the pros and cons of providing support to the Nicaraguan Contras, or Freedom Fighters. To defend his claim that the United States should increase, rather than withdraw, its aid to the Contras, Kip uses a hypothetical example:

Kip: Imagine a Freedom Fighter, we will call him Juan. Juan is eighteen. He has lost many relatives to the war with the Sandinistas. Juan's father fought beside Nicaraguan President Daniel Ortega during the Nicaraguan revolution. He shared Ortega's dream of replacing Somoza's ruthless regime with a Democratic form of governance. But after the revolution, Juan's father was betrayed. Because he would not support Ortega's Marxist/Leninist ideology, Juan's father was ordered into exile. When he refused to leave his beloved country, Juan's father was killed.

Now Juan is fighting for his father's dream. He joins 16,000 other patriots in the fight for democratization of his native land. The United States must not let Juan down. We must continue to give aid to the Contras. In fact, we should give twice the money this year as we did last year. Only then will the Contras be able to realize Juan's dream.

As Scott listens to this hypothetical example, he finds that it does not match well with his conception of reality. Replacing Kip's image with his own, Scott reshapes the hypothetical example:

Scott: Suppose that Juan's Contra companions, José and Franco, share Juan's zeal for overthrowing Ortega's Marxist/Leninist government. But their reasons are different from Juan's. They hope to regain the power lost by their fathers, members of land-owning elite. Their dream is to reclaim their empire and to continue the long tradition of despotism associated with the political right in Central America. Historically, the United States has provided military might and dollars to help the elite control the masses in Central America. The many atrocities associated with the Contras provide strong evidence that Juan will have little say about the future of Nicaragua's government if the Contras achieve their goal. Juan's ruthless friends, supported by rich American corporate leaders, will much more likely take control if the Contras overthrow the Ortega government.

By their very nature, hypothetical examples can be reshaped with ease. To make the most effective use of hypothetical examples, advocates need to seek the closest match to reality as is possible. Although potentially useful to argumentation, hypothetical examples should be carefully developed and used.

Statistics also provide potentially valuable sources of support. Statistics are numerical compilations of specific instances. Statistical evidence may include raw numerical data or data that has been tabulated and evaluated. For example, in the fall of 1986, Ohio State University had 1,083 full professors, 945 associate professors, 1,040 assistant professors, and 282 instructors. Of the full professors, 68 were women. Among the associate professors, 183 were women; among the assistant professors, 339 were women. There were 171 female instructors at the university at that time. These are raw data about the distribution of male and female faculty by rank and tenure.

Calculations show that in fall, 1986, 6.28 percent of full professors at Ohio State University were women, 19.37 percent of associate professors were women, 32.60 percent of assistant professors were women, and 60.42 percent of instructors were women. These data have been tabulated for the purposes of argument.

In a fall, 1986, speech to the Ohio State University Faculty Women's Club, the university's provost discussed the university's record for hiring women faculty members. He argued that "the Ohio State University has had a good record for hiring women faculty members." To support his claim, the provost used the following evidence:

▼▼▼▼▼▼

In comparison to the CIC institutions—that is, the Big Ten plus the University of Chicago—the Ohio State University ranks first in percentages of the number of faculty women who are tenured and the number of faculty women who are tenure eligible. At least as important, Ohio State ranks near the bottom of this group in the number of women who are hired on non-tenure eligible positions. This means that Ohio State tends to hire women into normal tenure positions and not on a temporary basis, the traditional abusive category for women faculty.[12] ▼▼▼

The provost effectively used available statistics to support his claim. Listening to his speech, however, were people uncomfortable with the provost's use of data. They were concerned, for example, that the provost's presentation did not consider the distribution of faculty by rank. These people believed that this omission may have led the provost to draw an unwarranted conclusion. To address this concern, someone asked the provost to consider

---

12.   From the transcript of a speech presented to the Ohio State University Faculty Women's Club, October 1986.

the fact that women comprised only 6.28 percent of all full professors at Ohio State University in fall, 1986. Recognizing the import of this additional fact, the provost concluded that while the university has an overall good record in hiring women, "There is room for improvement."

Statistical evidence by its very nature may be used, either unintentionally or intentionally, to mislead. This misuse of statistical evidence is so common that Darrell Huff has written a book entitled *How to Lie With Statistics.*[13] To effectively serve argumentation, statistical data should satisfy at least the following standards: It should come from the *most reliable sources;* rely on *valid measurements;* be *current;* and be *representative.* Later chapters provide more discussion about these guidelines for the use and evaluation of statistical evidence.

A third type of evidence is *testimony.* In most cases, testimonial evidence is used to give greater credibility to a claim. There are two types of testimony: *testimony of fact* and *testimony of opinion.* In a criminal trial, witnesses are often asked to give testimony of fact. Was the defendant at the scene of the crime? Did the witness see the defendant use the stick to hurt the child? Testimony of opinion is also often used in criminal proceedings. For example, psychiatrists are often asked to provide their opinion of whether a defendant was criminally sane at the time a crime was committed.

These uses of testimony help provide substantive evidence to support an advocate's claim. But the value of testimonial evidence is directly tied to the witness's *credibility.* How believable is the witness? How reliable is the witness's testimony likely to be? The widespread use of testimony in advertisements illustrates this point. Consider the actor who plays a doctor on a popular daytime television series. When this actor testifies that he favors one brand of aspirin over another, he lacks credibility with critical viewers. Unfortunately, some less critical viewers might attribute to the "doctor" (clad in professional medical clothing) a kind of medical expertise. This example graphically illustrates the importance of carefully assessing a testimonial source's credibility.

The value of testimony is not only tied to the *general* credibility of the source, it is also tied to the source's *topical* credibility. Is this person an expert on the relevant topic? How reliable is the witness's expertise on the relevant topic? Chief Justice Rehnquist would be a reliable source for testimonials about the constitutionality of capital punishment. After all, the Supreme Court has the final say on questions of constitutionality. Chief Justice Rehnquist would not, however, be a particularly reliable source for testimony about whether capital punishment in fact deters crime. He is neither a trained criminologist nor an expert sociologist. Thus, although Chief Justice Rehnquist would have high general credibility in testifying on the deterrent ability of capital punishment, his testimony would have low topical credibility.

---

13.   New York: W. W. Norton, 1954.

Finding and using testimonial evidence requires, then, a sensitivity to the source's general and topical credibility. Additionally, advocates need to be aware that overreliance on testimonial evidence has the potential to weaken the value of an argument to the critical thinking process. Arguers quickly discover that for every expert who argues that capital punishment deters crime, there is likely to be an equally reliable expert who argues that capital punishment does not deter crime. Controversial issues by their very nature call forth studies whose outcomes directly conflict with one another. Testimonial evidence, then, should be used primarily to supplement other forms of evidence.

▾ ▾ ▾
INFERENCES

Once evidence has been acquired, arguers are ready to make use of it. They are now ready to draw inferences. Recall from previous chapters that inferences move arguers from what is known, or believed to be true, to what is not known, or not believed to be true.

There are many forms of inference, each with its own potential strengths and weaknesses.[14] However, we will be primarily interested in distinguishing *demonstrative* from a number of *nondemonstrative* alternative forms of inference.

Demonstrative Forms

Formal logicians—specialists who study the structures or forms of inferences—have developed criteria for determining what they call the *formal validity* of argument forms. Their interest is in determining the logical relationships between various claims

Formal logicians are primarily interested in *demonstrative* argumentation. That is, they are interested in arguments that demonstrate with *certainty* that a conclusion follows from a set of premises. Because they are primarily interested in this type of argument, they use some version of the following criterion for determining whether an argument form is *valid:*

▾▾▾▾▾▾

An argument form is valid if and only if it is not possible for the conclusion of the argument to be false when all the premises are true. That is, *if* it is possible

---

14. For detailed analyses of many argument forms, see Perelman and Olbrechts-Tyteca's *The New Rhetoric.*

for the premises to be true while the conclusion is false, then an argument form is invalid.[15] ▼ ▼ ▼

This concept is usually referred to as *formal validity*. Formal validity is accompanied by a technical analysis of the difference between *deductive entailment* and *inductive inference*. To the formal logician, a conclusion is deductively entailed from premises if and only if the conclusion follows with certainty from the premises. Deductive arguments are, therefore, either valid or invalid. In contrast, inductive inference is a relationship based on probability. The following examples illustrate the differences between these two forms of demonstrative inferences:

Deductive Entailment

All cats like mice.
Larissa is a cat.
Therefore, Larissa likes mice.

Inductive Inference

Most cats like mice.
Larissa is a cat.
Therefore, Larissa likes mice.

In the example of deductive entailment, it would not be possible for the conclusion to be false if the premises were true. The argument form in this example would therefore be considered formally valid. In the example of inductive inference, it may not be the case that Larissa likes mice even though most cats like mice and Larissa is a cat. This argument form would not be considered formally valid.

Nondemonstrative Alternative Forms

But as we learned in previous chapters, argumentation always occurs in the realm of the *probable*. If we were able to demonstrate our conclusions with certainty, there would be no need for argument. As a result, the inferences that arguers make do not satisfy the formal logician's criteria for formal validity.[16]

Additionally, demonstrative arguments are primarily directed toward determining or discovering *truth*. Arguments that help people make better decisions or judgments are primarily concerned with guiding *action*. Whereas demonstrative arguments serve the purposes of demonstration, practical arguments serve the purposes of *deliberation, justification,* and *persuasion*.

---

15.   This standard definition for formal validity may be found in most traditional symbolic logic textbooks. See, for example, Irving Copi, *Symbolic Logic* (London: Macmillan, 1967), pp. 4–5.

16.   For a discussion of these and related issues, see Stephen Toulmin, *The Uses of Argument* (Cambridge: Cambridge University Press, 1958), esp. pp. 94–146.

Premises and inferences serving these functions are those adapted to the demands of *rhetorical probability,* not those addressed to meet the challenges of *mathematical probability.* Rhetorical probability is measured by the degree to which reasonable people capable of following extended argument accept the inference. In contrast, mathematical probability is tested empirically and statistically.

Columnist Ellen Goodman's discussion of people's willingness to take risks speaks to the differences between rhetorical and mathematical probability:

▼ ▼ ▼ ▼ ▼ ▼

In California, a family cuts back on sugar in the decaffeinated coffee they drink in their house—on the San Andreas fault. In Pennsylvania, a man goes jogging—against the backdrop of the Three Mile Island nuclear reactor. In Maine, a woman rides to aerobics class—on her motorbike, without a helmet.

A friend decides that after the recent crop of air crashes he will fly only in emergencies. He explains that earnestly, while chain-smoking cigarettes. Another friend drinks only bottled water, eats only meat untouched by steroids and spends weekends hang-gliding.[17] ▼ ▼ ▼

Two years after publishing this column, Goodman wrote a companion essay. In this piece she spoke of the Ray brothers, three boys with hemophilia, all of whom were exposed to the AIDS virus through blood transfusions. In an effort to prevent the boys from attending the local public school, people in their hometown burned the Ray home to the ground. Although Goodman makes clear that she does not agree with this and related actions taken to prevent the Ray brothers from attending school, she understands the motivation behind these terrible acts. She writes:

▼ ▼ ▼ ▼ ▼ ▼

In the face of a disease like AIDS, we all become risk assessors. We want guarantees, and all we can get are odds.

If one of the Rays bled, if a classmate with open sores touched that blood, he could conceivably contract the virus. Three health workers came down with AIDS in similar ways.

Such risks are remote, perhaps infinitesimal, but they exist.

Smith's son [a child whose concerned mother removed him from the Ray brothers' school] incurs a much greater risk riding in a car to his new private school than from going to class with the Rays. The risk from these three boys,

17. "People Play it Safe While They Take Risks," *Columbus Citizen-Journal,* October 3, 1985, p. A-4. © 1985 The Boston Globe Newspaper Company/Washington Post Writers Group. Reprinted with permission.

none of whom have active AIDS or behavior problems, is almost non-existent. The uncomfortable "almost" is what we have to live with.

"If this were a disease that parrots carried and this year three parrots were found to have the virus, I wouldn't hesitate to have the birds removed no matter how small the risk," says Harvey Fineberg, dean of Harvard's School of Public Health. "The problem is that you're dealing with other lives. You can't balance a clear and present harm done to three youngsters against infinitesimal risk."

That is what happened in Arcadia. The risk of infection became the reality of community violence and disruption. Here is another entry into the annals of our risk anxiety. But not the last. Not by a long shot.[18] ▼ ▼ ▼

As these examples illustrate, mathematical probability tells only a part of the decision-making story. People's reactions to the AIDS crisis in particular graphically illustrate that rhetorical probability goes beyond the scope of mathematics and into the realm of human emotion.

Sometimes, however, rhetorical probability adds to the credibility of mathematical probability. Sharon's decision to wear a seatbelt provides an example. Sharon wears a seatbelt because she has read the statistical data on the lives saved by wearing seatbelts. For Sharon, learning these data helped motivate her decision. Decisions of this kind are often based in part on mathematical probability. But even in these cases, rhetorical probability determines the final outcome. Had Sharon not found the statistical data persuasive, or had her interest in moving freely about the car taken precedence, she would not have decided to wear the seatbelt.

A number of nondemonstrative alternative forms of inference are directed toward achieving rhetorical probability, rather than either the certainty of formal deductive entailment or the probability of formally inductive arguments. Although many of these nondemonstrative forms work with the basic inductive and deductive forms associated with formal logic, they do not rely on the formal logician's validity criteria.

Arguments that inform action rely on probable premises and draw probable inferences. These arguments do not satisfy the formal logician's criteria for validity. And because nondemonstrative forms of inference do not satisfy these criteria, the logician's distinction between deductive entailment and inductive inference is of little help to arguers. As you can see from the discussion above, most inferences in practical arguments make probable moves from premises to conclusion, and therefore few (if any) practical inferences meet the logician's standard of formal deduction.

---

18.   Ellen Goodman, "On Aids, We Want Guarantees, Not Odds," *Columbus Dispatch,* September 9, 1987, p. A-11. © 1987 The Boston Globe Newspaper Company/Washington Post Writers Group. Reprinted with permission.

Inductive and Deductive Nondemonstrative Forms

Because the formal logician's uses of the terms are too restrictive for our purposes, we will use the terms *induction* and *deduction* in a different sense. Inferences that follow a particular-to-general pattern will be called *inductive*. And arguments that move from the general to the particular will be called *deductive*. According to our definition, then, the following argument uses an inductive form:

▾ Misia is a cat who likes mice.
▾ Runt is a cat who likes mice.
▾ Mopsey is a cat who likes mice.
▾ Lientje is a cat who likes mice.
▾ Etc.
▾ Larissa is a cat.
▾ Therefore, Larissa likes mice.

Deductive *quasi-logical* inferences employ a general-to-particular form similar to demonstrative argument forms but are nonetheless not deductively valid (in the formal sense discussed earlier). Recall that by our definition, the following is a deductive argument:

▾ Nearly all cats like mice.
▾ Larissa is a cat.
▾ Therefore, Larissa likes mice.

This argument uses the most common deductive form, which is modeled after the classical syllogism:

▾ All people are mortal.
▾ Socrates is a person.
▾ Therefore, Socrates is mortal.

But in the case of our quasi-logical argument, the first premise replaces the term *nearly all* for the term *all*. As a result, the conclusion ("Larissa likes mice") does not follow with certainty (as does the valid argument form's conclusion that Socrates is mortal). Later chapters provide guidelines for drawing and evaluating quasi-logical inferences adapted to this deductive form.

Among inductive nondemonstrative inference forms, perhaps the most widely used are arguments by comparison. *Arguments by comparison* argue from "resemblances of relation"[19] between objects, persons, situations, and

---

19. Perelman and Olbrechts-Tyteca, *The New Rhetoric*, p. 372.

so on. Arguments by *analogy, metaphor, simile,* and *example* are four commonly used types of arguments by comparison.

Analogies use terms from four different spheres. The logical pattern for argument by analogy is:

▾ **Analogy:** *A* is to *B*   as   *C* is to *D*

The following passages from President Woodrow Wilson's Pueblo speech in support of the League of Nations illustrate this analogical form:

▾ ▾ ▾ ▾ ▾ ▾

I had a couple of friends who were in the habit of losing their tempers, and when they lost their tempers they were in the habit of using very unparliamentary language. Some of their friends induced them to make a promise that they never would swear inside the town limits. When the impulse next came upon them, they took a street car to go out of town to swear, and by the time they got out of town they did not want to swear. . . . Now, illustrating the great by the small, that is true of the passion of nations.[20] ▾ ▾ ▾

Wilson's analogy, intended to persuade people that the League of Nations would help prevent future wars, not only compares individuals (A) with nations (B), but it also compares the desire to utter profanities (C) with the desire to make warfare (D). Implied is the assumption that the League of Nations would help delay people's desires to make war, thus leading to the conclusion that the League of Nations would prevent war.

Arguments by analogy, like all arguments by comparison, work best when they help people relate what they know well to what is more remote to them. Tristan made effective use of this strategy during a faculty discussion of the value of students' evaluations of their instructors. James had suggested earlier in the discussion that students' evaluations more precisely monitored teaching effectiveness than did any other indicator. Tristan argued that students' evaluations may measure how much students like their instructors, but they do not necessarily measure teaching quality. Tristan's colleagues strongly disagreed with his assertion; they agreed with James's views. Then Tristan tried a different strategy: He made use of analogical argument.

Tristan's argument began with a reference to a popular experience, dining out. Suppose, he suggested, that you have just enjoyed a delicious meal at your favorite restaurant. You ate a cream soup, a pasta dish loaded with cholesterol, a delicious three-layer chocolate cake smothered with hot fudge, a double espresso coffee, followed by a heated brandy. When asked whether you enjoyed the meal, you exulted that it was one of the finest meals you'd

---

20.   Cited in William J. Brandt, *The Rhetoric of Argumentation* (New York: Bobbs-Merrill, 1970), p. 129.

ever eaten. But the fact that you enjoyed the meal does not necessarily mean that the meal was good for you. Similarly, when students say that they enjoyed a class, that does not necessarily measure whether the class gave them what they needed. Thus, concluded Tristan, whereas students' evaluations may provide some evidence of teaching skills, they do not accurately measure an instructor's overall teaching effectiveness.

Tristan's argument by analogy had an impact on his colleagues. Tristan had effectively compared attending class (A) with dining out (B) and evaluating a teacher's effectiveness (C) with assessing the nutritional value of a meal (D). Because Tristan's colleagues were able to relate closely to his selected comparison, he was able to persuade them that the measurement of student affection for an instructor is not necessarily a measure of the instructor's overall effectiveness.

Arguments by *metaphor* and *simile* have much in common with arguments by analogy. All three types of argument rely on comparisons between objects in two different *spheres* (or categories). However, unlike analogies, metaphors and similes compare only one set of objects, in two different spheres. The logical forms of the central claim, or underlying assumption, in these two types of arguments are:

▾ **Metaphor:** A *is* B
▾ **Simile:** A is *like* B

The metaphor "involves the juxtaposition of two terms that come from apparently different realms or classes of experience."[21]

Well-crafted metaphors have significant persuasive potential. First of all, they have the potential to dramatically reshape people's perceptions. As philosopher Monroe Beardsley notes, "Metaphors give us new meanings, enlarge the capacity of our language to express subtle differences and name qualities of the world for which we may hitherto have had no words."[22]

Metaphors can be used to enlighten, educate, persuade, or to do any combination of these. A popular metaphor used to help socialize people, for example, is to urge them to "build bridges, rather than walls." Teachers might use the following extended metaphor, attributed to Aristotle, to inspire children to learn: "Learning is an ornament in prosperity; a refuge in adversity; and a provision in old age." To help people understand the importance of considering public consequences of their actions, moralists have been known

---

21.   Dana Cloud, "Metaphor as Argument: Some Definitions and Implications for Critics." (Paper presented at the 1988 SCA Convention, New Orleans), p. 4. Cloud cites as her source, Michael Leff, "Topical Invention and Metaphoric Interaction," *Southern States Communication Journal* 48 (1983): 216–17.

22.   Monroe Beardsley, *Thinking Straight,* 4th ed. (Englewood Cliffs, N.J.: Prentice-Hall, 1975), p. 164.

to say, "No person is an island." And how many parents teach their children that they will "reap what they sow"?

The film *Raintree County* provides an interesting example of this use of metaphor. In the film, a professor is shown using the following extended metaphor to teach young people how to live productive and fulfilling lives:

▾▾▾▾▾▾

About greatness, we Americans measure greatness in simple terms, in terms of money. We're always hunting for the tree of life whose fruit is pure gold. . . . But there's another tree, the tree of fulfillment whose flower is accomplishment, whose fruit is love, whose ways are the ways of pleasantness, whose paths all lead to peace. Find that tree and you will find greatness. ▾▾▾

Although the preceding examples easily illustrate the use of metaphors to enlighten at the same time that they are designed to persuade, the examples in the paragraph to follow illustrate more common uses of metaphor not so readily identified as persuasive in intent.

Many history instructors explain the dependent and controlled role of some leaders and administrations by referring to them as "puppets" or "puppet governments." Leaders who have questionable authority are said to be "lame ducks." Police refer to suspects who are fast fleeing the scene as "rabbiting." When a person's anger is out of control, he or she may be referred to as a "rabid dog." A remark that inflicts unjustified emotional pain is commonly referred to as a "low blow." Story lines that leave people waiting urgently for the next episode or chapter are referred to as "cliffhangers." Similarly, when someone stops in the middle of a story about a crisis or something of urgent interest to a listener, they are said to be leaving the listener "hanging." And research that keeps pace with rapid change is referred to as "on the cutting edge."

These commonly used metaphors appear to be primarily designed either to enhance understanding or to otherwise instruct. But even these influence audiences by shaping perceptions. Viewing a leader as a puppet creates a perceptual framework that influences decisions about that person. Referring to research as on the cutting edge encourages a highly competitive, aggressive attitude toward the search for knowledge, and so on. Sometimes, such seemingly benign uses of metaphor have the potential to significantly influence our thinking about important issues.

Often, metaphors are designed to persuade. A popular way to get funding and support for a cause is to refer to it as a "war against" something most people fear, dislike, or oppose. The "war against poverty," "war against drugs," "war against inflation," "war against disease," and "war against pollution" are but a few examples. The director of efforts to clean up Alaska's Prince William Sound after the well-publicized oil spill of spring, 1989, referred to his group's cleanup effort as "a war" and vowed to "get troops" behind the effort. In part, his use of the metaphor was intended to help persuade the public both of his sincerity in confronting the problem and of the severity of conditions facing his crew.

Use of the war metaphor might seem, on the surface, to simply invite interest in a cause, or to gain support for it, or to emphasize its importance. But when we consider the perceptual framework encouraged by adoption of the war metaphor, we see the importance of carefully assessing its appropriateness and validity. Consider, for example, the war on drugs metaphor. Use of the term "war" might encourage readers and listeners to support killing people who are on the "wrong" side of the battleground. "War" connotes circumstances that justify suspending ordinary boundaries of conduct. During war, countries often suspend such rights as the right to privacy, free expression, and a fair trial. Use of the war metaphor in the context of the drug problem in America has the potential, then, to influence the public's assessments of policies about the situation.

In the preceding examples, metaphors have been designed to enlighten, to persuade, or to achieve both of these ends. Metaphors are also used to create or sustain interest and to simplify complex concepts. Wide use of sports metaphors during media coverage of political campaigns often serves these related purposes. Journalists Germond and Witcover write:

▼▼▼▼▼▼

The political jargon is awash in the cliches of sports: winning or losing the game, campaign teams and their managers, public-opinion polls handicapping the horse race, candidates (often called "horses") jockeying for position and so on.[23] ▼▼▼

A candidate may be referred to as the "leader of the pack" or a "dark horse" or the "front runner." During a political debate, one of the candidates may be said to have delivered a "knockout punch" to an opponent. Or the "match" might be said to have been "more even," with no one "knocking out" any other "contestant."

These sports metaphors do help simplify otherwise complex issues or events for viewers, listeners, and readers. However, sometimes the price paid for such oversimplification may be great. In the case of presidential debates, for example, viewers may be encouraged to view the event in highly simplified win/loss terms. Such a perceptual framework discourages critical assessment of the rich variety of arguments presented during this public exchange of ideas.

The use of metaphors in advertisements may also sometimes discourage critical assessment. The American car manufacturer's description of its prod-

---

23. J. Germond and J. Witcover, *Wake Us When It's Over: Presidential Politics in 1984* (New York: Macmillan, 1985), p. xvi.

uct line as the "heartbeat of America" may encourage some consumers to assume that the product was produced exclusively for and by Americans. Yet a brief investigation reveals that many of the product's parts are produced overseas. Some of the company's products are even assembled outside the United States.

Linguist George Lakoff and philosopher Mark Johnson have written a book devoted to such common uses of metaphor. They argue that "metaphor is pervasive in everyday life, not just in language but in thought and action."[24] Because metaphors have the potential to significantly shape beliefs, and because this power is often hidden, metaphors challenge critical thinkers to carefully assess their appropriateness, acceptability, and value.

In her provocative book, *Illness as Metaphor*, Susan Sontag takes such a look at prevalent uses of illness metaphors. She begins her work by offering a metaphor of her own:

▼ ▼ ▼ ▼ ▼ ▼

Illness is the night-side of life, a more onerous citizenship. Everyone who is born holds dual citizenship, in the kingdom of the well and in the kingdom of the sick. Although we all prefer to use only the good passport, sooner or later each of us is obliged, at least for a spell, to identify ourselves as citizens of that other place.[25] ▼ ▼ ▼

Sontag goes on to discuss the widely used "cancer metaphor." Among the many examples she gives of this metaphor are the following:

▼ ▼ ▼ ▼ ▼ ▼

Trotsky called Stalinism the cancer of Marxism; in China in the last year, the Gang of Four have become, among other things, "the cancer of China." John Dean explained Watergate to Nixon: "We have a cancer within." . . . The standard metaphor of Arab polemics . . . is that Israel is "a cancer in the heart of the Arab World"; and I once wrote, in the heat of despair over America's war on Vietnam, that "the white race is the cancer of human history."[26] ▼ ▼ ▼

Sontag then examines possible harms resulting from such uses of the cancer metaphor. She points to the pain inflicted on people who actually have cancer. She notes that they may be seriously hurt by "hearing their disease's name constantly being dropped as the epitome of evil." Perhaps even more harmful is the oversimplification associated with these uses of this

---

24.   George Lakoff and Mark Johnson, *Metaphors We Live By* (Chicago: University of Chicago Press, 1980), p. 3.

25.   Susan Sontag, *Illness as Metaphor* (New York: Vintage Books, 1978), p. 3.

26.   Sontag, pp. 81–82.

metaphor. Sontag notes that such oversimplification often invites self-righteousness, if not fanaticism.[27]

Beardsley's discussion of a different but equally interesting historic use of metaphor further illustrates the importance of critically assessing the appropriateness and utility of these rhetorical figures. Beardsley assesses the potential rhetorical impact of Thomas Jefferson's letter describing the First Amendment's religious exercise clause as a "wall of separation between church and state." Beardsley asks:

▼▼▼▼▼▼

What is conjured up when we picture this situation as a "wall of separation"? A wall is opaque and impermeable; it marks areas off decisively and definitively; it is more solid and enduring than, say, a fence; the parties on both sides might not even be aware of each others' existence; etc.[28] ▼▼▼

Beardsley goes on to suggest that this type of image may, if unquestioned, jeopardize the quality of a person's decision making. He notes, for example, that adopting Jefferson's metaphor could give readers a false sense of security neither intended nor implied by the First Amendment's freedom of religion clause. As with most metaphors, Jefferson's requires readers to carefully consider its implications before succumbing to its persuasive power.

In sum, metaphors may serve valuable purposes to decision makers, teachers, and advocates. However, as with other arguments by comparison, metaphors need to be presented with great care, sensitivity, and wisdom, and received with caution and critical awareness.

Similes also need to be used with awareness and care. Like metaphors, similes have significant power to influence audiences. During his trial, for example, Oliver North said, "I felt like a pawn in a chess game being played by giants."[29] This simile had the potential to influence jurors who had to decide whether North was a victim or a responsible culprit in the Iran-Contra affair.

Unlike the more hidden associations made by metaphors, the association made by this and most other similes is relatively evident. The term "like" makes evident the fact that a comparison or association is being made. It does not follow, however, that little care needs to be taken in evaluating a simile's acceptability and usefulness. Consider, for example, the following simile heard often during World War II: "A racially mixed person is like a syphilitic."[30] Although today most people see the horror, injustice, and dan-

---

27. Sontag, pp. 82–83.

28. Beardsley, *Thinking Straight,* pp.165–166.

29. Cited in *Newsweek,* April 17, 1989, p. 20.

30. Cited in Sontag, p. 83.

gerous implications of this simile, there was a time when its authors enjoyed a frighteningly large audience.

A fourth type of argument form that relies on comparison is the *argument by example*. Unlike arguments by analogy, metaphor, and simile, arguments by example develop associations between terms in the *same* sphere. The pattern of this form is:

▾ **Argument by example:** *A* is to *B*   as   *A* is to *C*

The field of law relies heavily on this form of argument.[31] The following case is representative:

▾▾▾▾▾▾

John Doe is on trial for assault with intent to kill. Doe's attorney, Poe, is able to show that Doe was under the influence of alcohol at the time he perpetrated the assault. Further, Poe finds a precedent—previous judicial ruling—in which a man under the influence of alcohol perpetrated an assault similar to that committed by Doe. The man in this previous case was found not guilty because he was held not responsible for his actions while under the influence of alcohol. Poe uses this precedent to build a comparison between the precedent and Doe's case. Poe compares the facts of Doe's case with the facts of the previous case and concludes that, as in the previous case, Doe should not be held responsible for his actions while under the influence of alcohol. ▾▾▾

If Poe succeeds at establishing her comparison, she will have made a strong case for finding John not guilty. But if the dissimilarities between Doe's case and the precedent are greater than the similarities, Poe's argument by example will be weak.

Arguments by comparison appear not only in law but in argumentation within every field. Few people would deny the "importance of analogy in the workings of the intellect."[32] We have seen further the major role that metaphors, similes, and arguments by example play in a wide variety of practical contexts.

Other nondemonstrative inference forms also play an important role in argumentation, debate, and decision making. Among these are argument from authority, argument from cause, argument by sign, argument by paradox, and argument by generalization. In some contexts, these types of arguments make use of quasi-logical deductive inference forms. In other contexts

---

31.   Noted legal scholar Edward H. Levi goes so far as to suggest that argument by example is the principal argument form in legal reasoning. See Levi's *An Introduction to Legal Reasoning* (Chicago: University of Chicago Press, 1949).

32.   Perelman and Olbrechts-Tyteca, p. 371.

they are shaped inductively. Regardless of context, the usefulness of quasi-logical inference forms depends on their satisfaction of rigorous evaluation standards. Later chapters will provide detailed discussions of these standards.

▼ ▼ ▼
SUMMARY

Claims are the most fundamental elements of argumentation. Empirical or factual claims may usually be verified with data derived through experience. Value claims express aesthetic, value, and other types of judgments. Policy claims prescribe rules, regulations, laws, and so on.

Among the most important elements of argumentation are issues. An issue arises whenever there is a clash between two or more claims. Determining which issues are central and which are nonessential helps arguers make the most effective use of their time.

Whereas issues result from controversy, commonplaces are points of agreement. The more commonplaces—whether of value, fact, or definition—that arguers find, the more effectively they can use their limited time.

Presumptions also significantly influence the nature of argumentation. There are different types of presumptions. Technical presumptions are imposed on decision makers in an effort to protect the integrity of the decision-making process. In contrast, decision-making groups or communities select conventional presumptions. Some presumptions are ideal, others are both ideal and real, and still others are real but not ideal.

Every presumption—whether conventional or technical, ideal or real—is accompanied by a burden of proof. Regardless of the argumentation context, presumptions and burdens of proof play significant roles in determining the appropriateness and value of specific arguments.

Definitions are also important to effective argumentation. They help arguers find issues, commonplaces, presumptions, and burdens of proof by providing a sense of how terms are being used. Definitions help provide the common language needed to effectively use argumentation.

Evidence is also important to good argumentation. Evidence is the most common source of support for a controversial claim. Usually, when arguers are asked to prove or defend their claims, they are being asked to provide evidence.

Specific instances, statistics, and testimony are among the most commonly used types of evidence. Examples and illustrations are specific instances. To be useful, examples—whether real, or hypothetical, or illustrative—should be representative, sufficient in number, and well matched with the arguers' shared conception of reality. Similarly, statistics should come from the most reliable sources, rely on valid measurements, and be current and representative. The value of testimony is tied to the general and topical credibility of the source.

Drawing and evaluating inferences are also fundamental dimensions of good argumentation. Many forms of inference are available. Formal logicians—who study the structures of inferences—have developed formal criteria for determining whether a demonstrative argument is valid.

Arguments intended to help decision makers decide which action to take serve different purposes. They serve deliberation, justification, and persuasion. These arguments occur in the realm of the probable and address rhetorical, rather than mathematical, probability. These arguments rely on a variety of inductive and deductive nondemonstrative forms of inference.

Inductive inferences move from the particular to the general. And deductive forms move from the general to the particular. Deductive quasi-logical forms are adapted from the classical syllogism: "All people are mortal; Socrates is a person; therefore, Socrates is mortal." Analogies, metaphors, similes, and arguments by example are commonly used types of inductive inference.

Among the many forms of nondemonstrative argument inferences are argument from authority, argument from cause, argument by sign, argument by paradox, and argument by generalization. The usefulness of these inference forms depends on their satisfaction of the rigorous evaluation standards discussed in later chapters.

▾ ▾ ▾
EXERCISES

1. Select a controversial topic of national concern. Present your point of view on this topic to an opposing classmate. Through dialogue with this classmate, discover three major issues, define relevant terms, find as many commonplaces as possible, and find enough evidence to present persuasive arguments on the three issues. Finally, prepare the best arguments you can in support of your views on the three issues. Present these arguments to your opposing classmate.

2. List five facts and values currently accepted as commonplaces in the United States. Next, isolate a specific context and list five facts and values accepted as commonplaces by the argumentation participants in this context.

3. Listen to a televised discussion of a controversial issue (during a talk show or news program, for example). Identify and evaluate arguments by comparision employed by the participants.

4. Consider Tristan's analogical argument. Develop a refutation that you believe James could provide to overcome the persuasive impact of Tristan's argument.

5. Identify a decision-making group or community. Next, identify a topic they might discuss with interest. Finally, identify one technical presumption that would influence the nature of the discussion and two conven-

tional presumptions that would be likely to influence the outcome of the discussion.

6. Read the following passages from Tussman's *Government and the Mind.*[33]

▼▼▼▼▼▼

More fundamental and inalienable than even the war power stands the tutelary power of the state, or, as I shall call it, the teaching power.

The teaching power is the inherent constitutional authority of the state to establish and direct the teaching activity and institutions needed to ensure its continuity and further its legitimate general and special purposes. It is rather strange that a governmental power so visible in its operation and so pervasive in effect should lack a familiar name. The Supreme Court refers to the power of the state "to prescribe regulations to promote peace, morals, education, and good order of the people . . ."—a power, it adds casually, "sometimes termed its 'police power.' . . ." But it will prove useful if we separate out the school and call the power of government which comes to focus there by its own appropriate name. The teaching power is a peer to the legislative, the executive, and the judicial powers, if it is not, indeed, the first among them. ▼▼▼

a. Identify three factual claims and three value claims in these passages.

b. Find three assumptions that Tussman makes in these passages. Are these likely to be accepted or controversial?

c. Identify two issues that Tussman's passages address.

d. Find Tussman's conclusion, and identify two premises that he uses to support the conclusion.

e. Write two paragraphs arguing against Tussman's conclusion.

f. Find and evaluate Tussman's argument(s) by comparison.

7. Read the following excerpts from a newspaper editorial by science writer Earle Holland.[34]

▼▼▼▼▼▼

Bald Facts Are Enough to Throw You Off Your Feed

Most leaders in the field of risk communications will agree that fear of the unknown plays a major role in the public's misunderstanding of true risk. [National Resources Defense Council Senior Lawyer Al] Meyerhoff's presenta-

---

33. Joseph Tussman, *Government and the Mind* (Oxford: Oxford University Press, 1977), p. 54.

34. *Columbus Dispatch,* January 22, 1989, p. E-7. Reprinted with permission.

tion at the annual meeting of the American Association for the Advancement of Science committed the classic sin—it scared the heck out of the audience.

Instead of making a strong case for how hard it is to accurately portray the extent of chemical and pesticide poisoning in the country, he dumped out a mountain of toxic facts guaranteed to alarm, rather than inform, the public:

▼ Many of the 2 billion pounds of chemicals used by farmers are the byproducts of the nation's chemical warfare research after World War II. And only about 1 percent of the pesticides actually affect the pests they're aimed at.

▼ There are at least 200 different types of pesticides used on the food we eat, and many of them cannot be removed by simple washing of fruits and vegetables.

▼ The federal Food and Drug Administration, the policing agency charged with safeguarding our food supply, uses tests that can detect less than half of the chemicals used on foods.

[Meyerhoff] discussed at least 20 different species of crop pests that have mutated into forms against which no pesticides will work. And because of that, we lost about the same percentage of our crops to insects now as we did 40 years ago.

Only the price tag now is much greater. Not only are millions of dollars spent annually on buying these pesticides, farmers are now suffering much higher rates of certain cancers than would have been thought. Soft tissue sarcomas and particular lymphomas are on the rise among this group.

Meyerhoff played into the typical role of presenting frightening statistics, for the most part out of any rational context. In doing so, he played to the fear and ignorance of the audience and the public—just the same way this column has done. Surely, there must be a better way to inform and protect the public without having to scare the daylights out of them. But if there is, will the public pay enough attention to find out? ▼ ▼ ▼

a.   What contributions, if any, does this column make to our understanding of differences between mathematical and rhetorical probability?

b.   Find three assumptions that Holland makes in these passages. Are these likely to be accepted or controversial?

c.   Identify two issues that Holland's passages address.

d.   Find Holland's conclusion, and identify two premises that he uses to support the conclusion.

e.   Do you find Holland's argument persuasive? Why or why not?

f.   Write two paragraphs arguing against Holland's conclusion.

8.   Critically assess the following metaphors. What images does each evoke? How might each influence its readers' perceptions? In what contexts, if any, do you believe each might encourage or discourage thoughtful reflection?

    a.   That idea gave me food for thought.

    b.   This is the autumn of his life.

    c.   They have a May-December romance.

    d.   Judy is a dark horse in next week's election.

    e.   We must fight with all our might in this war against illiteracy.

9.   List and critically assess five commonly used metaphors.

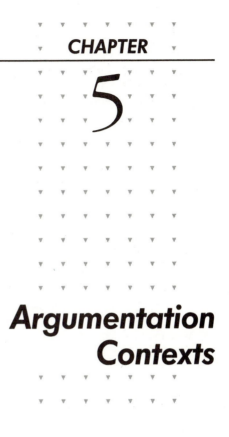

CHAPTER

5

Argumentation Contexts

Chapters 1 through 4 addressed the importance of critical thinking and the value of argumentation to the critical thinking process. These chapters also introduced the basic elements of critical thinking and argumentation.

Throughout the previous chapters, you learned that context plays an important role in argumentation. Chapter 5 directly discusses that role. This chapter shows that argumentation is only meaningful in relation to an *audience* and that thinking critically involves thinking about *something*. Argumentation and critical thinking cannot meaningfully occur outside a context.

Two types of audiences—*general* and *specialized*—are introduced in this chapter. We will also discuss a special category of audience that combines some features of generalized audiences and some features of specialized audiences. This *composite audience* includes openminded, interested, well-informed people who are capable of following extended argument.[1]

---

1. This definition is adapted from Carlin Romano's definition of Perelman's "universal audience" in "Rhetorically Speaking," *Voice,* May 1983, p. 47.

The chapter also introduces three types of argumentation contexts: those involving *two-way* communication, those involving *one-way* communication, and those involving both types of transactions. Two-way contexts include all *dialogic* contexts. One-way communication contexts include *public address* and *written communication* contexts. Most *special contexts* employ both two-way and one-way communication transactions.

▼ ▼ ▼

TYPES OF AUDIENCES

All argumentation addresses an audience. The *audience* is the *person or group of persons for whom argumentation is developed and to whom it is presented.* Whether written, presented over a radio broadcast, to a live audience, or on the television screen, argumentation is meaningful only in relation to a receiver. This is what argumentation theorists Chaim Perelman and L. Olbrechts-Tyteca have in mind when they write that "it is in terms of an audience that an argumentation develops."[2]

When you conceive arguments for a dialogue with your classmates, they are your audience. When you write a paper for your teacher, he or she is your audience. In these cases, the audience is evident. You are likely to have opportunities to learn something about these audiences' beliefs, expectations, and values, so that you can effectively develop your arguments for them.

Often, however, you will not be so fortunate. Sometimes, you will be unable to anticipate your actual audience; even more often you won't have opportunities to discuss issues with audience members. In these situations, you will be forced to imagine your audience and their beliefs, expectations, interests, values, and so on. Argumentation directed toward these elusive audiences can be difficult to construct. Similarly, when you evaluate argumentation, you sometimes have information that clearly establishes the nature of the work's audience. Arguments presented by classmates strictly for class consumption fit this category.

But often it is difficult to ascertain the nature of the audience for whom argumentation—especially written—was developed. In these circumstances, you can turn to historical sources for information about the context in which the argumentation was conceived and presented. You can also go to the actual text of the argumentation to find clues about the audience. These textual clues lead you to an *implied* audience.

---

2. Chaim Perelman and L. Olbrechts-Tyteca, *The New Rhetoric* (Notre Dame, Ind.: University of Notre Dame Press, 1969), p. 5.

Language style, examples used, commonplaces exploited, issues raised, all provide clues about the work's intended audience. How sophisticated is the text's sentence structure? What kinds of examples does the author or speaker use? What assumptions does the author or speaker expect the audience to grant? What is the nature of the controversy raised in the work? Answering these and related questions will help you characterize the work's implied audience.

As you develop your own arguments, you need to keep these same questions in mind. Argumentation serves its purposes best when it carefully anticipates its audience. *Sensitivity to audiences is a primary requisite of good argumentation.*

Just as a sensitivity to audience helps arguers develop effective arguments, the nature of the audience helps determine the value of the arguments to the decision-making process. There are many different kinds of audiences, each with its own characteristics. Argumentation developed for some of these kinds of audiences is more likely to serve good decision making than is argumentation designed for others.

General audiences include people with differing levels of expertise, but often sharing a common interest. Alex Pacheco, a coordinator for a national animal welfare organization, often addresses general audiences. When Pacheco presents arguments at public meetings, he is speaking to an audience that does not specialize in his subject. They do not come to the meeting with expertise about his subject, nor do they share a jargon for discussing it. They form a general audience.

One of Pacheco's industrial counterparts is American Farm Bureau Federation representative Hugh Johnson. In his discussions about the animal welfare movement, Johnson wisely admonishes his colleagues to direct their public relations campaign to a general audience. He writes, for example, "Emphasize your concern for your animals in interviews with the media."[3] Agricultural leaders understand the importance of using the media to bring their message to the general public.

Similarly, when 1988 presidential candidates George Bush and Michael Dukakis participated in two televised joint appearances, they addressed their remarks to the entire nation. Their campaign consultants carefully prepared these candidates to consider the values, interests, beliefs, and expectations of this general audience.

President Reagan's 1987 State of the Union address was directed to an even more general audience: members of Congress, the viewing American public, and people from other nations throughout the world. Although members of Congress form a specialized audience, the general nature of the rest

---

3.   Hugh S. Johnson, "Animal Rights Activists Harass Agriculture," *Buckeye Farm News,* September 1988, p. 21.

of President Reagan's audience allows us to conclude that he was addressing a highly general audience.

Other audiences are *specialized* as opposed to general. Specialized audiences come to a communication situation with their own language and expertise. Dr. Hogan's speech before an international meeting of fellow physicists provides an example. A noted nuclear physicist, Dr. Hogan presented arguments to support her latest thesis about nuclear fusion. Members of her audience share a specialized language that is foreign to most laypersons. The people in Dr. Hogan's audience also share a specific set of expectations and beliefs and specialized knowledge about nuclear physics. Dr. Hogan developed her speech for and presented it to a highly specialized audience.

Similarly, when a lawyer addresses the Supreme Court, the lawyer's audience is highly specialized. Supreme Court justices have a shared specialty language and expertise and a set of expectations not shared by the rest of the population.

Even members of community-based organizations can form a specialized audience. When Alex Pacheco speaks to his coworkers about a specific strategy, his audience is highly specialized. They share jargon, expertise, and a set of expectations not common to persons outside their group. Similarly, when factory-farming advocates discuss strategies with members of the Farm Bureau, they are most effective when their language and persuasive strategies are directed at this specialized audience.

While an audience may be specialized or general in nature, they may also be *informed* or *uninformed.* For example, Dr. Hogan's audience may be well informed about the study of nuclear physics and hence specialists in Dr. Hogan's topic. But they may not be well informed about the political and ethical implications of implementing some of their proposed programs for defense.

Additionally, audience members' critical thinking, listening, and reading skills may be more or less developed. As a result, members may have varying degrees of expertise at making critical judgments about the information available to them. The more audiences develop their critical thinking skills, the more sophisticated the argumentation available to them may be. In this important sense, the careful development of audiences' critical thinking, listening, speaking, and reading skills significantly improves the speaker's or writer's possibility for meaningfully using argumentation.

John Stuart Mill writes accordingly:

▼▼▼▼▼▼

The greatest orator, save one, of antiquity, has left it on record that he always studied his adversary's case with as great, if not still greater, intensity than even his own. What Cicero practiced as the means of forensic success requires to be imitated by all who study any subject in order to arrive at the truth. He who knows only his own side of the case knows little of that. His reasons may be good, and no one may have been able to refute them. But if he is equally unable to refute the reasons on the opposite side, if he does not so much as know what they are, he has no ground for preferring either opinion.

So essential is this discipline to a real understanding of moral and human subjects that, if opponents of all-important truths do not exist, it is indispensable to imagine them and supply them with the strongest arguments which the most skillful devil's advocate can conjure up.[4] ▾ ▾ ▾

▾ ▾ ▾
THE COMPOSITE AUDIENCE

What Mill has in mind is a kind of *composite audience*. This is an audience, either imagined or real, that includes people whose critical thinking skills permit them to make reasoned decisions about controversial issues. Members of the composite audience also have enough information on the particular topic to make an informed judgment about it.

A composite audience may be specialized or general. For example, those in Dr. Hogan's audience who were both familiar with her topic and adept at critical thinking formed her composite audience.

Often, composite audiences are not specialized at all. For example, most people viewing the televised Bush-Dukakis debates were not specialized. Yet many viewers were well informed about the issues the candidates raised. Many were also adept critical listeners, viewers, and thinkers. These people formed the debaters' composite audience.

In practical contexts, where policy choices affect specific groups of people, decision makers must take great care to help potentially affected groups develop the critical thinking skills they need to become members of the composite audience. Policy makers in a democracy such as ours also fulfill their roles most effectively when they help their constituents gain enough information about even the most complex proposal to be able to make a reasonable assessment of competing perspectives on the proposal. In this way, decision makers help ensure that the people affected by their decisions become an important part of their composite audience.

Through such an audience-enhancement process, decision makers are able to acquire vital information otherwise unavailable to them. For example, the tragic oil spill that devastated Alaska's once pristine Prince William Sound in March, 1989, directly affected not only thousands of animals, but thousands of people as well. The area's fishermen suffered particularly difficult losses. Less direct, but no less severe, was the loss felt by people who viewed Prince William Sound as one of the nation's last wilderness preserves. It is difficult

---

4.   John Stuart Mill, *On Liberty* (1859; reprint Indianapolis: Bobbs-Merrill, 1956), pp. 45–46.

to estimate the sadness these people felt as they saw the "vast sheet of oil" that "could set records for loss of birds, fish and mammals."[5]

This tragedy led some policy makers to reevaluate the soundness of our nation's Alaskan oil exploration program. A decision maker whose only knowledge of the topic came from scientific reports and expert testimonials would be unlikely to have an understanding of the relevant issues adequate to form a reasoned judgment about them. What would be missing for this decision maker, among other things, would be an understanding of the perspective of those affected by the policy in question. But this perspective is only available if the people affected by a policy are included in the debate about it. And to be included, these people must be offered the requisite information and the opportunity to develop necessary critical thinking skills.

At the same time, lay citizens in this country will serve their interests best if they make the extra effort needed to become well-informed members of the composite audience. Learning to reason, to critically read and listen, to speak persuasively, and to make effective use of available information helps prepare even the least formally trained citizen to play an active role in public policy making.

Learning to imagine a composite audience is one of the most helpful tools for the development of these skills. As Mill has pointed out, an ideal audience is rarely available for one's arguments. Often, we must create this ideal in our own minds. When manifest in an actual person or group, this type of audience usually appears in the context of a meaningful dialogue with reasonable and well-informed peers. But an ideal audience may also be manifest as a *concept* that we generate when we imagine the most ideal opposition. To envision this ideal audience, we ask ourselves why reasonable, informed people would disagree with us. Good dialogue with an actual audience provides direct input into the process of conceiving this ideal composite audience.

Use of this critical thinking tool is particularly valuable when you are asked to make hasty decisions. How often have you been told by a sales agent, for example, that a "special deal" will only be available to you if you decide to purchase the product or service "on the spot," without further consideration? Have you ever been urged to buy a condominium, car, travel opportunity, or piece of furniture without taking time to consider your options? In these and other high-pressure situations, you may find yourself confronted with someone who has a strong self-interest in selling you the product or service.

If possible, it is wise to simply walk away from such a situation so that you can take the time to critically evaluate your options. However, sometimes leaving is not an option. In these situations, imagining a composite audience

---

5. Malcolm W. Browne, "In Once-Pristine Sound, Wildlife Keels Under Oil's Impact," *New York Times,* April 4, 1989, p. Y-17.

can save you the consequences of making a poor decision. Taking the time to ask yourself how a reasonable, well-informed person might argue against the sales agent's position will afford you the opportunity to critically assess the strengths and weaknesses of the seller's arguments. Based on this assessment, you will be in a much stronger position to make your decision, even if you have not left the site of the potential sale.

Use of an imagined composite audience can be even more valuable when you have time to make a considered judgment. Suppose that you have to decide whether to go to law school, to go to business school, or to assist your mother in developing her business. If you are leaning in a particular direction on this decision, imagine a composite audience that would argue on behalf of an alternative position. Formulate the most persuasive arguments you can for this audience, anticipating their best reasons for disagreeing with you. This process will significantly contribute to the quality of your overall decision making.

Although sometimes ideal, this audience can be real for you as you formulate your arguments. Preparing a speech or written text for this audience helps you consider likely predispositions toward your topic. This process will show you that even the views of an imagined composite audience are shaped by underlying assumptions, values, beliefs, and interests.

▼ ▼ ▼

TYPES OF CONTEXTS

Just as argumentation is developed for different types of audiences, it is also developed for and presented in at least three types of contexts. These types of contexts are distinguished by their use of different types of communication transactions. In some situations, the audience is made up of one or more persons who actively and directly contribute to the development of arguments. This type of transaction is called *two-way* communication.

Other times, arguments are developed for oral or written presentation to an audience who will listen to or read the arguments, but who will not *directly* participate in the development of the arguments. This type of communication is called *one-way* communication.

There are also contexts in which arguments are developed through both two-way and one-way communication. Usually, this type of argumentation occurs in specialized contexts, such as in the legal sphere.

Dialogic Contexts

Effective *dialogue* plays a vital role in most two-way argumentation contexts. But making effective use of dialogic communication first requires an understanding of the many functions that dialogues potentially fulfill. This understanding is best acquired by asking, What is a dialogue?

Most of us intuitively understand that dialogues involve *exchanges be-tween at least two people.* Less obvious is the fact that there are many different kinds of dialogues, motivated by differing goals and serving different functions. Some dialogues are intended to instruct or teach. Others are intended to reveal something previously unknown, either about the topic under consideration or about one or more participants in the exchange. A related group of dialogues is designed to help generate understanding. Still others are intended to help resolve conflicts, while a fifth group is used primarily to persuade either one or more participants in the dialogue, or an audience, of the communicator's viewpoint.

The type of dialogue most often associated with teaching is the *Socratic dialogue.* This type of exchange acquired its name from a Greek philosopher, Socrates. One of this philosopher's best-known students, Plato, immortalized his teacher's thoughts through a series of philosophical works. Plato and his mentor cared deeply about helping young philosophers develop their *dialectical* skills. For the Socratics, dialectic involved the use of dialogue in the form of questions and answers designed to uncover important social, moral, and factual truths.

Teachers employing the Socratic method use a question-and-answer approach to help students arrive at "the truth" on their own. Some teachers believe that when students actively participate in their own learning through Socratic dialogue, they will be more likely to retain their acquired knowledge than are students who passively acquire the same knowledge. These teachers also believe that classroom use of Socratic dialogue helps students acquire the questioning habit so crucial to effective decision making.

The Socratic method of teaching is often employed by teachers who have specific answers in mind. For example, a history teacher who asks students how the American Constitution was formulated may well have a specific answer or set of answers in mind. Some teachers, however, view the classroom as a kind of forum and use creative dialogue to seek an understanding and meaningful resolution of complex social, political, and ethical issues. Professor Harrison, for example, uses dialogue to seek solutions to ethical problems that afford no simple or obviously correct answer. He opens questions for dialogue in the hope that the students will help him find new, creative answers for these challenging problems.

Teachers are not alone in their instructional and creative uses of dialogic communication. Counselors and therapists often use dialogue to help clients understand their problems in new, more constructive ways. They hope that this new understanding will help clients more effectively deal with the challenges in their lives. Counselors and therapists also use dialogue to learn more about a client's psychological state. And medical doctors often make similar use of dialogic communication. In an effort to make the most accurate diagnosis of a patient's medical condition, doctors use dialogue as a tool of discovery.

Dialogues are not only used for the purposes of instruction and discovery, however. They may also be effectively used to persuade. Consider, for example, dialogues between television journalists and spokespersons for government agencies or businesses. The journalist may be using the dialogue to uncover a "truth" about the spokesperson's agency or business. But in most instances, the spokesperson is using the dialogue to persuade audiences of the agency's integrity, innocence, quality of performance, or other desirable qualities. For the spokesperson, the dialogue has been successful if the audience is persuaded to accept his or her portrayal of the agency or business.

Written dialogues, though not technically dialogic because they are written rather than spoken exchanges, nonetheless illustrate how dialogues may be used to persuade audiences. Plato's written dialogues, for example, can be seen as efforts to persuade readers of his philosophical theses. The philosopher David Hume used dialogue to persuade readers to accept his philosophical perspective in his *Dialogues Concerning Natural Religion.* In *Walden Two,* B. F. Skinner, a well-known advocate of the behaviorist school of psychology, uses dialogues to cleverly mask his effort to persuade.

In contrast, dialogic communication between members of the composite audience is designed primarily to enhance the quality of participants' decision making. Dialogic communication in this specific context has the potential to serve important critical thinking functions. Through dialogue, decision makers are able to directly challenge each others' points of view. In this way, dialogic exchanges help expose flaws in our own as well as in our colleagues' reasoning.

In the following example, Jeffrey enters a dialogue believing that homosexual persons should not be permitted to teach in public schools. Through dialogue, he discovers that some of his reasons for maintaining this belief may have been ill-founded:

Jeffrey: Homosexual persons should not be allowed to teach in public schools because they might molest the children.

Joan: But approximately 88 percent of all child molesters are heterosexual men. Less than 10 percent are homosexual men, less than 3 percent are heterosexual women, and less than .05 percent are homosexual women. Yet the population is made up of at least 51 percent women, and at least 10 percent of those women are homosexual.

Martha: Joan is right. By your analysis, Jeffrey, we should permit only women to teach in public schools and we should be comfortable hiring homosexual women.

Jeffrey: I see your point. But there is another more important reason that we should not permit homosexual persons to teach in public schools. Because children admire their teachers, they might decide to follow their homosexual teacher's role model and opt for a homosexual life style. This would seriously hurt our children.

Joan: But Jeffrey, as you probably know, it is not at all clear that a person's sexual orientation is chosen. Scientists are not sure whether a person's sexual orientation occurs at or before birth, whether it is socialized or learned, or whether it is a combination of the two. We do know, though, that at least 10 percent of the population is homosexual and that nearly all of these homosexuals had heterosexual parents. We also know that people are seldom able to decide who they will find sexually attractive. Many of the great tragedies of the world have resulted because someone fell in love with the wrong person. If we can't decide *who* we will be attracted to, what makes you think we can decide *what type* of person we will find attractive?

Martha: Exactly! Besides, what makes you think that one positive role model would have greater influence on a child than the child's parents, peers, other teachers, religious leaders, the media, the community, and so on? The whole country is completely oriented toward heterosexual behavior. Children see men and women kissing each other in the park, on the street, and so on. Television programming leads them to believe that male-female romance is proper and even magical. They certainly have many more heterosexual role models than homosexual role models.

Joan: Yes, and that makes having at least one positive homosexual role model itself important. We know that at least 10 percent of the children attending school are homosexual. It is important for them to be given at least one positive homosexual role model in their education. Not having such a role model can seriously harm these children. It can also hurt relationships between the heterosexual and homosexual children who must live and work together for the betterment of everyone's future.

Jeffrey: But children do not know the sexual orientation of their teacher, so how could a homosexual teacher be a positive role model?

Martha: If children do not know the sexual orientation of their teacher, what is the problem in the first place?!

This dialogue helped Jeffrey to evaluate the reasons behind his claim. Through this exchange, Jeffrey learned that his thinking may have been influenced by inadequate or dubious information. He was not previously aware of the data regarding child molestation. Nor was he familiar with studies related to the nature of sexual orientation. The dialogue also helped him see an inconsistency in his reasoning. Martha revealed that Jeffrey's concerns stemmed from the assumption that children would know the sexual orientation of their teacher. Yet later in the dialogue he maintained that children would not know the sexual orientation of their teacher.

Based on the insights he gained in this dialogue, Jeffrey can now consider what other reasons he might have for his view that homosexuals should not be allowed to teach in public schools. Perhaps his religious allegiance leads him to his conclusion. Or perhaps he has more deeply personal, emotional reasons for his beliefs about homosexuality. Perhaps further dialogue will help Jeffrey discover yet some other basis for his views. Or, perhaps as a result of this dialogue, Jeffrey will find himself reconsidering his position. In either case, while of little benefit to either Martha or Joan, the dialogue was of great benefit to Jeffrey.

The most valuable dialogues, of course, are those in which all participants gain insights from the exercise. In these dialogues, issues of fact, policy, and value are discussed at length. Such dialogues uncover areas of agreement, establish points of controversy, and reveal underlying value and interest hierarchies. Above all, successful dialogic exchanges between critical thinkers help participants reevaluate the reasons on which they have based their initial opinions on a given topic.

But dialogues are not the only valuable type of argumentative interaction. Shaping good arguments for one-way communication may also be valuable for both the presenter and the receiver of the arguments.

Written Communication Contexts

Books, essays, commentaries, and even political cartoons are but a few examples of the forms through which authors present arguments to audiences. These forms of written communication are considered one-way transactions because the reader does not *directly* participate in the making of the text. Yet it does not follow that the reader is not an important *indirect* participant in the text's development.

The most obvious role for the audience occurs before a single word is written. Authors of arguments must first *conceive* of their audience. What are the audience's beliefs, expectations, and values? How can I best present my arguments to them in light of their predispositions? These are but a few of the questions that authors ask themselves before they develop their written arguments.

After the text is written, the audience again plays a fundamental role in influencing the text. Recall, for example, that reading always involves the process of *interpretation*. In Chapter 2, you learned that this complex process dramatically shapes our perceptions of the written or oral message. Through this complex process, readers give texts *meaning*.

The audience's indirect, but active, participation in the development of written texts helps written communication serve several important critical thinking functions. First, because writing convincing arguments requires the arguer to consider how his or her ideas will be received by others, the arguer is forced to consider what objections the audience members might construct as they read these arguments. At the same time, the presentation of good arguments helps readers to consider alternative perspectives and to evaluate their own ideas about the topic under consideration. In some cases, the author may introduce a concept that a member of the audience had not previously considered. In other instances, written arguments expose fallacies in an audience member's thinking process.

Public Address Contexts

The same may be said of public address contexts. Just as the author of written arguments must consider the audience before writing, the public address communicator must consider the audience before preparing his or her speech. And just as the reader's interpretation of the text gives it meaning, so does the audience's interpretation of a speech give the oral text meaning.

For example, when President Reagan's speech writers helped him prepare his 1987 State of the Union address, they first considered the values, beliefs, underlying assumptions, concerns, interests, and expectations of his audience. Their audience analysis led them to believe, for example, that the president should focus most of his attention on the favorable dimensions of his presidency. Little time should be spent discussing the president's role in, for example, providing the Iranians with weapons or providing underground money for the Contras against the will of Congress. Instead, the president should remind the American public of the blessings that America's freedoms give them and of the value of patriotism.

Following the president's address, leaders of the Democratic party gave a response. When these spokespersons were preparing their speeches, they too engaged in audience analysis. But their analysis required them to ask an additional layer of questions. Because they were responding to the speech of a popular president, their task was to pose questions that the audience would find reasonable and meaningful. Because President Reagan was known to be loved by many, and because he was known to have millions of faithful followers, the Democratic spokespersons had to find a way to constructively criticize the president's remarks without alienating these viewers and listeners.

Upon listening to these public presentations, the audience created new texts through their interpretations of what the president and the Democratic party leaders said. Audience members who listened with open and active minds were presented with much to consider. The Democratic response challenged the president's position on a number of issues. Similarly, the president's speech posed difficult questions for the Democratic leadership.

These are but a few of the ways in which public address contexts may contribute to the critical thinking process. Whether communicators present arguments in a dialogue or prepare arguments for presentation to a listening or reading audience, the process of shaping arguments for an audience contributes meaningfully to the decision-making process.

Legal Argument

The role of the audience in shaping good arguments is especially obvious in contexts that combine one- and two-way communication. The legal sphere provides useful examples of this type of communication.

The lawyer's job is to persuade a judge or jury to accept the client's point of view. In a criminal trial, for example, the defense attorney represents the defendant. This advocate's job is to persuade the judge or jury that the client should not be convicted. The prosecuting attorney represents the public and attempts to persuade the judge or jury that the defendant should be convicted. Ideally, these two advocates will present the best arguments possible for both sides. These arguments then equip the judge or jury to decide whether the defendant should be convicted.

The assumption underlying this system is that the truth will prevail when both advocates do their jobs well. This assumption is realized only when both advocates effectively present their cases to an open, reflective, and enlightened judge or jury. Central to the success of this process is the judge or jury's ability to evaluate the quality of the reasons given, to place the relevant facts and issues in an appropriate context, and to weigh the relevant values before making a decision. The case of Leroy Reed illustrates this point.

Leroy Reed was an ex-convict who had not violated his parole for nine years. Experts placed Leroy's literacy skills and intelligence at about second-grade level. In Leroy's home state, it is illegal for any convicted felon to own a firearm. Persons are to be convicted of this crime if they meet three conditions: (1) They are convicted felons (2) they own a firearm, and (3) they are aware that they own a firearm.

Leroy had been unemployed for many years. Watching television portrayals of private investigators led him to pursue that profession. Making use of his limited reading skills, he entered a mail-order class for private investigators. One of the requirements for completing this class was that the student purchase a gun.

Leroy met this requirement by purchasing a gun at the local gun shop. The gun he purchased looked much like the gun advertised in his mail-order class. Although he did not carry this gun with him, Leroy believed that owning the gun now qualified him to be a private investigator. He also believed that he should spend time at the county courthouse. Here he might find clients or otherwise serve the community.

One day, an official at the courthouse asked to see Leroy's identification. He showed the official the bill of sale for his gun. Later, the official discovered that Leroy was a convicted felon. He therefore asked Leroy to go home, get his gun, and take it to the district attorney's office. Leroy eagerly complied and turned the gun into the office. At that point, Leroy was arrested. He was a convicted felon who knowingly owned a gun.

The jury asked to decide Leroy's fate did not face disputed facts. Leroy's defense attorney admitted that Leroy did knowingly own a gun. However, he was able to prove that Leroy was neither aware of the law nor aware that he was considered a convicted felon. The prosecuting attorney conceded these facts but argued that they were not relevant to Leroy's conviction. The law in question, he argued, did not require Leroy to be aware either of the law or of his status as a convicted felon. The law only specified that Leroy had to know that he owned a gun.

In his closing statement, the prosecuting attorney emphasized these facts to the jury. And he reminded the jurors of the promise that each of them had made during the court's interviews of them. Each had promised to look as objectively as possible at the facts of the case. As the prosecuting attorney said:

▼ ▼ ▼ ▼ ▼ ▼

There's an old saying in the law that ignorance of the law is not a defense. You indicated that you—none of you—would speculate. You wouldn't be looking for some sympathetic reason or some conjured-up reason to avoid your responsibility.

That, in fact, the same law applies to everybody, but there—if there's a statute or if there's a law as the court gives it to you, you would apply that law to those facts, no matter who the person was, whether they're short, tall, black, or white. None of those kinds of things, like race, weight, height, mental ability, would be a factor in your mind.

A person who has possessed a firearm, with knowledge that they possessed a firearm while being convicted of a felony, has violated that statute. The person is guilty.[6]   ▼ ▼ ▼

The jury's task was complex. On the face of it, they had an open-and-shut case before them, because Leroy had clearly violated the letter of the law. But a jury's job is not simply to determine whether the letter of the law has been violated. Juries are asked to consider what is just and fair in a given situation. They are required to assess whether the law should be applied in any given case and whose interests will be served by finding a defendant guilty or innocent.

The defense attorney emphasized this dimension of the jury's responsibility in his closing argument. He told them:

▼ ▼ ▼ ▼ ▼ ▼

You have the power, despite all the technical legality, to find Leroy Reed not guilty. You're not violating the law by doing this. You are using the full power

---

6. This quote, and the others that follow in Leroy Reed's case, are from the transcript of the proceedings provided by the producers of *Frontline: Inside the Jury Room* (Boston: WGBH Educational Foundation, 1986), pp. 2, 7, 14, 15, 25.

given to you by the constitution and by the laws of the state of Wisconsin. You know why you have that power? Because you're not just twelve people of any sort. You are a jury. You've been sworn as a jury. You've heard the testimony and the evidence as a jury. And, as a jury, you're an independent body of citizens from this community, and you speak with the voice of the community. You're independent of the judge. You're independent of the Milwaukee County District Attorney's office. And nobody's guilty, or not guilty, until you say so. ▾▾▾

This closing statement emphasized the grave responsibility jurors face in cases such as this. The jury's decision would, to some degree, seal this person's fate. It would also send a message to other Leroy Reeds, as well as to future district attorneys with similar cases.

Making a decision in Leroy Reed's case would require the jury to use all of the elements of good reasoning. They were given facts and reasoning by competing advocates, as well as instructions by the judge. Their task was to reach a unanimous verdict based both on these data and on their shared conceptions of justice and fairness.

Leroy Reed's jury struggled to competently fulfill their functions. Representative comments included one juror's question:

▾▾▾▾▾▾

I wonder if we could find room in the law—for those of us that feel we need to follow the letter of the law—that perhaps he didn't, in the full sense of the word, "know" he was a felon, and didn't, in the full sense of the word, "know" that he possessed a firearm. ▾▾▾

In response, another juror argued:

▾▾▾▾▾▾

The hang-up seems to be in the word, "Did he 'know.' " He knew he had to register it [the gun], which he did. He knew he had to have a permit for it. So, on one hand you're saying, "Well, he knew this and he knew that, but he didn't know he had the gun." ▾▾▾

After one and a half hours of passionate but reasoned deliberation, the jury took a vote: three votes guilty, nine not guilty. In the absence of a unanimous decision, they had to continue their deliberations. Two hours later, another vote was taken. This time the vote was eleven not guilty and one guilty. At this point, the majority tried to persuade the one "holdout" that Leroy should not be convicted. To accomplish this task, one of the majority jurors asked the minority juror what appeared to be the deciding question:

▼▼▼▼▼▼

Do you think that he was able to . . . keep these two thoughts and link them together at the same time when he bought the firearm, that he was a convicted felon and that he was not supposed to own a firearm? Do you think he was able—do you think he had the—enough capacity to understand the ramifications of that? ▼▼▼

After two hours and twenty-eight minutes, the jurors unanimously decided that Leroy Reed should not be convicted. By the rules of our legal system, Leroy was therefore ruled innocent of the crime.

This example illustrates the diversity of intentions and accompanying roles that interact in our legal system. The defense and prosecuting attorneys seek to persuade the judge or jury. Although each presents only one side of the case, she or he does so knowing the other side will receive an equal opportunity to be heard. Thus, although the immediate goal of each advocate is to persuade the audience of a specific point of view, the ultimate goal of the exchange of arguments is good decision making.

Similarly, each juror enters the jury deliberation room predisposed toward a point of view. Yet, because their unifying goal is to make a reasoned decision, all of the jurors are expected to be open to each other's arguments. Each is asked to provide reasons for believing that the defendant should or should not be convicted. And all are receptive to these arguments.

Combining the two-way communication of cross-examination and jury deliberation with the one-way communication of lawyers' arguments to the judge or jury, the legal sphere makes effective use of argumentation.

This combination of communication styles is perhaps most evident, however, in Supreme Court deliberations. In more than 80 percent of the cases heard by the Supreme Court, the justices have the discretion not to hear the case. To help them decide to hear a case, advocates present written appeals. These appeals are then privately reviewed by each justice and then openly discussed by all of the justices.

Once a case is given the opportunity to be heard, advocates from competing sides present written briefs and oral arguments. During the oral argument phase, they may be questioned by any or all of the justices. Then the justices meet to openly discuss the case. At this time, vigorous dialogue helps shape each justice's position on the case. But the decisions are not always made here. Often, justices are asked to present written arguments to support their positions. These are then distributed, read, and discussed.

Finally, the justices make their decision. The chief justice then appoints someone representing the majority view (that is, the decision shared by at least five of the Court's nine members) to write the majority opinion. Dissenting justices—those not agreeing with the majority decision—may also write their own personal or joint opinions. Justices who agree with the decision but who do not agree with any aspect of the majority opinion may submit concurring opinions as well.

As you can see from the preceding example, the complex process of argumentation involves a wide variety of communication transactions, from dialogue, to written communication, to public address. Despite their differences, these types of transactions have in common their use of argumentation to assist decision making. This highly specialized context makes use of argumentation serving all of its possible functions, from persuasion, to deliberation, to justification. Yet all of these uses of argument are guided primarily by the shared goal of reaching the best decision possible.

In this book, we are exploring argumentation primarily as a tool for reasoned deliberation. In an important sense, we are approaching argumentation from the standpoint of the judge or jury. We come to the argumentation process because we want to test the quality of our reasons before we make judgments. We ask ourselves what arguments other jurors might give to oppose these perspectives or decisions. Whatever the topic, whatever the context, we attempt to envision the most reasonable arguments that other enlightened and informed jurors might pose against our point of view.

When we have an audience, we try to engage them in meaningful dialogue. Participants in these dialogues act as members of a jury, unified in the purpose of reaching the best judgment. These dialogues are used to find out exactly what beliefs, expectations, interests, values, and other reasons lead other reasonable, informed people to disagree with our point of view.

At the same time, we must recognize the vital role that persuasiveness plays in the decision-making process. Without the lawyers' persuasive presentation of competing sides, judges and jurors would not have access to the full range of views they need to make reasoned decisions.

Similarly, effective advocacy in other deliberation contexts enhances the value of argumentation to the reasoning process. Seeking the most persuasive arguments available, for as many sides of the issue as possible, is therefore central to all deliberation. Through the search for persuasive arguments we enlighten ourselves, and through the presentation of competing persuasive arguments we enlighten others. Whether in one-way communication or in two-way communication, the presentation of persuasive arguments plays a vital role in reasoned deliberation.

▾ ▾ ▾
SUMMARY

Argumentation is only meaningful when developed for and presented to an audience. There are many different types of audiences. The degree to which argumentation is able to effectively serve decision making depends, to a large degree, on the nature of the audience.

Specialized audiences have a shared language and expertise. A physicist speaking to other physicists is speaking to such a specialized audience. More general audiences do not share a specialized language or expertise. Presidential debates and State of the Union addresses are directed toward such general audiences.

In addition to being specialized or generalized, audiences may be informed or uninformed. There is more than one sense in which they may be informed, however. Audiences have varying degrees of knowledge about the topic under discussion. But they also have varying degrees of training in critical thinking, listening, and viewing.

The composite audience includes openminded, interested, well-informed people who are capable of following extended arguments. Designing arguments for the composite audience significantly contributes to the development of critical thinking skills and helps decision makers carefully consider the options available to them.

Just as there are many types of audiences, there are types of contexts, distinguished by their use of different types of communication transactions. Dialogic communication contexts make use of two-way communication. Written communication and public address contexts employ primarily one-way communication. Most special contexts, such as legal argument, employ both one-way and two-way communication.

In this book, we are exploring argumentation primarily as a tool for reasoned deliberation. We come to the argumentation process because we want to test the quality of our reasons before we make judgments.

At the same time, we should not overlook the valuable role that persuasiveness plays in deliberation. Through the search for persuasive arguments we enlighten ourselves, and through the presentation of competing persuasive arguments we enlighten others. Whether in one-way or in two-way communication, the presentation of persuasive arguments plays a vital role in reasoned deliberation.

▼ ▼ ▼

EXERCISES

1. Describe in as much detail as possible the audience to whom this book is addressed.

2. Write a short speech intended to persuade a poorly informed audience whose members have not yet developed their critical thinking skills. Next, write a short speech on the same topic intended to persuade a composite audience. Compare the quality of each speech.

3.   Review the following excerpts from an editorial by Universal Press syndicated columnist Mary Anne Dolan.[7]

▼ ▼ ▼ ▼ ▼ ▼

Conversation Becoming A Dying Art

The art of conversation, gradually enfeebled by too much talking technology and too few quiet walks in the woods, is now dangerously hovering on the brink of death.

When a perfectly good friend interrupts you with a gruff Sam Donaldson "Hold on there," and proceeds to create a lecture on the public right to know out of a simple chat regarding the local mail delivery, you smell the whiffs of a funeral pyre.

Curiously, at the same time that TV-addicted Americans listen 24 hours a day to people speaking extemporaneously with other people, we seem to be forgetting how to do it.

Television has changed the very pace of conversation. Which is to say, there is none. What was once the round-table rhythm of a strong waltz is a free-for-all cacophony, a contest to win by talking loudest and longest.

Questions, tools for broadening and probing the hands of deft conversationalists, are not questions anymore. Questions are statements, sometimes Koppelized with princely preliminaries such as, "With all due respect . . ." or "But surely Miss Vinderscratz, you don't believe . . ." or "Let's be fair here, Harvey. I'm sure you meant to say . . ."

Television isn't the only culprit in this conspiracy. The telephone—now available in cars, airplanes, bathrooms and on a pack you carry down the street—has people talking all the time. Nothing is stored up, mulled over, honed, shaped, made ready for articulate presentation.

We all end up sounding like combination political pollsters, White House analysts and pop psychologists all spouting instant analysis from the sidelines of life. Combination Bob Novaks, John Maddens and Oprah Winfreys.

But convenience foods have something to do with it too. A meal isn't cause for good conversation; it's what you eat when you watch the tube—if you're home—or what you play with while you're making a deal—if you're out.

I am in favor of a national day of silence. Not to commemorate anything or anyone in particular. But in the hope that if we all shut up for a while, we might find some things to really say to each other again. Not quotes from someone else's sound bites. Real things—thought and shared—between real people.   ▼ ▼ ▼

---

7.   *Columbus Dispatch,* August 8, 1988, p. A-11. Copyright 1988 Universal Press Syndicate. All rights reserved. Reprinted with permission.

a. Use critical analysis to make inferences about Dolan's implied audience and intention. To whom is this editorial addressed? What values and interests does Dolan seem to assume the readers have? What does she hope to achieve with this editorial?

b. Write a brief response to Dolan, using an imagined composite audience to formulate your thoughts.

4. Read the following description of Marlene's difficult decision:

▼▼▼▼▼▼

Marlene, a business school junior at a major university in California, is faced with a difficult decision. She has to decide whether to borrow money from the bank to purchase a new computer. Buying the computer now will greatly assist her in completing difficult school assignments. This is likely to improve her grade-point average, thereby giving her an edge when she applies to graduate school. However, if she buys the computer now, rather than waiting another year, she will pay a much higher price for it (the same model is likely to be available at a much lower price next year). Furthermore, she will be paying a great deal of interest to the bank. This will create a serious financial burden on Marlene for a number of years to come. Marlene already has a large debt waiting for her when she finishes her schooling. It is possible that adding to this debt now will leave her so financially strapped that she may have to work off the debt before she can start graduate school. ▼▼▼

a. Based on the facts available to you, develop the best arguments you can for and against buying the computer at this time. As you develop the arguments, imagine a composite audience's response to them.

b. Imagine that Marlene asked you to help her make the decision whether to buy the computer at this time. Develop an imaginary dialogue you might have with her. What questions would you ask her? What arguments would you develop to help her with this decision?

Argumentation and Communication Ethics

Chapter 5 stressed the importance of context in practical argumentation. The role that audience plays in shaping and evaluating practical arguments raises important ethical questions. For example, if arguments are to be evaluated in relation to an audience, should success be the primary criterion for assessing an argument's quality? On this view, wouldn't Hitler's arguments be among the best samples of argument available? And if persuasion is as central to good argumentation as previous chapters suggest, how far should an advocate go to try to persuade an audience?

This chapter addresses these and related questions of communication ethics. The chapter begins with an overview of relevant ethical considerations. This is followed by a discussion of guidelines for ethical argumentation.

The chapter suggests that successful use of cooperative argumentation requires advocates to satisfy rigorous ethical guidelines. Arguments addressed to a composite audience must strictly adhere to the *principles of fidelity and veracity.* Composite audiences demand argumentation that *reasons with,* rather than manipulates, them. These critical audiences expect advocates to *share* information and perspectives and to avoid *misstating opposition.* Arguments addressed to a composite audience are also expected to satisfy the rigorous criteria discussed in Chapter 8. Among other things, these arguments are expected to be *consistent, relevant,* and *coherent.*

By the end of this chapter, you will understand the ethical foundations of cooperative argumentation. You will also learn how valuable the tools of cooperative argumentation are to the resolution of ethical problems.

▼ ▼ ▼

ETHICAL CONSIDERATIONS

Communication ethicist Richard Johannesen writes that "potential ethical issues are inherent in any instance of communication between humans to the degree that communication can be judged on a right-wrong dimension, involves possible significant influence on other humans, and to the degree that the communicator consciously chooses specific ends sought and communicative means used to achieve those ends."[1]

As the discussion below will demonstrate, effective argumentation meets all of these conditions. To influence other humans, advocates choose argumentation strategies that will help them achieve their chosen ends. As such, argumentation "can be judged on a right-wrong dimension."

Because argumentation is a form of public communication, it is subject to the same ethical considerations as other forms of communication. How far should an advocate go to try to persuade an audience? If persuasiveness is important to deliberation, should advocates use only the most effective means to persuade their audiences? At what point does persuasiveness cease to be a help and begin to become a hindrance to the decision-making process?

These and other questions have important ethical dimensions. Skilled orators are able to manipulate audiences into accepting dangerous views. History provides numerous accounts of tragedies that resulted from such rhetorical effectiveness. Recall, for example, the Reverend Jim Jones, who persuaded his adult flock to kill themselves and their children. Remember Mussolini's ability to rouse audience passions. These orators' appeals to fears, prejudices, and biases were very effective, with devastating consequences.

---

1.   Richard L. Johannesen, *Ethics in Human Communication,* 2nd ed. (Prospect Heights, Ill.: Waveland Press, 1983), pp. 1–2.

In our daily lives, most of us have at one time or another become upset over the consequences of a skilled orator's unscrupulous tactics. Perhaps a great uncle expended valuable savings to purchase a worthless insurance policy because an actor he trusted gave public testimony on behalf of the policy's value. Or perhaps you lost a cherished friend to a manipulative group that exploits his talents and resources. Or consider your own disappointment at purchasing a flawed and overpriced product after listening to an intense sales pitch at the local discount appliance store. What about the money you sent to a local charity because you believed the spokesperson's impassioned testimony about it? How disheartening it is to later learn that the money you sent went into the pockets of an already rich fund-raising specialist.

Ethical considerations come into play whenever advocates use tools of persuasion to achieve their ends. Do the ends justify the means in communication? Which strategies of persuasion are ethical? Which are not? What guidelines should communicators use to determine whether their persuasive appeals are ethical? What role does a speaker's intention play in evaluating the speech's ethics? Should we measure a communicator's ethics by the effects of his or her messages?

These challenging questions are especially relevant to today's political and social climate. Some would describe this as an era of widespread cynicism, and there is strong support for this characterization. Studies of popular opinion during the 1988 presidential campaigns are especially telling. When asked whether they believed candidates were "mostly giving honest views on issues," a startling majority of people (74 percent) said that the candidates were "saying what they need[ed] to in order to get elected." Only 20 percent of those polled believed that the candidates were being "mostly honest."[2] This mistrust appears in other contexts as well. How many people in our society trust our public servants? How much faith do people have in the ethical intentions of business leaders? The popularity of "lawyer jokes" speaks to a growing mistrust in legal advocates as well.

These concerns are directly relevant to argumentation practitioners. We learned in Chapter 5 that argumentation takes place in a wide variety of contexts, with different types of audiences, and for a variety of purposes. A breakdown of trust in these contexts makes it difficult to find forums for cooperative argumentation. We have seen throughout this text that such forums play an important role in preserving democracy and in improving the quality of people's lives. Preserving these forums requires a sensitivity to standards for ethical argumentation. The remainder of this chapter will focus on these standards.

---

2.   Larry Mark (with Margaret Garrard Warner, Howard Fineman, Eleanor Clift, and Mark Starr), "The Smear Campaign," *Newsweek,* October 31, 1988, p. 19.

▼ ▼ ▼
GUIDELINES FOR ETHICAL ARGUMENTATION

Argumentation is a social process, the success of which depends on participants' understanding of and adherence to *mutually accepted norms.* These norms provide *standards for proper conduct* or *rules for right action.*[3] Norms for ethical argumentation differ in the various contexts discussed in Chapter 5. Argumentation addressed to specialized or generalized audiences, in one-way, dialogic, or varied communication settings, is governed by both general and particular norms. These norms help make effective and ethical communication possible.

This text has focused on cooperative argumentation addressed to a composite audience for the purposes of assisting reasoned decision making. As the discussion in the next section will demonstrate, this type of argumentation is governed by the most rigorous ethical standards. In this sense, adopting this approach to argumentation helps advocates learn the habit of ethical interaction.

The heart of this type of argumentation is its cooperative nature. You learned in Chapter 3 that cooperative arguments are usually more likely than competitive arguments to enhance the quality of dialogue and critical thinking. Cooperative argumentation promotes the open exchange of ideas and information needed to make reasoned judgments.

▼ ▼ ▼
COOPERATIVE ARGUMENTATION AND TWO PRINCIPLES OF COMMUNICATION ETHICS

General principles of communication ethics affect the quality of cooperative argumentation. Fulfillment of these principles builds the trust so fundamental to successful cooperative argument. The principles of fidelity and veracity play such a role.

The *principle of fidelity* deals with making promises and the role that keeping promises plays in maintaining the trust so fundamental to effective communication. This principle holds that *bona fide promises are to be kept.*[4] The *principle of veracity* deals with truth-telling and the role that honesty

---

3. These definitions appear in the *Dictionary of Philosophy* (Totawa, N.J.: Lisslefield, Adams, 1962), p. 212.

4. From John Rawls, *A Theory of Justice* (Cambridge: Harvard University Press, 1971), pp. 344–348.

plays in maintaining trust. This principle *gives strong presumptive weight to truth-telling.*[5]

The principles of fidelity and veracity derive from commonsense understandings about human communication. Philosopher Richard Brandt records such a commonplace when he writes that making a promise creates "a prima facie obligation."[6] The term prima facie, meaning "on the face of it," refers here to the presumptive nature of the promise maker's obligation. Most people recognize this presumption. For them, making a promise entails having an obligation to keep that promise, unless doing so would require violating a higher obligation, such as saving a human life or preventing a tragedy. The principle of fidelity expresses this commonplace.

When applied in actual circumstances, this principle affords flexibility and adapts to the many situations people confront in their everyday lives. According to the principle, making a promise entails obligations only if the promise is bona fide. To be *bona fide,* a promise must be made in appropriate circumstances and without any excusing or releasing conditions.

Appropriate circumstances include the promisor's sanity, consciousness, competence, intent to be taken to be making a promise, intent that the promisee believe the promisor intended to fulfill the promise, and the absence of duress when making the promise. The most prominent *excusing condition* is any extreme, unanticipated cost. *Releasing conditions* include the unanticipated inability to fulfill the promise, unanticipated radically changed circumstances, mutual knowledge that neither the promisee nor the promisor have an interest in fulfillment of the promise, and the promisee's explicit release of the promisor from making the promise.

Releasing conditions release communicators from their promises, whereas excusing conditions only change the intensity of their obligation. When excusing conditions are mutually understood to overshadow the obligations of the promise, then the promise maker is fully released.

On Saturday, Dan promises his mother that he will take out the garbage Monday morning. According to the principle of fidelity, Dan has a prima facie obligation to take out the garbage Monday morning. But his promise must be bona fide to be obligatory. At first, Dan's promise meets this condition. He was sane, conscious, and competent when he made his promise. He gave no indication to his mother that he was not serious about keeping his promise, nor was his promise made under duress. However, Sunday evening Dan broke his arm while helping his mother move furniture. On Monday morning, he is no longer able to keep the promise, and his mother excuses him

---

5.   From Sissela Bok, *Lying: Moral Choice in Public and Private Life* (New York: Vintage Books, 1979), pp. 32–33, 88–91.

6.   Richard R. Brandt, *Ethical Theory: The Problems of Normative and Critical Ethics* (Englewood Cliffs, N.J.: Prentice-Hall, 1959), p. 388.

from fulfilling it. Dan's promise is no longer bona fide; he is freed from its obligations.

As this example illustrates, the circumstances surrounding promise making determine whether the promise is bona fide. Dan's situation was relatively simple. Few would argue that he remained obligated to fulfill his promise after he broke his arm while helping his mother, particularly given that his mother released him from the obligation.

Sometimes, however, deciding whether a promise remains enforceable is more complex. Kara's difficult experience illustrates this complexity. On his deathbed, Kara's grandfather asked her to promise that she would never sell the family farm. Kara made the promise, confident that she could keep it in good faith. A number of years after making the promise, Kara faced a complex decision. Her own two children were grown and had decided to move to the city many miles from the family farm. Kara's husband had died, leaving only a small pension behind for her support. Although Kara had enough financial resources to keep the farm going, she was growing increasingly tired from all of the work that she had to do to maintain the farm. And there were no other family members to whom Kara could turn for help with this work.

One day, a "new-age" corporation offered to purchase the farm from Kara. They promised to take good care of the land and to maintain the conditions she had created to ensure the land's protection. They assured her that they would protect the interests about which her grandfather cared so deeply. Knowing of Kara's promise, they assured her that their company's policies would satisfy the "spirit" of her promise to her grandfather.

Despite these assurances, Kara knew that if she sold the farm, she would violate the "letter," and perhaps even the "spirit," of her grandfather's wishes. The question she had to ask herself was whether her promise was still enforceable. Could she have reasonably predicted the consequences of keeping the promise at the time she made it? Was she still obligated to fulfill her promise to her grandfather after all of these years? What other interests were involved at this point? Were these relevant to her decision making?

This example illustrates the complexity of satisfying the principle of fidelity. Cooperative argumentation requires mutual trust, which is jeopardized when promises are broken. Yet communicators sometimes find themselves in situations in which they must choose between keeping a promise and satisfying other important interests. Recognizing this danger, advocates should take great care before making promises that they may be unable to keep.

When confronted with a situation in which they have to choose between keeping a promise and satisfying another worthwhile purpose, advocates should use the critical thinking techniques discussed throughout this book. Assessing which values and interests should have primacy in these difficult situations requires communicators to consider their options and the outcomes available to them. In this sense, the process of communicating ethically depends, in part, on the communicator's willingness and ability to use the tools of cooperative argumentation.

The relationship between ethical communication and effective argumentation is perhaps even more evident in cases involving application of the second principle of communication ethics: the *principle of veracity*. Like the fidelity principle, this norm for ethical communication derives from commonplaces regarding the importance of trust in communication and the role that honesty plays in maintaining mutual trust. Ethicist Sissela Bok expresses a commonplace related to the veracity principle when she writes that "trust in some degree of veracity functions as a *foundation* of relations among human beings; when this trust shatters or wears away, institutions collapse."[7]

Bok draws a distinction between deception and lying. *Deception* is the broader category, including *any message meant to mislead,* whether it is stated, disguised, photographed, or presented in any other communication form. *Lying* is a form of deception that involves *any statement which communicates an intentionally deceptive message, a message meant to make others believe what we ourselves do not believe.*[8]

Cooperative argumentation depends on strict adherence to this principle. As we have seen in previous chapters, the quality of decisions influenced by cooperative argumentation depends on the advocates' willingness to *share information* and to *avoid misstating opposing views. Accuracy, relevance,* and *understandability* are all important to successful cooperative argumentation. Any form of deception, however apparently innocent on the surface, can undermine the decision-making process that argumentation is designed to enhance.

Yet the diversity of circumstances in which communicators find themselves often makes adherence to the veracity principle difficult. Just as promise keeping may require sacrificing other laudable interests, truth telling must often be balanced against other interests.

Bok's extensive study of lying supports both the importance of truth telling and the complexity of issues surrounding adherence to the veracity principle. The discussion below demonstrates the strong presumption in favor of truth telling required by cooperative argumentation. At the same time, the discussion illustrates the value of cooperative argumentation in resolving ethical conflicts.

Bok describes different kinds of lies, each with its own rationale. *White lies* are falsehoods "not meant to injure anyone, and of little moral import." Common uses of white lies are to avoid hurting feelings, to be polite, to

---

7. Bok, *Lying: Moral Choice in Public and Private Life,* p. 33.

8. Sissela Bok, cited in Gillian Michell, "Women and Lying: A Pragmatic and Semantic Analysis of 'Telling it Slant,'" *Women's Studies International Forum* 7 (1984): 375.

flatter, "to throw cheerful interpretation on depressing circumstances, or to show gratitude for unwanted gifts."[9]

Although these types of lies seem harmless on the surface, they often do harm. Bok points out, for example, that "disagreeable facts come to be sugar-coated, and sad news softened or denied altogether."[10] Earlier discussions of group and personal decision making emphasized the hazards of inaccurately assessing risks in any given circumstance. Not only are people who have been told white lies likely to miscalculate the consequences of their decisions, they are deprived of the freedom that comes from being fully informed.

The harmful effects associated with white lies therefore need to be carefully considered before choosing this communication strategy. As with situations involving conflicts between the need to keep promises and the desire to satisfy other interests, situations in which communicators must choose between telling a white lie and satisfying other interests require careful reflection. In sum, before telling even a white lie, communicators need to use the tools of critical analysis to assess their options.

Paternalistic lies and lies told to protect the sick and dying provide additional examples of seemingly justifiable kinds of deception. These types of lies are told with "the intention of guarding from harm," yet they often lead, "both through mistake and through abuse, to great suffering. The 'protection' can suffocate; it can also exploit."[11]

Consider the case of Adam's attempt to protect his sister by telling her a paternalistic lie. When Adam was sixteen years old, his parents decided to adopt an infant girl. After much discussion, Adam and his parents decided that the child would be happier and more secure if she didn't know that she was adopted. All of her life, Roxanne believed that Adam and she were biological siblings. Never did Roxanne question her biological heritage.

Shortly after her fiftieth birthday, Roxanne learned that she had developed a potentially fatal form of bone-marrow disease. She was told that she would need to find a family member who could donate bone marrow to her. Already burdened with this painful illness, Roxanne was devastated when Adam informed her that he would be unable to provide the bone marrow because he and Roxanne were not biologically related. Imagine her anger at discovering that she had been deprived of the opportunity to consider investigating her biological heritage. Consider the emotional trauma of learning that her parents and brother had conspired to lie to her all of these years. In this, as in many cases involving a paternalistic lie, the person being "protected" was seriously hurt by the lie.

---

9. Bok, p. 61.
10. Bok, p. 64.
11. Bok, p. 216.

Just as white lies prevent decision makers from accurately assessing their options, lies told in an effort to protect someone often result in hurting the people they are intended to help. When you avoid telling someone the truth as you know it, you deprive them of making informed judgments. Although Roxanne might have decided not to track down her biological family, she was not given this choice. She was deprived of the opportunity to consider this option, despite its potential importance to her.

Sometimes, otherwise ethical practitioners succumb to the temptation to deceive on behalf of a "good cause." Legal advocates are particularly vulnerable to this problem. Audiences expect legal advocates to present impassioned pleas on behalf of their clients. Yet our system of justice can serve its purposes only if legal advocates adhere strictly to the principle of veracity. Manipulating juries or using deceptive means during a legal proceeding, no matter how successful, endangers the delicate thread on which our system of justice depends.

The Leroy Reed case discussed in Chapter 5 illustrates this point. Fortunately, both the prosecuting and defense attorneys in this case reasoned with the jurors. The prosecutor's arguments stressed the importance of basing legal decisions on the available facts. The defense attorney reasoned with the jurors about the importance of including considerations of justice and fairness in their deliberations.

These competing arguments permitted the jury to make a reasoned, well-informed decision. Suppose, however, that the district attorney had chosen to *manipulate,* rather than reason with, the jury. Suppose, for instance, that before presenting his arguments, the district attorney had made sociological assessments of the jurors to learn their fears, prejudices, and biases. Suppose he had discovered that many of the jurors suffered from irrational fear of mentally retarded people and that six of the jurors were prejudiced toward blacks, while ten were biased against ex-convicts.

If the district attorney had been primarily motivated by winning for its own sake, he might have preyed on the jurors' fears, prejudices, and biases. Yet in doing so, he would not have been serving the system of justice. Rather than contribute to the jury's deliberations, the district attorney's manipulative strategies would have diminished the quality of these deliberations.

Equally destructive to the quality of decision making is argumentation that "suppresses facts or arguments, misstates elements of the case, or misstates the opposition."[12] This type of argumentation creates an image of balance, while jeopardizing the true balance of perspectives needed for reasoned decision making. Had either or both of the competing advocates in the Leroy Reed case succumbed to the temptation to misrepresent the elements of the case, the jurors might have been deprived of the insights needed to make their important decision.

---

12. John Stuart Mill, *On Liberty* (1859; reprint Indianapolis: Bobbs-Merrill, 1956), p. 25.

Other types of seemingly justifiable lies are just as damaging on close analysis. Lies in a crisis, lies protecting peers and clients, and lies for the public good all seem justifiable on the surface. Yet critical analysis of the long-term consequences of these types of lies, particularly from the perspective of the deceived, reveals that even these types of misrepresentations may do more harm than good in the long run.

Before deciding to tell a lie intended to protect someone, communicators should evaluate the circumstances from the standpoint of the deceived. Ask yourself, if you were the person being deceived: Would you consent to the deception if given a choice? Would you consider the deception to be to your long-term advantage? Would you believe that the deceiver had the right to deceive you? On what grounds? Answering these questions honestly will help prevent many of the harms that result from telling paternalistic lies. Respected author Adrienne Rich neatly sums up the "truth" about most seemingly innocent deceptions: "Lies are usually attempts to make everything simpler—for the liar—than it really is, or ought to be."[13]

Despite the veracity principle's strong admonition against lying, the principle does allow for circumstances in which varying degrees of deception are expected and therefore accepted. Bok discusses some of these circumstances. People, she writes, sometimes play "mutually deceptive roles" in "certain bargaining situations":

▼▼▼▼▼▼

In a bazaar, for instance, false claims are a convention; to proclaim from the outset one's honest intention would be madness. If buyers and sellers bargain knowingly and voluntarily, one would be hard put to regard as misleading their exaggerations, false claims to have given their last bid, or words of feigned loss of interest. Both parties have consented to the rules of the game.[14] ▼▼▼

The field of advertising provides interesting examples of situations in which communicators might consider themselves exempt from the strong presumption for truth telling imposed by the veracity principle. Asking an advertiser to present a balanced perspective is asking the advertiser to defeat his or her purpose. And, advertisers might add, the public fully expects advertisements to be aimed at misleading them.

But Bok explains that there are three conditions which must be met before deception is justified even in these circumstances: mutual knowledge of the "rules" of the game, mutual consent, and mutual freedom. If one of the parties is not fully aware of the rules, or not in a position to fully consent,

---

13. Adrienne Rich, "Women and Honor: Some Notes on Lying," in *On Lies, Secrets, and Silence: Selected Prose 1966–78* (New York: Norton, 1979), pp. 187–188.

14. Bok, pp. 138–139.

or not fully free to negotiate the rules, then communicators remain obligated to avoid deception.

When advertising to children, or to other people who do not have knowledge of the rules of the marketplace, these communicators must carefully consider the audience's perspective. Even in the hard realities of a marketplace in which *caveat emptor,* meaning "buyer beware," is a widely accepted credo, public communicators have a responsibility to consider the consequences of violating the public's trust. In these and related situations, public communicators have the responsibility to apply the principles of critical thinking to the resolution of their ethical dilemmas.

▼ ▼ ▼
THE COMPOSITE AUDIENCE AND ETHICAL CONSIDERATIONS

Unlike advertising, which is usually addressed to uninformed general audiences for the sole purpose of persuading them to purchase a service or product, cooperative argumentation addressed to a composite audience services good decision making. Given its purpose, cooperative argumentation *requires* fulfillment of the principles of fidelity and veracity.

Fortunately, composite audiences are trained to look for omissions, misrepresentations, and other forms of deception. Composite audiences are usually unmoved by efforts to use manipulative tactics. Arguing before a composite audience requires adherence to the principles of fidelity and veracity because the audience will be intolerant of abuses.

Among the standards that composite audiences use to evaluate arguments are the demands that arguments be *relevant, consistent,* and *coherent,* which will be extensively discussed in Chapter 8. Fulfilling these and other rigorous criteria for good argumentation seriously limits the possibility that advocates addressing composite audiences will successfully employ unethical communication practices.

In this sense, learning to participate in cooperative argumentation with and for composite audiences helps advocates learn the habit of ethical interaction. Perhaps more than any other kind of communication interaction, cooperative argumentation addressed to a composite audience meets the rigorous challenges posed by basic guidelines for ethical communication.

At the same time, we have seen throughout this chapter that resolution of complex ethical problems requires cooperative argumentation. Consider the complex choices that communicators must make in applying the principles of fidelity and veracity to specific situations. Deciding whether to keep a promise at the expense of another important interest or deciding whether to tell painful truths to the sick and dying are but two types of circumstances whose effective resolution depends on skillful use of critical thinking tools.

In sum, application of the principles and tools discussed throughout this book enables communication practitioners in a wide variety of contexts to effectively confront their ethical challenges.

▼ ▼ ▼
SUMMARY

Because argumentation is a form of public communication, it is subject to the same ethical considerations as other forms of communication. Successful argumentation takes place when participants understand and adhere to mutually accepted norms. Cooperative argumentation addressed to a composite audience is governed by rigorous norms.

The heart of this type of argumentation is its cooperative nature. Cooperative argumentation promotes the open exchange of ideas and information needed to make reasoned judgments.

General principles of communication ethics affect the quality of cooperative argumentation. The principle of fidelity deals with promise making and the role that promise keeping plays in maintaining the trust so fundamental to effective communication. The principle of veracity deals with truth telling and the role that honesty plays in maintaining trust. This principle gives strong presumptive weight to truth telling.

Sometimes, communicators must choose between keeping a promise, telling the truth, or fulfilling other important purposes. Yet effective communication depends on the trust that promise keeping and truth telling help maintain. Advocates should take great care before making promises they might be unable or uninclined to keep. Similarly, advocates need to recognize the significant role that truth telling plays in ethical and effective communication. The fulfillment of the goals associated with cooperative argumentation depends on full disclosure, accurate representations, and honest characterizations. Even seemingly harmless "white lies" or well-intentioned "paternalistic lies" intended to protect someone may result in great harm. These forms of deception jeopardize reasoned decision making and deprive decision makers of the tools they need to critically analyze their situation. Advocates should therefore carefully weigh the cumulative costs before employing any form of deception.

Resolving these and other ethical challenges requires advocates to make effective use of cooperative argumentation. Application of critical thinking principles and tools to the resolution of these conflicts helps communicators make the most ethical decision available to them.

Fortunately, composite audiences are trained to look for omissions, misrepresentations, and other forms of deception. They are unmoved by efforts to manipulate, rather than reason with, them. They expect strict adherence to the principles of fidelity and veracity and are intolerant of arguments that are irrelevant, inconsistent, or incoherent.

In this sense, learning to participate in cooperative argumentation with and for composite audiences helps advocates learn the habit of ethical interaction. Perhaps more than any other form of communication, cooperative argumentation addressed to a composite audience meets rigorous standards for ethical communication practice.

At the same time, resolution of complex ethical problems requires cooperative argumentation. Application of the principles and tools discussed throughout this text enables communication practitioners in a wide variety of communication contexts to effectively confront their ethical challenges.

▼ ▼ ▼

EXERCISES

1. Discuss the public's disenchantment over the advertising strategies used during the 1988 presidential campaigns. Using the tools of critical analysis discussed so far in this text and the insights provided by this chapter, consider the long-term implications to a representative democracy when political candidates employ slick advertising techniques in their campaigns. Discuss this issue with friends and classmates. Finally, develop some ethical standards for political campaigns.

2. Apply the principles of fidelity and veracity to the following sets of circumstances:

   a. Ingrid has promised her brother Vic that she will call him on Thursday. When Ingrid made her promise, she fully intended to keep it. Her promise was bona fide.

      However, on Thursday morning Ingrid unexpectedly got the opportunity to audition for a play. She had waited many years for this opportunity. Ingrid knew that auditioning would mean she would be unable to fulfill her promise to call Vic on Thursday. She knew, for instance, that Vic would not be near a phone until 2:00 in the afternoon, and by then she would be involved in the audition. Because she would be unable to leave the auditorium at any time between 2:00 and midnight, and because the auditorium does not have a phone, Ingrid believed that going to the audition would mean violating her promise to Vic.

      Based on these facts, what advice would you give Ingrid? What additional information do you believe would help you advise Ingrid?

   b. Consider the circumstances facing Kara and Adam in the examples developed in this chapter. Based on the facts given, how would you advise them to respond to their respective ethical conflicts? Why? What additional information would you need to more effectively advise them?

c. Janet has spent hours dressing for a job interview. Looking "just right" is crucial to her. When she finally enters the room, her mother is disappointed with how Janet looks. Somehow, the dress doesn't quite look right on Janet, and her makeup doesn't do her justice. But Janet only has a few more minutes to get ready, and her mother wants her to go to the interview feeling relaxed and confident. Would you advise Janet's mother to tell Janet the truth about how she sees her daughter's appearance? Why or why not?

d. Henry, an eight-year-old child, is known for his poor appetite. When it comes to fried chicken, however, Henry has an excellent appetite. He will eat about as much fried chicken as his parents are willing to give him. Henry is a gentle and sensitive child. He would not knowingly hurt anyone—not even an animal. One day, Henry came home from school worried. He had heard that the chickens his family buys from the local store were raised under cruel conditions. Because Henry lives in a suburban neighborhood, he doesn't understand what this might mean. He knows nothing about factory farming or about how poultry, cattle, swine, and sheep are raised on those farms. Henry's father thinks it's important to tell him the truth about modern methods of poultry production, even if this may mean that Henry will no longer want to eat chicken. Henry's mother disagrees. She thinks Henry is much too young to learn about such complex and potentially upsetting matters. Besides, she argues, Henry should be allowed to continue enjoying the pleasure of eating his favorite food without having to worry about it. He should be sheltered from the truth.

What advice would you give Henry's parents? Why? What additional information would help you advise his parents?

e. Lt. Col. Oliver North knowingly told members of Congress lies about matters related to the so-called Iran-Contra affair. He also lied to leaders of Iran and to Central American leaders during his work on behalf of Nicaragua's freedom fighters. North justified his lies on the grounds that telling the truth to Congress and the American people would have kept him from being as effective in his work for the Contras. He also argued that he needed to tell lies in order to protect his commander-in-chief, President Reagan.

Using search strategies developed earlier in this text, research the circumstances surrounding North's testimony before Congress. Next, discuss the Oliver North case with friends and family. Based on your research and discussions, do you believe North's ends justified the means he used? Why or why not?

f. The Fifth District Court of Appeals ruled in October, 1988, that "as a matter of law, it is not in the best interest of a seven-year-old male child to be placed for adoption into the home of a pair of adult male homosexual lovers." The child in question, Charlie, had been a ward of Licking County Children's Services since he was abandoned by his parents at the age of three. Charlie is a victim of leukemia, though his disease was believed to be in remission at the time the court made its ruling. He has also been diagnosed as suffering from learning disabilities and other effects of fetal alcohol syndrome. He has lived in five foster homes during his five years as a ward of the county.

Melvin Lee Balser, a psychologist who served as Charlie's therapist, had the consent and encouragement of the county children's services agency to take the boy home for weekends and holidays. He was the only person to file for adoption of the boy.

In his application for permanent custody of Charlie, Balser made no attempt to hide his three-year live-in relationship with another man. Had he hidden this relationship, Balser might have been granted custody of Charlie. Because he told the truth about his life style, Balser was denied custody, and Charlie was denied a permanent home with Balser.

Ronald, a homosexual who wishes to adopt a five-year-old handicapped child in the same state, has read the details of the Balser case. He knows that the Supreme Court would be likely to uphold the district court's ruling. Under current laws, homosexual persons are afforded no constitutional protection against discrimination based on their affectional preference. Ronald has good reason to believe that the child he wishes to adopt will have trouble finding another permanent home. The child is mixed race, disabled, and five years old and is therefore considered difficult to place. Ronald believes that he can give the child a loving, secure environment. He has been in a thirteen-year relationship with the same man, and they share a "normal" family life style in every respect other than their affectional preference for one another.

The case worker handling Ronald's adoption case enthusiastically supports Ronald's petition. She has seen Ronald, his lover, and the child interact, and has never seen the child happier or more responsive than when he is in the two men's company. She also believes that current laws fail to consider all of the circumstances surrounding adoptions. She has studied such issues as child abuse and molestation and has learned that the vast majority of abuse and molestation cases involve heterosexual men abusing children. She is aware of the stigma likely to be experienced by children whose adoptive parents are homosexual. But she believes that a mixed-race disabled child will have a much greater chance of happiness in a loving, secure home, despite this stigma, than he would have if he moves from foster home to foster home.

Because the case worker feels so strongly about these issues and because she believes that Ronald will be denied permanent custody if he speaks openly about his life style, she urges Ronald to not reveal that he is homosexual.

Do you agree with her advice? Why or why not? What advice would you give Ronald? On what grounds? What additional information do you believe you would need to adequately advise Ronald?

g. Suppose that a number of major banks are in such serious trouble that they run the risk of financial collapse. The only hope for their survival is the preservation of public trust in them. If anyone leaks information about the seriousness of the problem, people will begin withdrawing all of their funds, and this will ensure the banks' collapse.

You run a local paper, whose revenues are closely tied to one of the banks in question. You have a reputation for providing the public with accurate information about local and national events. You have good reason to believe that no one else is going to leak the truth about the banks' problems. Hence, if you faithfully represent the facts as you know them, you would consider yourself at least partially responsible for the banks' almost certain collapse and for the likely demise of your own paper. In your opinion, many innocent people would suffer as a consequence. Local businesses would fail. And townspeople would no longer have access to an honest source of local news.

Should you report your information as honestly as possible? Why or why not? What additional information do you need before you would be in a position to make a reasoned decision on this matter?

h. Suppose you are deeply committed to the Right-to-Life movement. You believe that every abortion which takes place involves the murder of an innocent child. You realize that the "system" is against you. The courts have legalized abortion, and states are not likely to challenge their decision.

You are a respected expert on fetal development. Somehow, without intentionally deceiving anyone, you have managed to keep your personal beliefs about abortion to yourself.

Now you have access to film footage which seems to show a fetus suffering during an abortion. Your own research indicates that this is not what the film actually shows. But you believe that what the film *appears* to show could have a powerful impact on the public. You are an ethical person, in both your professional and personal life, who is devoted to truth and to fulfillment of the principle of veracity. But you believe that the rights of the unborn justify using deception to persuade in this instance. You plan to distribute the film to members of Congress, religious leaders, influential politicians, educational leaders, and to as many television news outlets as possible.

What arguments might someone make in an effort to dissuade you? How are you likely to reply? Which of these sets of arguments is most persuasive? Why?

i. You are a district attorney prosecuting someone for the rape and murder of a young child. You are absolutely convinced of the defendant's guilt, but are afraid that you might not have enough evidence to convict. The state has provided you money to purchase a psychological profile of each juror. Based on these profiles, you will be able to develop arguments that take advantage of each juror's fears and prejudices. Although you are committed to truth, you are equally committed to justice. And you believe that manipulating the jury in this case will help ensure a just outcome.

What arguments might someone make to discourage you from (1) getting a psychological profile of each juror and (2) relying on information you have regarding each juror's fears and prejudices? Would you find these arguments convincing? Why or why not?

j. The late Reverend Jim Jones believed that faith has strong healing power. He was convinced that if people had faith that he could heal them, he would be able to heal many of them. In the service of his mission, several of Jones's followers agreed to act as if they were healed by Jones's hands during religious gatherings. After one such gathering, one of these followers expressed some doubts about Jones's methods. She was concerned about the deception involved in acting as if she were healed, when in fact there had been nothing wrong with her. Jones replied that deception was necessary to strengthen the congregation's faith and thereby make actual healing possible. He reasoned that without complete faith, the followers would not be healed. In his mind, the deceptive means were justified by the ends.

Do you agree with Jones? What advice would you give his concerned follower? What reasons would you provide to support your advice?

What additional information would you need to provide more adequate advice to Jones and his followers?

3. Ghandi once said that the "means are the ends in the making." What would acceptance of this view entail? How does this concept relate to issues of communication ethics? Argumentation ethics? Do you agree with Ghandi? Why or why not?

4. Discuss the role that critical thinking plays in completing all of the preceding exercises. How do the tools developed in this text help communication practitioners resolve their ethical dilemmas? Why is cooperative argumentation with and for a composite audience so valuable to practitioners faced with ethical dilemmas?

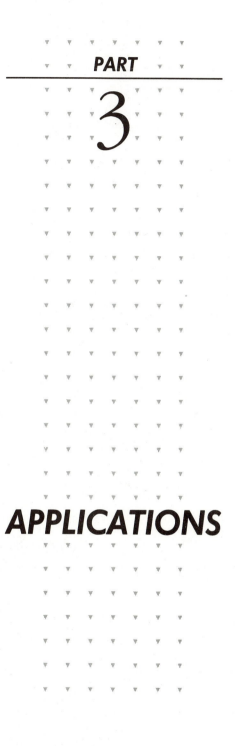

PART

3

APPLICATIONS

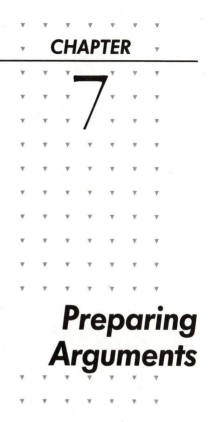

CHAPTER

7

Preparing Arguments

Chapter 5 introduced a variety of contexts in which argumentation effectively contributes to decision making. This chapter provides tools for preparing effective arguments in these different types of contexts.

The chapter begins with a brief recapitulation of relationships between *deliberation* and *advocacy*. Next, the chapter provides discussion, exercises, and examples designed to help advocates prepare oral and written arguments for a variety of argumentation contexts. Particular attention is given to preparation of the *issues brief,* a tool for enhancing the quality of deliberative and persuasive argumentation. The chapter ends with discussion and exercises designed to help advocates develop and present persuasive arguments.

▼ ▼ ▼

RELATIONSHIPS BETWEEN DELIBERATION AND ADVOCACY

As we have seen in previous chapters, effective decision making is a dynamic process that involves interaction between deliberation, justification, and persuasion. Decision making on public policy issues is particularly illustrative of the dynamic nature of this process.

Consider the issue of whether human fetal tissue should be used in scientific research and medical procedures. In the fall of 1987, increased medical use of fetal-cell implant surgery drew international attention to the debate over whether such surgery should be permitted. Surgeons in Sweden, Mexico, and the United States were stepping up efforts to use fetal-cell implants in the treatment of Parkinson's disease. The increased popularity of this and other medical procedures using human fetal tissue motivated advocates on competing sides of this controversial issue to present their arguments to the public.

Representatives of the research community used print and electronic media to convey their finding that human fetal tissue could be used to treat a variety of major health problems, including Parkinson's disease and Alzheimer's disease. Spokespersons for the research and medical communities reported that human fetal tissue could be used to restore the health of other fetuses, helping prevent genetic defects such as sickle-cell anemia, hemophilia, or Tay-Sachs disease. Dr. John Sladek of the University of Rochester Medical Center appeared on a special edition of the ABC news program "Nightline" that was devoted exclusively to the debate over medical uses of human fetal tissue. Dr. Sladek stated that "every one of the neurological models of disease, Alzheimer's, Huntington's, stroke, epilepsy, even some birth defects—as far as lack of development of certain parts of the brain—have been improved or reversed in the laboratory, using fetal nerve cell grafts."[1]

Not everyone shared the research community's enthusiasm, however. Abortion foes were especially concerned about the prospect of widespread medical use of human fetal tissue. National Right to Life Committee President Dr. John Wilke, for example, argued that "we are now destroying tiny lives and using their tissues."[2] Opponents of human fetal tissue use joined Dr. Wilke in urging the government to impose a moratorium on the scientific and medical use of human fetal tissue.

In March, 1988, the Department of Health and Human Services "halted new federally supported research on fetal tissue transplants obtained from

---

1. From the transcript of "Nightline," January 6, 1988, p. 3.

2. Matt Clark (with Mariana Gosnell and Mary Hager), "Should Medicine Use the Unborn?" *Newsweek,* September 14, 1987, p. 62.

elective abortions until an advisory committee could review the scientific and ethical issues."[3] Even more dramatic was the proposed executive order drafted by Gary L. Bauer, President Reagan's assistant for policy development. Bauer sent his draft to Dr. Otis R. Bowen, Secretary of Health and Human Services. If adopted, this order would make it federal policy "that an unborn or newborn child who has died as a result of an induced abortion shall not be used for purposes of research or transplantation."[4] Bauer told reporters that he sent the document to Dr. Bowen "to stimulate comment from his department on a very complicated issue."[5]

While advocates from competing sides of the controversy about human fetal tissue use presented their arguments to the public, medical ethicists entered the debate by calling for great care in the deliberation process. They urged policy makers to carefully consider such fundamental questions as: Who should decide whether an aborted fetus should be used for research or medical treatment, and if the mother is permitted to decide, could this not lead some women to become pregnant and abort for the purposes of providing fetal tissue to help themselves or loved ones? Arthur Caplan, director of the Center for Biomedical Ethics at the University of Minnesota, reflected the view of many ethicists when he stated that "the worst possible ethical evil of all this would be to create lives simply to end them and take the parts."[6]

In response to these and related calls for caution, Dr. Hans Sollinger of the University of Wisconsin stated, "If ethical issues sidetrack this research, and the tissue cannot be used, it could cause tremendous harm to these patient groups [who could benefit from this research]."[7]

Eventually, legislators will be forced to make decisions on these and related issues. Relying on their assessments of the many competing arguments, but especially more related to values, legislators will draft laws regulating the use of human fetal tissue that will potentially affect millions of lives. Once these laws have been enacted and enforced, some of them will be likely to face challenges of their own. Of these, some will inevitably reach the Supreme Court, whose decisions will significantly influence the outcome of the issue.

Chapter 5's discussion of Supreme Court decision making revealed that judicial decisions are influenced by a variety of oral and written arguments, presented before and during the formal deliberation process. Advocates from competing sides present written briefs supporting their controversial posi-

---

3.   "Use of Fetal Tissue from Abortion May Be Halted," *Columbus Dispatch,* September 9, 1988, p. A-4.

4.   Ibid.

5.   *Columbus Dispatch,* September 9, 1988, p. A-4.

6.   Reported in *Newsweek,* September 14, 1987, p. 63.

7.   David Lore, "Doctors Say Fetal Transplants Promising, Urge End to Ban," *Columbus Dispatch,* September 15, 1988, p. D-1.

tions. Justices then listen to oral arguments that are based on information provided in the written briefs. Justices are expected to base their tentative initial decisions on their assessments of the arguments and information available to them. However, research reveals that judicial decision making, like decision making in most other practical contexts, relies heavily on each justice's own philosophy, interests, and value hierarchy, as well as on arguments presented during court proceedings. To help justify individual judgments, the justices write opinions that support their initial decisions. These opinions are first distributed among the justices. Later, revised versions of these written documents are submitted to the public.

We learned in Chapter 5 that cooperative argumentation designed to enhance reasoned decision making follows this judicial model of reasoning. Like the Supreme Court, we attempt to make the best possible decision on any given issue. And, like members of the Court, we seek to employ persuasive arguments to justify our choices, first to ourselves and later to others. Like the justices, we must develop the ability to persuade reasonable opponents that ours is a justified, reasonable decision based on the available information.

Determining where advocacy begins or ends, or when deliberation replaces advocacy, and so on, is difficult, if not impossible, in most practical contexts. Nor is it always possible to exactly determine how these related processes interact with one another. However, we do know that there are some tools which significantly contribute to the quality of both effective advocacy and good deliberation. One of the most useful and practical tools is the *issues brief.*

▾ ▾ ▾
THE ISSUES BRIEF

The *issues brief* provides *an overview of commonplaces, issues, positions, and support designed to help structure effective argumentation.* The discussion below will explain the value of writing the issues brief.

Chapter 5 stressed that effective advocacy significantly enhances the value of argumentation to the reasoning process. The quality of deliberation on controversial issues depends, in large measure, on the arguers' ability to thoughtfully consider as many alternative perspectives as possible.

Accordingly, previous chapters suggested that the more honest and open interaction we are able to have with opponents, the more effectively we will be able to employ the tools of argumentation. Similarly, the more attention we give to our effort to imagine reasoned opposition, the more likely we will arrive at the most reasonable decision possible.

Related is the need to be willing to take a stand on issues, even when doing so leaves us vulnerable to opposing arguments. Previous chapters have shown that exposure to persuasive arguments in support of alternative perspectives helps advocates and their audiences effectively consider available options. As we have seen throughout this text, people in group settings, or in dialogues with only one other person, or even reflecting about a topic alone, learn much from the experience of taking a stand on an issue.

Preparation of the issues brief helps critical thinkers effectively participate in discussion, deliberation, and debate on controversial topics. Once written, the brief helps shape opinion and correspondingly provides valuable material for reasoned advocacy in support of a specific point of view. Writing this document can therefore play a valuable role in the overall critical thinking process.

The issues brief has much in common with its legal counterpart, the legal brief. Both documents isolate issues, expose commonplaces, and provide extensive support for controversial claims. Both indicate sources for each claim's support, and both attend to the audience's predispositions on the relevant issues.

However, the issues brief differs from the lawyer's brief in one important respect. Recall that lawyers present arguments in an adversarial, competitive climate. They begin their work with a clear idea of the outcome they hope to achieve. The lawyer's brief provides an issues overview calculated to lead readers to one conclusion. In contrast, the issues brief serves as preparation for cooperative argumentative exchanges. As such, this brief is expected to present at least two competing sides of as many central issues as possible. Readers of an issues brief *should be unable to detect the author's biases* on the topic.

When successful, the issues brief assists advocates and audiences alike in their efforts to effectively employ the following five *strategies of reflection.*

Strategy 1: Discovering Commonplaces and Issues

▼ We have learned throughout this text that one of the first tasks for effective argumentation is discovery of points of agreement and disagreement. Determining centers of controversy on a topic is of critical importance to productive dialogue on that topic. Similarly, effective argumentation requires shared starting points, with common understandings of terms, as well as some shared assumptions.

Strategy 2: Considering Alternative Perspectives

▼ Once the issues have been defined to the satisfaction of participants in argumentation, alternative perspectives on these issues need to be developed. Throughout the text we have seen the importance of this phase of argumentation. Advocates and audiences alike benefit most through an exploration of as many alternative perspectives as possible.

Strategy 3: Taking a Stand on Central Issues

▼ This is one of the most difficult phases in the argumentation process. Because careful reflection often leads thinkers to question the validity of their initial views on a topic, they sometimes become reluctant to take a firm stand on complex issues. Yet *effective deliberation requires advocates to take stands and risk having their positions exposed to forceful opposition.* This process of advocacy and opposition is the heart of productive argumentation.

Strategy 4: Anticipating Opposition

▾ In an ideal situation, once an advocate has taken a stand he or she has opportunities to expose this position to reasonable people who disagree with it. However, as we have seen in previous chapters, this ideal situation rarely exists. We are often left with the limits of our imaginations, which is one of the reasons that development of critical thinking skills is so important in today's complex world. We must often act as our own composite audience. The effectiveness of our critical thinking depends, therefore, on our ability to imagine a reasonable audience's most rigorous opposition to our views.

Strategy 5: Responding to Reasonable Opposition

▾ We have seen throughout this text that only the ability to effectively respond to forceful and rigorous opposition justifies the belief that we have reached the best judgment available to us. John Stuart Mill writes accordingly:

▾ ▾ ▾ ▾ ▾ ▾

Complete liberty of contradicting and disproving our opinion is the very condition which justifies us in assuming its truth for purposes of action; and on no other terms can a being with human faculties have any rational assurance of being right.[8] ▾ ▾ ▾

The issues brief helps authors employ these strategies of reflection by requiring thoughtful exploration of the topic. The brief—much longer than its name implies—provides an overview of major issues, support for competing responses to these issues, definitions of key terms, and a review of commonplaces. An effective issues brief allows readers to scan issues, from competing perspectives, with little effort. Completing this document requires care, diligence, and sensitivity to alternative points of view.

The format of the issues brief is as follows:

The Issues Brief Format

1. Designation of central issues, presented in question form:

    Issue 1: _____ ?

    Issue 2: _____ ?
    etc.

---

8. John Stuart Mill, *On Liberty* (1859; reprint Indianapolis: Bobbs-Merrill, 1956), p. 24.

2. Statements of commonplaces:

   Commonplace 1: _____

   Commonplace 2: _____
   etc.

3. Definitions of key terms:

   Term 1: _____ :   *Definition 1:* _____

   Term 2: _____ :   *Definition 2:* _____
   etc.

4. Overview of competing claims and support (note that each of the issues designated earlier on the brief should be represented by at least one claim and one counterclaim):

I. Claim I _____ :
    (affirmative response to
    Issue 1)

    A. Support Claim 1
       1. Evidence for support
          (with source)
          a. further support
             (with source)
       2. Evidence for support
          (with source)
          a. further support
             (with source)
    B. Support Claim 2
       etc.

II. Claim II _____ :
    (affirmative response to
    Issue 2)

    A. Support Claim 1
       1. Evidence for support
          (with source)
          a. further support
             (with source)
       2. Evidence for support
          (with source)
       etc.

I. Counterclaim I _____ :
    (negative response to
    Issue I)

    A. Support Claim 1
       1. Evidence for support
          (with source)
          a. further support
             (with source)
       2. Evidence for support
          (with source)
          a. further support
             (with source)
    B. Support Claim 2
       etc.

II. Counterclaim II _____ :
    (negative response to
    Issue 2)

    A. Support Claim 1
       1. Evidence for support
          (with source)
          a. further support
             (with source)
       2. Evidence for support
          (with source)
       etc.

Designation of Central Issues

This feature of the issues brief helps shape dialogue. Effective characterization of issues has the potential to enrich reflection on the topic. In contrast, inadequate characterization of issues is likely to constrain thoughtful consideration of the topic.

We have seen throughout this text that the discovery of "true" issues plays a fundamental role in helping decision makers recognize and effectively consider their choices. Careful delineation and precise description of the issues help prevent decision makers from relying on "tunnel" vision, while helping them focus on the most viable alternatives available to them.

Designation of issues also assists advocates as they prepare persuasive arguments to support their perspectives. Advocates whose claims respond to the audience's central concerns are usually more effective in reaching the audience. This accomplishment in turn encourages audiences to seriously consider the advocate's controversial point of view.

The overview of Michael's and Maria's concerns described in Chapter 4 serves to illustrate the complex process of designating and characterizing central issues. Recall that Michael and Maria found themselves disagreeing on a number of issues related to animal experimentation in laboratories. Michael was unimpressed by scientific arguments favoring the use of animals in medical, military, and industrial research. Maria was similarly unmoved by Michael's arguments against the use of animals in such research.

At first, it might seem that Michael's and Maria's main concerns center on scientific progress as a result of animal experimentation in scientific, military, and industrial laboratories. However, further discussion could reveal a broader disagreement between them. It could be that Michael and Maria base their initial arguments on a larger set of concerns regarding animal welfare. That is, perhaps their "true" disagreement centers on considerations of animal welfare generally. Or perhaps the real center of their topic isn't animal welfare at all. Recall that much of their discussion centered on concern about whether expenditures of time and money on animal models proved to help or hinder efforts to improve the overall quality of human life. Perhaps this is the central concern that drives their discussion.

More discussion would be needed to determine the core of their concerns. Where there is doubt about the actual locus of controversy, it is usually wise to construe central issues in broad terms. This type of construction provides decision makers the opportunity to consider a more encompassing set of concerns. Decision makers can then narrow the topic.

In the case at hand, Michael and Maria discover through discussions on broader issues that most of their attention centers on disagreements about the prevalence of animal models in scientific, military, and industrial research. They learn that their reasons for addressing this topic range from general concerns for human and animal welfare to a specific concern for efficient use of resources. As they discuss the topic further, they discover that much of their disagreement on the topic centers on the question of whether existing laws adequately protect human interests and animal welfare. Related is their disagreement about whether the costs associated with animal experiments are justified by the accomplishments attributed to them.

Like many of us, Michael and Maria do not have the time, energy, or resources to fully explore the many issues that underlie their concerns. Finding the "true" locus of their disagreement helps them to make the best use of their limited time. Based on their discussions, Michael and Maria decide to focus their attention on the two issues that seem most central to their concerns:

▾ **Issue 1:** Do existing laws regulating the use of live animals in scientific experimentation adequately protect human interests and animal welfare?

▾ **Issue 2:** Do the achievements associated with experimentation on live animals justify the human costs and animal suffering invested in these experiments?

In the ideal situation, these issues would be construed more broadly, allowing a wider array of responses. For example, during informal discussions on the topic, Michael, Maria, and other discussants would learn much from framing Issue 2 in broader terms, as follows:

▾▾▾▾▾▾

To what extent do the achievements associated with experimentation on animals justify the investments of scientific energy, public funds, and animal suffering required by the experiments? ▾▾▾

Note that, whereas Issue 2 asks for an affirmative or negative answer, this broader construction of the issue asks for responses that reflect degrees of affirmation or negation. Framing the issue more broadly would therefore permit Michael, Maria, and other participants in the discussion to consider the many plausible responses available to them.

We have seen throughout this text that most issues are represented by *more than two* competing perspectives. In the case of Issue 2, some people believe that the commercial interests protected by cosmetic and other commercial testing on live animals do not justify the animal suffering associated with industrial experiments. These people also believe that the benefits to a few people as a result of exotic disease research fail to justify the millions of tax dollars and thousands of animal lives invested in this research. However, these same people believe that the use of animals in research designed to eliminate certain birth defects and life-threatening infectious diseases are justified by the wide-ranging benefits resulting from this research. For these people, framing the issue in black or white terms limits exploration of the topic's more subtle but significant dimensions.

At least two other groups have more clearly defined, "either-or" stances on the issue. The first group believes that no alleged benefits can justify the great suffering of animals during the course of experiments performed on them. These people call for alternative approaches to medical, industrial, and scientific inquiry, from ethnographic and computer studies to tissue culture and related alternative research methods. On the other end of the spectrum, a second group of people believes that the medical, scientific, and technological achievements attributed to experiments on animals justify the energy, public funds, and animal lives invested in these experiments.

These opposing groups have more clearly defined disagreements about whether animal experiments are justified than have their less "absolute" counterparts. Yet they too would benefit from framing the issue more broadly. Such a construction would encourage them to explore more fully the issue's many sides.

Ideally, then, Michael and Maria would characterize Issues 1 and 2 in broad terms, permitting a wide variety of responses. During the informal initial stages of discussion described throughout this text, they and other discussants would benefit by formulating their issues as broadly as possible.

However, in order to prepare themselves to present competing arguments before an audience, it is necessary for Michael, Maria, and other advocates to pose issues in terms that permit pro and con (or affirmative and negative) answers. Although this method of narrowing issues runs the risk of inhibiting fuller exploration of available options, it provides advocates the opportunity to introduce structured sequences of their competing positions to each other as well as to other audiences. These more structured presentations help both advocates and audiences take a position on the issues.

Recognizing the need to take a position is particularly important for legislators and other policy makers faced with the difficult task of making decisions on complex issues. Legislators responding to Issues 1 and 2 in Michael and Maria's case will ultimately be forced to decide, for example, whether to maintain or revise existing policies, replace old policies with new ones, or simply abandon existing policies and hope the problems are resolved through other vehicles. In 1989 alone, representatives in both houses of Congress will be asked to consider at least three pieces of legislation related to Issues 1 and 2: H.R. 1708, which sets up restrictions and stipulations for animal experimentation; S. 1457, which would restrict the use of pound animals being used by research facilities; and H.R. 5154, the Research Accountability Act, which is intended to prevent redundancy and waste in scientific experiments. An issues brief providing an overview of Issues 1, 2, and other relevant issues would assist legislators as they confront these and related policy decisions.

This discussion of only two of the many issues central to Michael and Maria's discussion reveals the importance of constructing issues as broadly as possible, yet with a sensitivity to advocates' and audiences' needs. We have seen throughout this text the importance of recognizing and acknowledging the diversity of alternative perspectives available to decision makers. Carefully and precisely designating an argument's central issues directly addresses this challenge.

▾ **Exercise 1:** Based on the descriptions of Michael's and Maria's concerns provided here and in Chapter 4, designate at least two additional issues that you believe are central to their discussions.

▾ **Exercise 2:** Select a topic of your own. Discuss the topic with friends, colleagues, classmates, or any others who generally disagree with your position on the topic. Designate three issues that you believe are central to your discussions.

Statements of Commonplaces

Related to the designation of issues is the second feature of the issues brief, the statement of commonplaces. As Chapter 4 indicated, commonplaces of fact, value, and policy play a central role in effective argumentation. They serve as the starting points of an argument, thereby permitting participants to address issues of controversy and allowing communication on these issues to proceed from what is accepted to what is not.

Recall that Michael and Maria share a number of commonplaces. They both value medical progress. Both place a high value on the quality of human life, and both believe that scientists should strive to provide knowledge and technical innovations that will help improve the human condition. They also agree that the public spends approximately 4 billion dollars annually to fund animal experimentation. However, they do not agree on the number of animals actually used in American labs each year. Michael believes that 40 million animals are used annually in these labs, whereas Maria puts the figure closer to 20 million. Because the government requires an accounting of only about 20 percent of animals used in labs, Michael and Maria are unlikely to find a definitive answer to this question. They would therefore be likely to agree on a figure that is somewhere between 20 and 40 million. Neither Michael nor Maria disputes the fact that many of these animals suffer emotional stress or physical pain while experiments are being performed on them, though they strongly disagree on the nature and extent of this suffering. They also agree that less than 20 percent of the animals used in labs are protected by federal legislation, though they strongly disagree about the implications of this fact. Although they disagree about the overall success rate of scientific experiments on animals, Michael and Maria agree that at least some of these experiments have provided information of major benefit to humans, whereas others have led to false assumptions that have threatened human well-being. These commonplaces may be listed on the issues brief as follows:

1. Medical, military, and industrial experiments should be directed at the acquisition of knowledge that will improve the quality of human life.

2. The American public spends approximately 4 billion dollars annually on animal experimentation.

3. Between 20 and 40 million animals are used by American medical, industrial, and military researchers each year.

4. Many animals suffer emotional stress and physical pain while experiments are being performed on them.

5. Some experiments on animals have furthered medical progress, which has improved the quality of human life.

6. Some experiments on animals have led to false scientific assumptions that have in turn threatened human well-being.

7. Current federal laws protect approximately 20 percent of animals used in laboratory experiments.

These commonplaces of value, policy, and fact are but a few of the assumptions that Michael and Maria share. Listing as many shared assumptions as possible helps participants in discussion and debate clarify their points of controversy. In this way, Feature 2 of the issues brief plays an important role in preparing participants to argue effectively.

> ▾ **Exercise 3:** Review the characterizations of Michael and Maria's discussions provided here and in Chapter 4. List previously unspecified commonplaces that you believe Michael and Maria are likely to share.
> ▾ **Exercise 4:** Select a topic of your choice. Discuss this topic with people who disagree with your views on it. Next, list commonplaces you believe you share with the other participants. If possible, ask these participants if they agree with your analysis.

Definitions of Key Terms

The third feature of the issues brief is less complicated than the first two, though it also requires careful reflection. The main purpose of this feature is to provide a common vocabulary to participants in discussion and debate. In this sense, the definitions provided on the issues brief are extensions of the commonplaces listed earlier. They are commonplaces of definition.

To determine which terms need definition, the advocate needs to answer two questions:

> ▾ What are the key terms needed to effectively discuss the topic?
> ▾ How may we characterize the shared definitions of these key terms?

In Michael and Maria's discussion, key terms would probably include: *animal, animal models, military research, industrial research, medical research, scientific progress, human well-being, animal welfare, emotional stress, physical pain, justified,* and *adequately protect.* Of these, only "animal models" and the three types of research are likely to produce shared definitions. Discussion on the term "animal" is likely to lead to a distinction between humans and other animals, so that remaining discussion centers on uses of "nonhuman animals" in research. Definitions of such terms as "emotional stress" and "physical pain" are likely themselves to be issues. What constitutes *human well-being* and *animal welfare* are likely to be in dispute as well. Efforts to define "scientific progress" are likely to be fascinating, but not without major disagreement. And such terms as "justified" and "adequately protect" are likely to generate as much controversy as any other central issue.

As discussion continues, participants are likely to discover new key terms. Michael and Maria are likely to discuss alternatives to animal experiments, including mathematical modeling of the structure-activity relationship and computer graphics; mathematical modeling of biochemical and physiological processes; human studies; in vitro techniques; exchange and use of computer-stored information; and other alternatives. Finding commonplace definitions of these terms will assist dialogue on the topic.

Recall from Chapter 4 that there are at least six different types of definitions: formal, by example, by common usage, operational, by negation, by comparison or contrast, and by a combination of two or more of these types of definitions. Once participants have a common understanding of what the key terms are, the process of defining them is eased considerably by this variety of definition types.

> ▾ **Exercise 5:** Provide definitions for at least two of the key terms listed above.
> ▾ **Exercise 6:** Select a topic. After discussing the topic with people who disagree with you, identify at least three key terms. Finally, provide definitions for these terms. If possible, ask the other discussants if they accept your definitions.

Overview of Issues, Competing Claims, and Support

The final feature of the issues brief—an overview of issues, competing claims, and relevant support—requires the most meticulous and sometimes even painstaking effort for the advocate. However, this effort offers two valuable rewards: A detailed issues overview provides excellent material for the development of persuasive arguments and provides both advocates and their audiences some of the most useful tools for reasoned deliberation. Decision makers equipped with this type of overview are able to quickly and effectively consider at least two competing sets of options.

Preparation of the issues and support overview requires participation in extensive discussions on the topic (where possible), the type of research described in earlier chapters (when possible), and careful reflection about the issues. Ideally, the final feature of the issues brief provides a coherent overview of competing views on the central issues, with an outline of support (in terms of both evidence and argumentative development) for each competing view.

In reality, however, authors of issues briefs often face limited time and resources. Sometimes extensive discussions are not possible. Or library and other research facilities are unavailable.

More often preparation time is limited. Given the vast amount of information available on a topic, a comprehensive issues brief would take much more time to prepare than most advocates have available to them. As a result, careful choices must be made. Which evidence is most likely to assist advocates prepare effective arguments for competing sides? What sources are likely to enhance each side's credibility? Which claims would enhance the audience's ability to assess the validity of each side's perspective? Responding to these questions will help authors make the difficult choices required in writing an issues overview.

The Sample Issue Overview on pages 153–160 illustrates this point. Although much more evidence is available than is presented for each of the claims on the brief, enough evidence is given to assist opposing advocates as they attempt to prepare persuasive arguments in support of their claims. As you read the sample overview, identify claims and support (if any) that you believe satisfy this goal and those which you believe fail to fulfill it.

- ▼ **Exercise 7**: Review the overview of Issue I on pages 153–160. Identify claims that you believe would effectively serve an animal welfare advocate who wants to argue on behalf of strengthening government regulation of experimentation on animals. Next, identify any claims that you believe would effectively serve an opposing advocate. How effectively are these claims developed in the Sample Issue Overview? What changes would you propose to strengthen the proposed arguments? Why?

- ▼ **Exercise 8**: Identify strengths and weaknesses in the Sample Issue Overview. How effectively would this overview of Issue I serve an audience attempting to assess the adequacy of laws that regulate animal experimentation? Why?

- ▼ **Exercise 9**: Determine whether each of the Sample Issue Overview's primary claims (I.A., I.B., I.C., I.D., and their counterclaims) are statements of fact, value, or policy. Next, evaluate the appropriateness of the types of support provided for each of these claims and counterclaims. Given the nature of the issue addressed, how appropriate were the claims? Should the author have considered different types of claims? Why or why not? Finally, in the case of each primary claim, imagine what types of support would have been appropriate if the claim had been a different type. For example, if the claim is factual, imagine the types of support that would have been appropriate had the claim been a value or policy claim.

- ▼ **Exercise 10**: In the Sample Issue Overview, there is relative parity between the claims and counterclaims presented. Does this relative parity help the reader to assess the strengths and weaknesses of each side? How important is a relatively balanced presentation to the decision maker's consideration of relevant issues? Why?

- ▼ **Exercise 11**: Applying the information provided in Chapter 4, identify the types of evidence provided to support competing claims on the Sample Issue Overview. Evaluate the persuasiveness of each type of evidence. How persuasive are the sources cited? Why?

Sample Issue Overview

Issue I: Do existing laws regulating uses of live animals in scientific experimentation adequately protect human interests and animal welfare?

I. Current regulation of experimentation on animals effectively protects human interests and animal welfare.

A. The Animal Welfare Act, as amended (effective December 23, 1986), effectively protects animals.

   1. Provision A of the act requires researchers to "ensure that animal pain and distress are minimized, including adequate veterinary care with the appropriate use of anesthetic, tranquilizing drugs, or euthanasia."

   2. Provision B of the act requires "the principal investigator" to consider "alternatives to procedures likely to produce pain or distress in an experimental animal."

   3. Provision C of the act requires consultation with a veterinarian, uses of pain inhibitors, and appropriate postsurgical procedures when adopting painful practices.

   4. Provision D of the act prohibits using animals in more than one major operative procedure except in cases of "scientific necessity."

B. Government regulations are supplemented by other regulatory mechanisms.

   1. Funding agencies provide their own screening of research proposals.

      a. Most funding agencies require certification of laboratory animal facilities by the American Association for Accreditation of Laboratory Animal Care (AAALAC).

I. Current regulation of experimentation on animals fails to adequately protect human interests and animal welfare.

A. The Animal Welfare Act, as amended (effective December 23, 1986), fails to adequately protect animals used in military, industrial, and medical labs.

   1. The vast majority of animals used in labs are not even covered by the Animal Welfare Act. Less than 20 percent of all animals used in laboratories receive protection from this legislation.

   2. Provisions A–D of the act give complete discretion to researchers to determine the nature of care and the "necessity" of painful methods used.

   3. The act requires only semiannual inspections of animal areas and permits inspectors to warn researchers before making their inspections. The law also permits the research community to participate in the selection of all members of the inspection team.

   4. All provisions of federal animal welfare regulations may be waived "when specified by research protocol."

B. So-called regulatory mechanisms fail to protect animal welfare.

   1. Funding agencies actually discourage research that attempts to minimize animal suffering.

      a. Agencies are uncomfortable with innovative approaches, preferring the "accepted mode of research in a particular field." As a result, "awards and grants that finance research" are "geared to animal experiments," even when alternatives are more reliable and more humane. (Peter Singer, *Animal Liberation: A New Ethics for Our Treatment of Animals* [New York: Avon Books, 1975], p. 67.)

Sample Issue Overview (*continued*)

b. The National Institutes of Health (NIH) insist that researchers adhere to the "NIH Guide for Care of Laboratory Animals."

c. Many agencies require adherence to the Guiding Principles of Animal Care promulgated by the American Physiological Society.

2. Many institutions have their own animal-care committees that screen protocols and inspect facilities.

3. Because abuses of animals in labs distort scientific findings, the scientific community is intolerant of such abuses. Peer reviews and other mechanisms carefully guard against such abuses.
   a. The Scientists Center for Animal Welfare in Bethesda, Maryland, publishes newsletters, guidelines for animal care, and other materials for use by scientists. This group also sponsors conferences on animal care in scientific laboratories.

C. Current regulations help scientists use effective methods to enhance the quality of human life.
1. "In biomedical, agricultural, toxicological, behavioral, and other biological studies intact animals perform a vital and irreplaceable function, often serving as models for man" (American Institute of Biological Sciences, "Statement Regarding the Use of Animals in Experimentation," presented to the U.S. House of Representatives Committee on Agriculture, September 19, 1984, p. 262).

b. NIH guidelines cover less than 40 percent of animals used in labs. Furthermore, NIH and other agencies seldom enforce their guidelines. For example, one of the nation's major research institutions, Ohio State University, has never received a spontaneous visitation by NIH officials.

c. Guiding Principles of Animal Care offer suggestions for ethical treatment of animals in labs. Researchers are left complete discretion to determine the actual care that animals receive in labs.

2. Animal-care committees are usually comprised of members of the research community and people selected by researchers, thereby providing no spokesperson whose primary concern is animal welfare.

3. Peer reviews are designed primarily to protect the credibility of the research community, not to protect the welfare of animals used by researchers.

C. Current regulations fail to protect human interests.
1. Regulations encourage studies that draw dangerously invalid inferences from animals to humans.

a. "Virtually every major biomedical advance can be traced back to original critical studies using animals. . . . The extension of the average life span from 45 years at the turn of the century to 70 plus years today is dependent in a major way upon animal studies." (John A. Krasney, *Buffalo Physician*, September 1984, p. 6.)

(1) Poliomyelitis, rheumatic heart disease, infectious diseases now treated with antibiotics, mental diseases treated with chlorpromazine and its tranquilizing derivatives, advances in immunological diagnostic procedures are among the many breakthroughs attributable to animal studies. (Krasney, pp. 6–13.)

b. "The discovery of insulin, which has proved so beneficial to diabetics, was accomplished in part through experiments on dogs." (Eugene Garfield, Institute for Scientific Information, *Current Contents*, January 30, 1984, p. 3.)

c. Dr. Zaven Khacharurian of the National Institute on Aging notes that "there has been incredible progress in Alzheimer's research concerning brain functioning. . . . [The] bulk of that research involved animals, and they hold the key to continued progress." (*The Washingtonian*, August 1986, p. 117.)

d. "The dog's cardiovascular and respiratory systems closely approximate that of a small man. Therefore, equipment to be used on man can be developed and tested on the dog. Modern animal surgery to treat clinical conditions in the dog is completely indebted to the development of this equipment." (William I. Gay, Director of the Animal Resources Program, National Institutes of Health, "Why the Dog as a Research Subject?" *Lab Animal*, March 1983, p. 37.)

e. "For every new vaccine produced, live-animal testing answers the questions 'Does it work?' and 'Is it safe?'" (*The Washingtonian*, August 1986, p. 117.)

a. Thalidomide, a sleeping pill that resulted in the birth of hundreds of severely deformed babies, was extensively tested on animals before it was released. Toxicologists have noted that "the toxicity tests that had been carefully carried out on thalidomide without exception had demonstrated it to be an almost uniquely safe compound." After the drug was proven dangerous in humans, further tests on pregnant laboratory dogs, cats, rats, monkeys, hamsters, and chickens failed to indicate the potential dangers of the drug to humans. (S. F. Paget, ed., *Methods in Toxicology* [Palo Alto, Calif.: Blackwell Scientific Publications, 1970], pp. 134–139.)

b. Insulin produces deformities in infant rabbits and mice, but does not have this effect in humans (Paget, p. 142).

c. "If penicillin had been judged by its toxicity on guinea pigs it might never have been used on man" (G. F. Somers, *Quantitative Method in Human Pharmacology and Therapeutics* [New York: Pergamon Press, 1959], p. 153).

d. Studies to determine weight loss in "smoking laboratory animals" are seriously undermined by the fact that "exposing laboratory animals to cigarette smoke requires a restraint apparatus since animals avoid cigarette smoke and will move away from the generating source." Unfortunately, "Restraint alone stresses the animal enough to alter food intake and weight gain." (*Physiology and Behavior* 32 [1984]:389–395.)

e. Swine flu and other vaccinations have proven to be so potentially harmful that vaccine manufacturers are unwilling to guarantee their safety. In 1977 alone, law suits concerning death and paralysis resulting from swine flu vaccine were estimated at $1.3 million. (Hannah Allen, *Don't Get Stuck! The Case Against Vaccinations and Injections* [Natural Hygiene Press, 1951].)

Sample Issue Overview (*continued*)

2. Human beings are part of the animal kingdom. Animal studies give us "more complete knowledge of the whole" animal kingdom, including ourselves. "The whole history of biomedical research tells us of the countless benefits to humans obtainable by asking the right questions of animal models." (Joe R. Held, "Appropriate Animal Models," in *The Role of Animals in Biomedical Research*, ed. Jeri A. Sechzer [New York Academy of Sciences, 1983], p. 19.)

   a. "Because primates share 95% of human DNA, they are irreplaceable models in the neurosciences." (Frederick Goodwin, Director of intramural programs for the National Institute of Mental Health, cited in *The Washingtonian*, August 1986, p. 17.)

   b. "Thousands of people owe their lives to the animals who made possible the initial research for many scientific advances such as heart-lung machines, vaccines, cancer therapy, and insulin." (Senator Orrin G. Hatch, "Biomedical Research," *American Psychologist*, June 1987, p. 591.)

   c. "Animal research will play an essential and integral role in the development of cures for Alzheimer's disease, cancer, heart disease, birth defects, acquired immune deficiency syndrome (AIDS), and other tragic ailments that strike so many people both in our country and around the world." (Hatch, p. 592.)

   d. "Only the study of behavior in animals can provide methods to study the efficiency of new treatments to improve the quality of patients' lives. Psychologists studying animal behavior can make important contributions to both rehabilitation and the development of cures, especially in the area of brain and spinal cord injury." (Dennis M. Feeney, "Human Rights and Animal Welfare," *American Psychologist*, June 1987, p. 594.)

2. Current regulations discourage the development of less costly and more reliable alternatives.

   a. Systematic acceptance of animal models discourages consideration of more reliable and less costly computer studies, mathematical modeling, tissue studies, ethnographic studies, and human studies.

   b. The discovery of propranolal, a commonly prescribed treatment for high blood pressure, is often attributed to animal research. In fact, this drug's antihypertensive effect was actually discovered by accident when the drug was used for treatment of anginal pain. (Brandon Reines, *Heart Research on Animals*. American Antivivisection Society publication, June 1985, p. 11.)

   c. Surgery for coarctation of the aorta and mitral stenosis was unsuccessfully attempted on animals. Proper techniques were developed through work on humans. (Reines, p. 11.)

   d. "Although thousands of animals have been forced to inhale tobacco smoke for months or even years, the proof of the connection between tobacco usage and lung cancer was based on data from clinical observations of humans." (Singer, p. 80.)

e. "Basic psychological research with animals has led to important achievements in the interest of human welfare." (Frederick A. King, Chair of the American Psychological Association's Committee on Animal Research and Experimentation, "Animals in Research: The Case for Experimentation," *Psychology Today*, September 1984, p. 56.)

f. Research on animals has led to biofeedback techniques, behavioral modification and behavioral therapies, programmed instruction, and the application of learning principles to educational tasks. (King, pp. 56–58.)

3. "We must recognize that progress is often slow, but necessarily so if we are to ensure that the integrity of science is not compromised." (Hatch, p. 592.)

4. "No matter what the model or simulation shows, it must be tested in the living animal if one is to understand behavior." (Feeney, p. 597.)

e. Current laws encourage cancer researchers to continue using animal studies, despite the fact that "carcinogen testing on candidate compounds can be performed within three months for approximately 1/10 or 1/20 the cost of a single rodent cancer study." (Toxicologist David J. Brusick, "The Use of Short Term *In Vitro* and Submammalian Tests as Alternatives to Large Scale Animal Bioassays," in *The Role of Animals in Biomedical Research*, p. 68.)

f. Current laws encourage continued use of the cruel and wasteful LD–50 test, which determines the lethal dose of industrial and other products for 50 percent of animals forcibly exposed to a product, despite the fact that this test is widely considered ineffectual. (Frank Bentayou, "Biology or Brutality," *The Plain Dealer Magazine*, June 5, 1988, p. 30.)

3. Current laws encourage needless repetition at a large expense to both humans and animals.

a. Between 1974 and 1988, P. Tornheim of the University of Cincinnati used a Remington head stunner to crush the heads of approximately 1,000 cats in experiments described by other scientists as "outdated, wasteful, and irrelevant." These experiments cost approximately 1 million dollars. (*Columbus Dispatch*, November 18, 1988, p. B-6.)

4. Current regulations encourage costly experimentation on animals at the expense of more effective scientific, medical, and social projects.

a. A transfer of funding from experiments on rare diseases to preventive medical care would ultimately help many more Americans have a better quality of life.

(1) Despite 4 billion dollars of funding per year, experiments on animals have failed to improve an American infant's chances of living to the age of one. The United States is currently ranked nineteenth among industrial nations in infant mortality. In fact, an infant born in Hong Kong has a better chance of reaching adulthood than an infant born in one of America's inner cities (ABC News, November 26, 1988).

Sample Issue Overview (*continued*)

D. Additional regulations are not needed to protect animals from needless abuse in labs.
1. Researchers are anxious to reach scientifically valid conclusions. Improper care of animals in labs distorts research results, thereby invalidating the investigator's painstaking efforts.
    a. The research community is intolerant of abuses of animals in labs. Journal review boards carefully screen journal submissions for evidence of poorly designed protocols and other scientifically unacceptable practices.
2. "Many experimental studies of animal behavior involve the use of positive rewards such as food. In many cases, especially with the higher animals such as cats, dogs, and monkeys, the use of food that is especially preferred provides enough motivation so that the animals do not have to be food-deprived in order to make them hungry enough to be motivated to work for the reward." (Neal E. Miller, "Understanding the Use of Animals in Behavioral Research: Some Critical Issues," in *The Role of Animals in Biomedical Research,* p. 113.)

3. Research on animals ultimately benefits animals. Much research helps veterinarians "understand the normal structure and function of animals, determine the etiology and pathogenesis of abnormal conditions, and provide pharmaceuticals and biologics

D. Current regulations fail to discourage severe and needless abuses of animals in military, industrial, and medical laboratories.
1. Harlow subjected numerous monkeys to total isolation in "pits of despair." After acknowledging the monkeys' severe depression and anguish, Harlow wrote that "the direct applicability of this research to human psychopathology seems somewhat limited." Nonetheless, these experiments continue to be replicated in American laboratories. (H. F. Harlow, "Learning to Love," *American Scientist,* September 1966, pp. 244–272.)
2. Cats are known by researchers to be "difficult research subjects." Experimenters have devised an "improved responding apparatus" for cats. To test the device, researchers starved cats to 80 percent of their normal weight. Next they stood the cats on a grid floor that could be electrified. The cats' heads were placed in a Plexiglas cylinder at the back of which was a key that they had to press to obtain food. "Each animal was trained to press the key between 1,500 and 2,000 times per hour. . . . Electric shock was then used to teach the cats not to press the key whenever a white light was turned on. This training continued for three months, during which period a certain percentage of 'unsignaled' shocks were also given, so that the cats were shocked whatever they did. The light was then dimmed to see what intensity the cats could detect. The results were very similar to those obtained by other investigators in 1952 and 1970. The report concludes: 'In conclusion we would like to put to rest the myth that the cat is a difficult behavioral S [subject], and offer this technique as a solution.'" (Singer, p. 59. This research is documented in *Behavior Research Methods and Instrumentation* 4 [1972]: 121.)
3. As early as 1946, Magnus Gregorson of Columbia University surveyed the literature on experiments involving the mental and physical shock that occurs as a result of serious injuries. He reported that over 800 papers dealt with such studies. Methods

used included "a tourniquet on one or more of the extremities, crush, compression, muscle trauma by contusion with light hammer blows, Noble-Collip drum [a device in which animals tumble repeatedly to the bottom of the drum and injure themselves], gunshot wounds, strangulation of intestinal loops, freezing, and burns." Gregorson notes that "hemorrhage has been widely employed" and "an increasing number of these studies has been done without the complicating factor of anesthesia." (*Annual Review of Physiology* 8 [1946]: 335. Cited in Singer, p. 55.)

a. Researchers have since noted that "animal investigations in the field of traumatic shock have yielded diversified and often contradictory results." They urge that "prolonged anesthesia is best avoided" and encourage "future experimentation in this field." (S. M. Rosenthal and R. C. Millican, *Pharmacological Review* 6 [1954]: 489. Cited in Singer, p. 55.)

4. Researchers have developed a restraining chair for long-term studies on baboons. "Noting that 'the difficulties of restraint increase markedly with the use of electric shock' researchers 'anchor' the baboon's arms so as not to allow the animal to straighten them. At the same time, they allow room for the 'considerable growth' to be expected in a long-term study. For the delivery of electric shock the baboon is fitted with an electrode around the waist, and other metal parts, including the seat itself, serve as a second electrode for the delivery of electric current." In one study of this device, twenty-two baboons and rhesus monkeys were "restrained in this manner for lengthy periods, several of them for one-and-one-half years of continuous experimentation." (J. Findley, W. Robinson, and W. Gilliam. *Journal of the Experimental Analysis of Behavior* 15 [January 1971]: 69. Cited in Singer, pp. 60–61.)

for animals. . . . There are many other research areas including nutrition, immunology, and behavior that have also aided animals." (Bruce H. Ewald and Douglas A. Gregg, "Animal Research for Animals," in *The Role of Animals in Biomedical Research*, p. 48.)

a. Examples of benefits to animals include pet vaccines for rabies, distemper, parvo virus, and infectious hepatitis; treatments for animal parasites; feline leukemia research; vaccines for livestock diseases; vitamin deficiency treatments; artificial joints for dogs with hip dysplasia; and pet cancer and heart research treatments.

4. Current regulations are consistent with international standards.
a. "No country prohibits painful experiments." (Franklin M. Loew, "Alleviation of Pain: The Researcher's Obligation," *Lab Animal*, September 1981, p. 36.)
b. "In Great Britain, in 1979, a total of 4,719,878 animals of all species were reported to have been used; anesthesia was not administered (because it was not judged necessary) to 3,873,955, or 82.1 percent of animals." (*Statistics of Experiments on Living Animals, Great Britain, 1979* [October 1980], Cmnd. 8069, H.M.S.O. Cited in Lowe, p. 36.)

Sample Issue Overview (continued)

5. Regulations actually lead some researchers to avoid using animals at the cost of human safety. Some researchers prefer to use human subjects because "access to suitable human subjects is often quick and convenient, whereas access to appropriate animal subjects may be awkward, costly, and burdened with red tape." More regulations would only further discourage work that needs to be done. "To maximize the protection of human subjects ... the wide and imaginative use of live animal subjects should be encouraged rather than discouraged." (Carl Cohen, "The Case for the Use of Animals in BioMedical Research," *New England Journal of Medicine* 315 [October 2, 1986]: 869.)

6. Efforts to "protect animals" "blocked the use of the rabies vaccination developed by Pasteur. It was not until the later development of diphtheria antitoxin, a vaccine to protect against the serious clinical consequences of a disease of epidemic proportion that threatened many more people than rabies, that the importance of animal research was generally accepted." (Feeney, p. 593.)

7. Science often effectively relies on serendipity. One scientist writes, "We were examining the effects of various drugs on reflexes in brain-injured cats (Feeney and Hovda, 1983). I had a new student who got very bored simply describing the behavioral recovery of hemiplegic rats. ... He had just taken his first course in physiological psychology and wanted to put something into the wound to stimulate neurotransmitters. ... I suggested that he try giving the rats the drugs we were using in the experiment with cats. I expected the rats to turn in circles, as had been reported after other unilateral brain lesions. ... Much to my surprise we observed the opposite effect. ... Based on this work with rats and cats, a treatment regimen has been developed for promoting recovery of function in stroke patients." (Feeney, p. 596.)

5. One scientific report summarizes experiments in which more than 700 beagles and other dogs were irradiated with X-rays. The authors of this report did their own study with 50 beagles, receiving results "typical of those described for the dog." The beagles were placed in "wooden boxes and irradiated with different levels of radiation. ... The irradiated dogs vomited, had diarrhea, and lost their appetites. Later they hemorrhaged from the mouth and anus." (K. Woodward, S. Michaelson, T. Noonan, and J. Howland, *International Journal of Radiation Biology* 12 [1967]: 265. Cited in Singer, pp. 28–29.)

6. A 1984 study involved 17 sheep implanted with tubes and burned over 25 to 50 percent of their body. Researchers poured hot water (203 degrees) over shaven skin "until the hide was blanched, indicating a full-thickness burn." The animals were then deprived of food for 24 hours and water for 48 hours, to observe resultant effects on burn-induced tissue swelling. No analgesics were provided to relieve suffering during this experiment. (*Surgery* 95 [1984]: 593–602.)

7. The ineffective Draize test continues to be used to test cosmetics, such as makeup and shampoos. In this test concentrated solutions of the product are dripped into rabbits' eyes. The damage is measured subjectively, according to "the size of the area injured, the degree of swelling and redness, and other types of injury." The "highest level of reaction" is described as "total loss of vision due to serious internal injury to cornea or internal structure. Animal holds eye shut urgently. May squeal, claw at eye, jump, and try to escape." To avoid this inconvenient outcome, rabbits are immobilized in holding devices. Many researchers use metal clips to keep the animals' eyelids apart thereby preventing the animals from receiving any relief from the burning irritation in their injured eyes. (*Journal of the Society of Cosmetic Chemists* 9 [1962]. Discussed in Singer, p. 48.)

▾ ▾ ▾
FROM DELIBERATION TO EFFECTIVE ADVOCACY

Whereas effective deliberation requires a kind of "suspension" of judgment, effective advocacy *begins* with a well-defined judgment. Advocates seek to persuade others to accept their points of view. The advocate's task, unlike the judge's, is to present arguments that *favor one* perspective or point of view.

We have already noted that the issues brief helps decision makers consider competing perspectives. The brief also helps advocates find and develop persuasive arguments. Writing the brief helps the advocate identify arguments most likely to be advanced by people who do not share the advocate's perspective. This identification of alternative perspectives helps advocates develop otherwise undefined views, strengthen existing views, or change their own views in light of reasonable alternative perspectives. This reconceptualization of perspectives helps advocates identify and develop persuasive arguments in defense of their points of view.

If successful, the brief provides commonplaces and shared definitions. The brief also designates central points of disagreement and lines of argument on behalf of competing views on these central issues. With this information in hand, the advocate is ready to respond to the *key questions* that shape the *four steps* needed to *develop and present persuasive arguments.*

Step 1: Discovering and Defining Your Position

- ▾ What are my beliefs on the topic?
- ▾ On what grounds do I base these beliefs?
- ▾ What are my central premises?
- ▾ What is my central conclusion?

Step 2: Defining the Audience

- ▾ Who is my audience?
- ▾ What are their beliefs on the topic?
- ▾ What are the grounds for their beliefs?
- ▾ What are their relevant values?
- ▾ What is the hierarchy of those values?
- ▾ What are their relevant interests?
- ▾ What is the hierarchy of those interests?
- ▾ In sum, what are the bases of the audience's disagreement with me?

Step 3: Defining Your Intention(s)

- ▾ What do I want from my audience?
- ▾ What do I hope to persuade them to believe as a result of reading my paper or listening to my oral presentation?

Step 4: Planning Your Argumentative Strategy

▾ How may I most effectively move the audience from their current views to the views I wish to persuade them to accept?

When developing arguments for a composite audience, advocates use responses to the first set of questions to shape the second set. Once an advocate has discovered and refined his or her views on a topic, his or her answers to the second set of questions, "Defining the Audience," should look something like this:

My audience is a group of people who share the information available to me and share my capacity to reason and to critically assess arguments, but who nonetheless disagree with me for the following reasons:

a. They have the following values: _____ with the following value hierarchy: _____

b. They have the following interests: _____ with the following interest hierarchy: _____

c. They currently believe _____ based on the following support: _____ etc.

Answering the third question follows from the first two, but requires careful reflection of its own. Precisely what do you hope to achieve by writing your argumentative paper or presenting your oral arguments? The more precisely you are able to define both your audience and your intention(s), the more care you will be able to give to the fourth step, developing strategies of persuasion.

Kacey's efforts to write a persuasive paper on prayer in public schools illustrate this process.

Step 1: Discovering and Defining Her Position Preparing a detailed issues brief on the topic helped Kacey reconsider this controversial topic. After careful consideration of many related issues, Kacey found the arguments in favor of school prayer more persuasive than those opposed.

Step 2: Defining the Audience Now that she knows her position, Kacey is ready to define her audience. Because she is writing to a composite audience, she is addressing reasonable, well-informed people who disagree with her perspective. At this point, Kacey does not have a group of people available for discussion. However, she did have access to an audience while she was writing her issues brief. She also has access to literature that describes opposing views on the topic.

Based on her knowledge about and understanding of the topic, Kacey must now imagine her specific audience's values, beliefs, and interests. Accordingly, she asks herself why reasonable people disagree with her. What are their beliefs on the topic? What are their relevant values? What is the hierarchy of these values? What are their relevant interests?

Kacey has learned from her reading on the topic that many opponents of prayer in public schools share her sense that religious faith is vital to mental and spiritual well-being. But these opponents' commitment to maintaining a separation of church and state takes precedence over their other related values. They fear any policy that jeopardizes this value. And they believe that prayer in public schools would ultimately endanger it.

Kacey has also learned that many reasonable opponents of school prayer want to preserve their parental autonomy as it relates to the development of their children's religious orientation. They are concerned that the operationalization of any policy that permits school prayer may result in indoctrination to one specific religious point of view.

Some people who oppose school prayer, Kacey has learned, base their opposition on the belief that a short period of prayer in school could potentially trivialize religious faith. They fear that their commitment to teaching children to value religion may be endangered by a trivialization of religion during school.

After many hours of discussion, research, and reflection, Kacey concludes that these values and beliefs play a primary role in her audience's opposition to prayer in public schools.

Step 3: Determining Her Intention(s)   Kacey's next task is to decide what she hopes to accomplish with her paper. What does she want to persuade her readers to accept? If successful, what will her arguments achieve?

Kacey decides that she wants her audience to reconsider their beliefs on school prayer. She hopes to persuade them to consider endorsing a compromise bill recently proposed by a U.S. senator. This bill would permit public elementary schoolteachers to provide a short voluntary period of silent prayer.

Step 4: Planning Her Strategy   Given Kacey's assessment of her audience and her designated intention, Kacey decides that her arguments will be most effective if they work *with* rather than *against* her audience's values, interests, and beliefs. After much thought, Kacey decides to adopt the following strategy:

1. Begin by acknowledging the importance of maintaining the separation of church and state.

2. Raise the apparent central issue: Will permitting a voluntary period of school prayer be more or less likely to maintain the separation of church and state?

3. Use acceptable premises, credible evidence, and reasonable inferences to show that school prayer will help *restore* the otherwise beleaguered

rights guaranteed by the First and Fourteenth Amendments to the Constitution.

Kacey plans to use considerable evidence in support of her basic premise:

> ▼ **Basic Premise:** The "secular humanism" currently taught in public schools jeopardizes First and related Fourteenth Amendment rights by teaching antireligion.

She plans to show that this antireligious indoctrination is a form of state intervention into religious training similar to any other such intervention, thereby violating the First and related Fourteenth Amendments' implicit admonitions against teaching religion in public schools. Kacey will conclude with an argument for her central claim:

> ▼ **Central Claim:** Providing a period of prayer in public schools will help restore the balance intended by the authors of the First and Fourteenth Amendments.

If Kacey has accurately assessed her audience's reasons for opposing school prayer, and if she is able to persuade her audience to accept her central claim, she probably will achieve her intention. Under these circumstances, she will have persuaded her audience that their primary values will be more effectively protected by endorsing prayer in public schools than by opposing it.

However, Kacey's success will depend on a number of factors, including the following:

Success Factors

> ▼ An accurate assessment of the source(s) of the audience's disagreement with the advocate
> ▼ The ability to anticipate audience responses
> ▼ The development of carefully structured arguments that make reasonable inferences from acceptable premises and from credible evidence derivable from reliable sources

As we have seen in previous chapters, Kacey's success will also depend on her sensitive and effective choice of language to describe the issues, the relevant facts, and the competing perspectives that she plans to address. Throughout her paper, Kacey will need to ask herself the most central question:

> ▼ **Central Question:** How will my audience respond to this label, this definition, this characterization of facts, this claim, this evidence, or this inference?

In short, the key to effective written advocacy is a sensitivity to the audience's beliefs, values, interests, and expectations.

▾ **Exercise 12:** Carefully review the information you have been given regarding Kacey's intention and her audience. Given this information, how would you assess her selected argumentative strategy? What suggestions would you make to Kacey? Why? What additional information would you need to better assess Kacey's strategy?

▾ ▾ ▾

REFUTATION

In the preceding example, Kacey is preparing written arguments for a specific audience. She hopes that her written presentation will persuade her audience to accept her point of view. As we have seen, the degree to which Kacey anticipates opposing arguments significantly contributes to the persuasiveness of her presentation. Sometimes, opposing advocates have the opportunity to both anticipate and directly respond to one another's arguments. Whether these advocates present their arguments in writing or orally, their presentations can make effective use of several *strategies of refutation.*

A common strategy is *direct refutation,* or a point-by-point response to each of the opposing advocate's claims. Sean is an opponent of prayer in public schools. He has carefully reviewed Kacey's arguments in favor of this policy, and he is ready to refute them. He directly challenges each of the points that Kacey makes. He argues, for example, that the so-called secular humanism taught in public schools today is not antireligious at all. Instead, he contends, this approach to religion emphasizes the importance of permitting people to practice their own chosen faith. He also challenges Kacey's interpretation of the purposes underlying the First and Fourteenth Amendments. He presents historical documentation to support his claim that this nation's founders worked hard to prevent the government from imposing a specific religious dogma on its citizens. Sean concludes his direct refutation by arguing that a period of prayer in public schools would seriously jeopardize the religious freedoms afforded by this nation's Constitution.

As part of his refutation of Kacey's arguments, Sean employs a second strategy, *source derogation.* That is, Sean challenges the credibility of some of Kacey's sources. Sean contends, for example, that Kacey has relied on fundamentalist testimony to defend her interpretation of the First and Fourteenth Amendments. Sean concedes that Kacey's sources may know much about biblical interpretation. However, their credentials do not support Kacey's reliance on them as constitutional experts.

To help further strengthen his case, Sean makes use of a third strategy of refutation. He asks the audience to take an *even if* stance. He argues that even if Kacey were correct in arguing that the secular humanism currently taught in public schools is antireligious and therefore a form of indoctrination that jeopardizes religious freedoms, and even if Kacey's sources were reliable, her conclusion still would not follow. According to Sean, replacing this allegedly dangerous antireligious indoctrination with a period of school prayer creates an even greater danger to people's religious freedoms. If there really is a problem with the way things are, he continues, then we should force teachers to take greater care in their explanation of why public schools may not endorse a particular religious perspective. This would help children appreciate the importance of religion, without imposing a particular perspective on them. In contrast, Sean concludes, allowing teachers to provide a period of school prayer encourages teachers to impose their religious perspective on children. Sean urges the audience to reconsider the arguments and to oppose Kacey's proposed policy.

Given Sean's views on prayer in public schools, he is not likely to propose a *compromise*. This strategy of refutation is useful when an advocate can find a middle ground that borrows the best from opposing perspectives. This very useful decision-making tool is not appropriate for Sean, because he so strongly opposes Kacey's premises and proposed policy. Nor is Kacey likely to favor a compromise position on this issue. It is important to note, however, that while neither Kacey nor Sean may propose a compromise, their audiences might imagine and eventually adopt a compromise position not presented by either advocate.

Kacey's arguments defended a general policy claim. She hoped to persuade her audience that some kind of prayer period should be provided in public schools. She did not, however, provide a specific proposal, detailing precisely how her policy would be operationalized. If she had provided such a proposal, Sean could have chosen a fifth strategy of refutation known as *counterproposal*. This strategy allows advocates to concede premises that lead to an opposing advocate's call for a general policy change, while rejecting the specific plan provided to operationalize the policy. Even if Kacey had provided a specific proposal, however, it is unlikely that Sean would have selected this strategy of refutation because he opposes *any* version of Kacey's policy. He fundamentally rejects the idea that there should be any kind of prayer period in public schools.

Once Kacey has become aware of Sean's selected strategies of refutation, she will likely wish to develop and present her own. As she prepares the *rebuttal* to Sean's refutation, Kacey has an additional strategy available to her: *supportive refutation*. This approach calls for defensive arguments to support her case in light of Sean's opposition to it. Perhaps she will present additional evidence to support her interpretation of the First and Fourteenth Amendments. Or perhaps she will find and present additional evidence to support her claim that current educational policies are antireligious and therefore inevitably threaten children's spiritual development.[9]

---

9. For further discussion of these strategies of refutation, see Richard D. Reike and Malcolm Sillars, *Argumentation and the Decision Making Process,* 2nd ed. (Glenview, Ill.: Scott, Foresman, 1984), pp. 176–190. Reike and Sillars note that in specialized argumentative situations, advocates may select yet a seventh refutation posture known as *denial*. This strategy is appropriate when someone has been accused of incompetence, negligence, or the commission of an offense.

Whatever strategies Kacey eventually adopts, she will need to continually remind herself that the persuasiveness of her presentation depends in large measure on her sensitivity to her audience's beliefs, values, and interests. Throughout her presentation, whether it is written or oral, Kacey must ask herself how a reasonable audience that does not share her views on the topic might respond to the arguments she is presenting to them. This audience orientation will significantly increase the chances that Kacey's audience will carefully attend to her arguments as they deliberate on the topic.

> ▾ **Exercise 13:** Evaluate the likely effectiveness of each of Sean's strategies of refutation. Next, consider how Kacey might most effectively respond to each type of refutation. Which of these sets of arguments would you find most persuasive? Why?
>
> ▾ **Exercise 14:** Identify the types of claims that Kacey and Sean present in defense of their positions. What types of evidence are appropriate to defend each type of claim? How do the types of claims interact with one another? How important is it for advocates to select support appropriate to the type of claim being defended?

▾ ▾ ▾
SUMMARY

Decision making is a dynamic process that involves interaction between deliberation and advocacy. The issues brief assists both advocates and their audiences effectively employ the five strategies of reflection. A well-prepared brief allows readers to scan issues, from competing perspectives, with little effort. At the same time, the process of completing the brief prepares advocates to effectively defend their views.

Effective advocacy requires meticulous preparation and a sensitivity to audience interests, values, and beliefs. Advocates who are preparing arguments for a composite audience need to discover and define their position, define their audience and intention, and carefully plan an argumentative strategy. A well-planned argumentative strategy includes selection of the most appropriate and effective method of refutation. Advocates must also find and present support, make inferences, and use language that is appropriate to the types of claims defended and adapted to the occasion and audience.

Above all, effective advocacy requires sensitivity to the audience. Whether advocacy is presented in writing, through oral presentation, or through both, successful advocacy requires consideration of how a reasonable audience that does not yet share the advocate's views on the topic might respond to the arguments presented to them. This audience orientation significantly increases the likelihood that audiences will carefully attend to an advocate's arguments as they deliberate on the topic.

▼ ▼ ▼

EXERCISES

1. Select a controversial topic on which you have a readily definable position. Next, prepare to write an argumentative paper that supports your position. Complete the four steps needed to develop persuasive arguments as described on pp. 161–162. As part of Step 2, identify commonplaces of value, policy, fact, and definition that you share with your audience. As part of Step 4, state your central premise(s) and claim(s). Finally, write your paper, carefully considering the "success factors" described in the steps.

2. Imagine an advocate who opposes the perspective presented in your paper from Exercise 1. What strategies of refutation should this advocate employ to persuade your audience to reconsider your arguments? How would you respond to this refutation? What types of refutation would you use in your rebuttal?

3. Select a controversial topic about which you do not have a readily definable position. Write an issues brief designed to help you and others reach a reasonable position on the topic. Next, plan to develop a persuasive oral presentation in support of your position on the topic. As you prepare your presentation, be sure to complete the four steps needed to develop persuasive arguments.

4. Imagine an advocate who opposes the perspective presented in your paper from Exercise 3. What strategies of refutation should this advocate employ to persuade your audience to reconsider your arguments? How would you respond to this refutation? What types of refutation would you use in your rebuttal?

5. Several court districts have begun permitting jurors to actively participate in criminal trial proceedings. The procedure permits jurors to write questions that they would like the judge to ask witnesses during the trial. The judge reviews each question in the presence of the prosecuting and defense attorneys. Both attorneys have the right to challenge any question. However, attorneys seldom exercise this right because they do not want to create the perception (among jurors) that they have anything to hide.

    Opponents of this innovative court procedure argue that active juror involvement during a trial leads jurors to become advocates, thereby jeopardizing the integrity of the proceeding. Supporters of active juror involvement contend that the procedure affords jurors the opportunity to gain information and insights they need to make well-informed decisions.

Develop the best arguments you can for and against permitting this type of juror involvement during criminal trial proceedings. What is your position on this topic? Why? What issues would you need to address to effectively defend your position? What commonplaces would you be likely to share with your audience? What terms would you need to define? What opposing arguments would you need to anticipate and overcome?

CHAPTER

8

Evaluating Argumentation

Chapter 7 emphasized the interaction between skillful deliberation and effective advocacy. Central to both is the ability to evaluate arguments. And evaluation is the key to effective argumentation. Recall from Chapter 1, for example, that D'Angelo defines critical thinking as "the process of *evaluating* statements, arguments, and experience. Listening, reading, viewing, speaking, and writing skills require well-developed evaluation skills.

This chapter provides guidelines for evaluating argumentation addressed to a composite audience. It presents an overview of the following standards for evaluating argumentation: *premise acceptability, relevance, adequacy of support, comprehensiveness, structural coherence,* and the avoidance of *basic fallacies.* In order to help critics apply these standards, the chapter ends with a list of five sets of questions that critics may apply to argumentation in a variety of practical contexts.

▼ ▼ ▼

THE ART OF CRITICISM

Evaluating argumentation is a complex process that requires sensitivity to the many elements of critical thinking discussed in previous chapters. Critical thinking depends on the ability and willingness to develop and maintain an open mind.

By definition, argumentation implies more than one possible and reasonable outcome. If reasonable people are unanimous in their position, there is no need for argumentation. Argumentation is meaningful and productive only in light of disagreement. And this disagreement, to be meaningful, is represented by at least two (and usually more) reasonable, yet differing, points of view.

Argumentation relies on underlying assumptions and values. Further, argumentation occurs in the realm of the probable, rather than that of certainty. Arguments in practical contexts cannot be expected to make airtight logical connections. As we have seen, this absence of certainty leaves practical arguments vulnerable to refutation.

But refutation that is hostile or intended simply to defeat someone else's argument does not serve the purposes of argumentation. Suppose, for instance, that you have been asked to serve as a member of city council. Your first assignment is to vote on whether your local government has a right to force people to protect themselves by wearing seatbelts. You tend to believe that the government does not have this right, but you need to discuss the matter further before you will feel prepared to make a decision. Through discussion, you learn that disagreements on this question depend in part on differing interpretations of what it means to be a citizen in a free country. You also learn that we cannot be certain about the correctness of any position on this issue. You realize that it will always be possible to refute any argument made. But refutation for its own sake, or hostile refutation designed only to discredit arguments, will not be much help to you in reaching a reasonable decision. William Brandt provides a useful summary of this problem. He writes, "An inveterately hostile audience can refute any argument whatsoever,"[1] but such refutation only inhibits useful dialogue and constructive deliberation.

Your vote on the seatbelt legislation will best be guided by cooperative debate. The most useful arguments will be those that help everyone on the council more fully and openly evaluate the evidence, discover and evaluate relevant questions of value, and otherwise address many of the issues involved in the complex question of whether the government should be permitted to compel people to protect themselves by wearing seatbelts.

---

1. William J. Brandt, *The Rhetoric of Argumentation* (Indianapolis: Bobbs-Merrill, 1970), p. 201.

Similarly, criticism does not simply involve finding "something wrong with" or "saying something bad about"; it is an exercise in intelligent judgment. "It is easy to find something bad to say about a book, a person, an institution, a society; but to allow that to pass as 'being critical' is to confuse hostility with understanding."[2] Useful evaluation of argumentation requires intelligence, understanding, and skill and is best pursued with an open, but critical, mind.

▼ ▼ ▼
THE ROLE OF CONTEXT IN EVALUATING ARGUMENTATION

An open, critical mind is not enough to effectively evaluate argumentation. Argumentation occurs within a context. And arguing effectively in a context requires knowledge about it. Scientific argumentation, for example, requires scientific knowledge and a sensitivity to the beliefs, values, and shared language of the scientific community to whom the argumentation is addressed. Legal argument addressed to a jury must take account of the legal system's formal rules, as well as the predisposition of the jury to whom the argumentation is addressed.

Evaluating argumentation in other, less specialized contexts also requires knowledge of the topic and about the context. To whom is the argumentation addressed? What formal and informal constraints characterize the context in which this argumentation appears? These are but two of the many contextual questions that must be answered before you begin evaluating arguments.

Even apparently universal criteria for evaluating argumentation must be adapted to specific contexts. The reasonableness of any argument is tied directly to the context in which it is conceived, delivered, and received. History has taught us that perspectives widely considered reasonable in one century are often considered unreasonable in another. There are many examples of social and political arguments that found greater favor in one era than in another. At one time, for example, the idea that women should have the right to vote seemed foolish to many Americans. The views expressed by early suffragettes were poorly received in most social circles. Today, most Americans value women's right to vote. These and other social, political, legal, scientific, and economic changes have taught us that context plays a fundamental role in determining the acceptability of an argument's premises.

But evaluating argumentation in its context makes it difficult to determine, beyond any doubt, what is a weak or irrelevant argument. We are left to wonder whether such questions are relevant to the audience or whether

---

2.   Joseph Tussman, *Government and the Mind* (New York: Oxford University Press, 1977), pp. 69–70.

they can then be determined objectively. For example, when we look at arguments for animal welfare today, should we look at them from the standpoint of today's audiences only? Or should we apply some universal philosophical principles in our analysis?

When we look for criteria to evaluate arguments, we are not likely to find universal, airtight rules. Instead, we need to "take account of the particular character of the audience, of its evolution during the debate, and of the fact that habits and procedures that prove good in one sphere are not good in another." Evaluation of arguments "must be able to adapt itself to the most varied circumstances, matters, and audiences."[3]

But this recognition of the importance of adapting criteria for evaluation to contexts does not leave us without standards for evaluating the quality of specific arguments. Despite the variability among contexts, evaluating practical arguments requires a method of analysis that "demands rigor from the critic even as it allows him or her the freedom to adapt to the changing demands of particular situations."[4] Criteria for evaluating argumentation addressed to a composite audience fulfill this need.

Recall that the primary purpose of argumentation addressed to a composite audience is to improve the quality of decision making on issues of public interest. In addition to satisfying the need for rigor, criteria for evaluating arguments addressed to a composite audience satisfy the need to be adaptable to a wide variety of practical contexts.

Application of these criteria in a specific context, however, requires knowledge of the relevant subject matter. A critic who wants to evaluate the quality of arguments presented in favor of limiting advertising during television programs directed at children will need to have enough knowledge about this topic to determine the quality of the arguments presented. Although these critics do not need to be experts on the topic, they do need to have enough knowledge and understanding of the topic to assess the acceptability of the premises presented, to determine whether central issues were addressed, and to assess the quality of the inferences made.

Walter Fisher's discussion of what it means to be rational provides a useful summary of the skills and knowledge required to apply these criteria, regardless of the topic area. He writes:

▼▼▼▼▼▼

Being rational . . . implies not only that one respects reasoning, it also indicates that one knows the nature of argumentative issues, the forms of arguments and their tests, and the rules that govern the particular kind of

---

3.   Chaim Perelman, *The New Rhetoric and the Humanities* (Boston: D. Reidel, 1979), p. 25.

4.   Michael C. Leff, "Interpretation and the Art of the Rhetorical Critic," *Western Journal of Speech Communication,* Fall 1980, p. 349.

argumentative interaction in which one may be an actor, whether scientific, political, legal, ethical, or whatever.[5]   ▾ ▾ ▾

Critics armed with this respect, knowledge of the subject matter, and understanding of the topic and context will be able to effectively use the criteria discussed in the next section whenever they evaluate argumentation intended to improve the quality of decision making.

▾ ▾ ▾
GUIDELINES FOR CRITICISM OF ARGUMENTATION

Unlike advocates, whose job it is to use argumentation for persuasive purposes, the critic is primarily interested in determining an argument's value in improving the quality of the audience's decision making on the subject. Guidelines available to the critic of argumentation addressed to a composite audience include:

- ▾ Acceptability of premises
- ▾ Internal consistency
- ▾ Relevance
- ▾ Adequacy of support
- ▾ Comprehensiveness
- ▾ Structural coherence

Acceptability of Premises

Chapter 5 discussed the nature of composite audiences. Recall that members of this type of audience are qualified to assess the *acceptability of premises* in the relevant argumentation context. They have a general knowledge of the topic, an understanding of the relevant issues, an interest in the topic, and a familiarity with the standards appropriate to the argumentation context. The credentials that these audience members bring to the discussion will, however, vary depending on the context.

For example, in a general discussion about what their family should have for dinner, Bonnie and Jim require only basic nutritional knowledge, as well as some knowledge about the family's culinary habits and preferences. But if one of their children gets sick, Bonnie and Jim will seek the guidance of a

---

5.   Walter R. Fisher, "Rationality and the Logic of Good Reasons," *Philosophy and Rhetoric* 13 (Spring 1980): 123.

trained professional. This medical practitioner will be expected to offer advice based on much more extensive knowledge.

Similarly, the ability to assess the acceptability of premises within a specific context varies significantly, as does the importance of determining acceptability. In most everyday contexts, participants in dialogue do not have the luxury of omniscience. Their knowledge is likely to be reasonably limited. Nor do decision makers always have the time, energy, and resources needed to determine with great reliability the acceptability of premises. In these situations, decision makers use their critical thinking skills to make the best assessment of acceptability they are able to make.

In any given context, acceptability is based on the best knowledge available to the composite audience. At one time, the claim that animals are unfeeling machines represented society's best knowledge. Today, scientists and laypersons alike believe that many species of animals have the capacity to reason and that most have the capacity to suffer physical pain and emotional stress. Many species of animals are now believed to grieve the loss of a companion. Primates have even been known to die as a result of grief. Based on this recently acquired understanding, the premise that animals are unfeeling machines is no longer culturally acceptable. Such a claim now carries a burden of proof with critical audiences.

In most contexts, conventional presumptions pass the test of acceptability. Recall from Chapter 4 that people who seek rejection of conventional presumptions bear a burden of proof with their audience. Fulfillment of this burden overturns the prior claim's status as a presumption and opens debate regarding its acceptability.

Commonplaces also often have the status of acceptability. However, unlike presumptions, commonplaces are more easily challenged. The discovery of new information or new interpretations of available information presents easy challenges to commonplaces. When audience members challenge a commonplace, the claim loses its status as acceptable. By definition, such challenged claims become issues.

Consistency

In addition to determining the acceptability of premises, critics must assess the adequacy of the *connections* between an argument's premises and conclusions. Connections between the premises themselves also must be evaluated.

In this regard, perhaps the most fundamental guideline for evaluating argumentation addressed to a composite audience is *internal consistency*. This term refers to maintaining a consistent line of argument. Internal inconsistency is acceptable only when it is used purposefully, for example, when an advocate uses inconsistency to expose a problem with the audience's thinking.

The reason for this standard is that internally inconsistent argumentation fails to provide a meaningful position. An advocate who tells the audience that the earth is flat and later leads the audience to believe that the earth is not flat leaves the audience no meaningful position for consideration.

There are different types of inconsistency, however, and it is sometimes helpful to keep these distinctions in mind. One popular schema for making these distinctions is the traditional *square of opposition:*

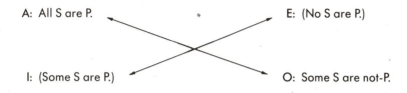

A: All S are P.   E: (No S are P.)

I: (Some S are P.)   O: Some S are not-P.

This square of opposition represents relations between types of statements. The diagonals on the square are *contradictory* to each other. According to traditional logic, statements that are contradictories *cannot have the same truth value.* If all banks offer certificates of deposit (A), then it is not the case that some banks do not offer certificates of deposit (O). Similarly, if some people are not bankers (O), then it is not the case that all people are bankers (A).

On the square, propositions A and E are *contraries.* This means that they *both cannot be true, but they both can be false.* If some people are bankers, whereas others are not, then both A (all people are bankers) and E (no people are bankers) would be false. Furthermore, if all people were bankers (A), then it would not be the case that no people are bankers (E) (and vice versa).

Finally, propositions I and O bear a *subcontrary* relationship. This means that they *both cannot be false, but they both can be true.* If it is not the case that some people are bankers (I), then it is the case that some people are not bankers (O). Yet it might be that some people are bankers (I), whereas others are not bankers (O).

The relations reflected by the square of opposition rely on acceptance of the *law of the excluded middle,* a basic tenet of elementary logic. According to this ancient law of logic, "A is either B or not-B." According to this view, Socrates is either mortal or immortal. It would not be possible for him to be neither mortal nor immortal. Furthermore, according to this basic logical tenet, every statement is either true or false; it is not possible for a meaningful statement to be either both true and false or neither true nor false. Although this basic tenet of logical theory is controversial,[6] it retains status as a technical and conventional presumption in Western philosophy.

---

6.   Some philosophers argue, for example, that it is possible for "some A to be neither B nor not-B" and for "some Statement P to be both true and false or neither true nor false."

When applying this law of logic to argumentation in ordinary language, keep in mind that words of ordinary or natural language often have more than one possible meaning. Sometimes what appears to be an inconsistency is simply a set of statements employing the same term, but *connoting* different meanings. If an otherwise reasonable person says, "When Suzie and Andy both dance they are not both dancing" or "They live in the same world, yet they do not live in the same world," you should look first for a meaningful interpretation to eliminate the incoherence. Constructive dialogue requires that we make a sincere effort to understand each other; we need to try to make sense of what we are each attempting to communicate.

If your analysis of argumentation reveals internal inconsistencies, be certain that these inconsistencies are inadvertent or otherwise unintended, real instances of logical incompatibility. In the event that the advocate did inadvertently propose incompatible claims, then you are justified in concluding that the argumentation is technically inadequate.

Complete analysis requires more than just a review of the argument's internal consistency, however. In Chapter 1 we learned that good reasoning considers not only statements made, but also statements assumed, inferred, and implied by argumentation. Similarly, useful criticism evaluates arguments not only in terms of explicit statements made, but also in terms of assumptions shared by the arguer and his or her audience. Evaluation of consistency therefore requires a review of statements implied by the arguer.

As you evaluate arguments on the basis of consistency, you will find that good advocates seldom *explicitly* make inconsistent claims. But you will also discover that even experienced advocates sometimes provide arguments that lead to conclusions which are inconsistent with assumptions shared by the advocate and his or her audience. The following argument in defense of the view that scientists are morally justified in using animals in psychological experimentation provides an illustration:

▼ ▼ ▼ ▼ ▼ ▼

Hamid wishes to argue that psychological experimentation on animals is morally justified. He is particularly interested in defending the practice of performing psychological experiments on animals capable of experiencing pain, stress, or anxiety. Below is a summary of his stated argument: ▼ ▼ ▼

▼ **Premise 1:** Whatever enriches our understanding of suffering and leads to its alleviation is morally justified.
▼ **Premise 2:** Psychological experimentation on human prototypes enriches our understanding of suffering and leads to its alleviation.
▼ **Premise 3:** Animals capable of suffering pain, stress, and anxiety are human prototypes.
▼ **Conclusion:** Therefore, psychological experimentation on animals capable of suffering pain, stress, and anxiety is morally justified.

Hamid's argument concludes that psychological experimentation on sentient creatures is morally justified. Yet suppose that in the course of discussion, Hamid concedes that he shares the audience's acceptance of the following three assumptions:

▾ **Assumption 1:** The success of psychological experimentation often depends on the intentional infliction of stress or pain on, or the induction of anxiety in, lab animals capable of experiencing such feelings.
▾ **Assumption 2:** Researchers know that laboratory animals suffer when they experience stress, pain, or anxiety.
▾ **Assumption 3:** All intentional infliction of suffering is morally reprehensible.

In conceding these three assumptions, Hamid has acknowledged that some types of psychological experimentation on laboratory animals involve the intentional infliction of suffering in those animals. If this is the case, Hamid must confront an inconsistency. On the one hand, Assumption 3 holds that all intentional infliction of suffering is morally reprehensible. Yet Hamid's original conclusion asserted that experimentation on laboratory animals is morally justified. By conceding that such experimentation intentionally inflicts suffering, Hamid has conceded that, according to his own standards, such experimentation is morally reprehensible. Analysis would quickly reveal that this inconsistency was inadvertent. In this instance, a review of assumptions accepted by the arguer revealed an inconsistency between these assumptions and the claims explicitly advanced by his argument.

In discussing internal inconsistency, we noted the importance of looking for an explanation that would overcome the problem. The presumption of reasonableness is equally useful when confronting an apparent inconsistency between a normally reasonable person's claim and some other justified belief.

Bonnie and Judy's recent exchange about legislating morality illustrates this point. Bonnie's assertion, "You can't legislate morality," proved to be inconsistent with beliefs that she and Judy share. Rather than simply rejecting the claim due to this apparent inconsistency, however, Judy sought an explanation for it.

In the course of their conversation, Bonnie and Judy agreed that marriage and divorce laws are examples of moral legislation. Bonnie conceded further that laws against suicide, laws protecting animals and children from abuse, laws regarding sexual practices, laws against polygamy, laws against prostitution, and so on, are also attempts to legislate morality. After some discussion, Bonnie concluded that probably most laws in some sense are legislations of morality. She acknowledged further that these laws have often prevented immoral acts. She recalled, for instance, a man who would have severely beaten his grandmother had he not feared legal retribution. Despite these acknowledgments, Bonnie maintained her stance: "You can't legislate morality," she repeated. But this time she added, "No law can change what is in a person's heart."

Judy suddenly understood what Bonnie had in mind when she made her original claim. For most speakers of English, the term *morality* involves action at least as much as it does thoughts. A person who thinks about prostitution, but never acts on these thoughts, is not usually viewed as immoral. Immorality, for most people in our culture, involves at least some conduct. Because of their dialogue, Judy now understands that Bonnie's statement was meant to refer only to moral thoughts. Although her statement seemed to imply that legislation could have no impact on moral conduct, Bonnie's use of the term *morality* was meant to encompass only moral consciousness. By presuming Bonnie's reasonableness, Judy was able to ascertain the actual intention of Bonnie's statement.

The resulting discussion taught Bonnie the common usage of the term *morality* and helped Judy consider an interesting idea: that laws do not have the power to influence moral consciousness. Bonnie and Judy will now be able to meaningfully consider this controversial and provocative concept. For them, the presumption of reasonableness was productive.

In sum, evaluation of an argument's internal consistency requires more than just a review of what an arguer actually says or writes. Statements implied by the argument, assumptions shared by the arguer and his or her audience, and alternative readings of the author's intent also provide important material for the analysis of consistency.

Relevance

Argumentation that meets the test of consistency may nonetheless violate basic standards of argument. The reasoning or the data provided to support central claims may not be relevant.

Relevance is of central importance in all argumentation, regardless of context. However, what is relevant to one context is often not relevant to another. In previous chapters, we discussed the importance of discovering points of agreement and controversy before attempting to develop arguments in defense of a position. We also discussed the importance of discovering underlying assumptions and values. Only after you have completed these preliminary steps will you be adequately equipped to determine whether the argumentation you are evaluating has satisfied the audience's reasonable expectation of relevance.

For example, suppose that the topic under discussion is capital punishment. Suppose further that informal dialogue reveals strong disagreement on the question of whether capital punishment deters crime. Suppose further that the discussants agree that deterring crime is an important goal of the criminal justice system. Having uncovered this information, an effective critic will find that argumentation specifically addressed to the question of whether capital punishment deters crime is relevant.

Now suppose, in contrast, that discussion reveals strong disagreement about whether persons on death row prefer long appeals or short appeals. Further discussion would undoubtedly show that resolving this question will make no substantive difference in discussants' views regarding capital punishment. The issue regarding inmates' procedural preference is not relevant to argumentation about capital punishment.

Skillful critics determine not only whether the issues discussed are relevant. They also evaluate the relevance of evidence. Karl supports capital punishment. In his presentation on behalf of maintaining capital punishment, Karl introduces the fact that, in 1980, 60 percent of all murders committed in the United States were committed by black persons against black persons. Although interesting, this statistic will initially be held irrelevant. Karl needs to illustrate the fact's relevance to the issue under discussion.

Perhaps Karl is anticipating an argument likely to be presented by Ian, an opponent of capital punishment. In an effort to show inherent problems with capital punishment, Ian is likely to argue as follows:

▼▼▼▼▼▼

In 1980, nearly half of all persons on death row in America were black. This fact provides prima facie evidence that the American system of capital punishment discriminates against blacks.   ▼▼▼

Karl may use the fact that in 1980, 60 percent of all murders in America were committed by black citizens against black citizens to combat Ian's claim that the system discriminates against black persons. He may first argue that *not* sentencing murderers of black persons to death row would be discriminatory because it would suggest that the black victims of murders are less important than white, Hispanic, Asian, or other murder victims. Furthermore, given that over 60 percent of all murders in 1980 were committed by blacks and given that most persons are placed on death row for murder, the fact that nearly half of all persons on death row in America in 1980 were black fails to provide prima facie evidence of the system's alleged discrimination toward blacks. A critic evaluating this line of reasoning will find that the evidence Karl provided is indeed relevant to the argumentation topic, regardless of the initial appearance of irrelevance.

This example illustrates that evaluation of relevance is fundamentally contextual. Only if you are equipped with an understanding of the topic, as well as knowledge about the context, will you be in a position to determine whether your argument has satisfied this second guideline for effective argumentation.

Adequate Support

Another consideration for evaluating argumentation is *adequacy of support*. When attempting to evaluate the adequacy of an argument's support, you will first need to determine the degree of controversy surrounding the relevant claim. As with determination of relevancy, your evaluation of support will depend on your knowledge of the topic and your awareness of the overall cognitive context of argument.

Let's return, for example, to our discussion of capital punishment. Ian opposes capital punishment. What arguments will he use to attempt to persuade the audience that the system does indeed discriminate against blacks? We saw earlier that the initial evidence Ian provided regarding the number of blacks on death row was inadequate support in light of Karl's persuasive interpretation of that evidence. Ian will need to provide more support for his claim that the system discriminates against blacks. Suppose that, to respond to this audience concern, Ian provides evidence to show that during the many years the United States has used capital punishment, the proportion of blacks killed for the murder of whites has been considerably larger than the proportion of black persons killed for the murder of other blacks. Suppose he shows further that the proportion of whites killed for the murder of blacks has been considerably lower than the proportion of whites killed for the murder of other whites. Without further opposition, this evidence might provide adequate support to at least lead audience members to question the equitability of current capital punishment law enforcement. Whether this evidence would be adequate support for the claim that the system in fact discriminates against blacks would depend on the amount and kind of additional data and arguments that Karl provides regarding the enforcement of capital punishment laws.

As with evaluation of relevancy, determining the adequacy of an argument's support requires careful consideration of the composite audience's reasonable beliefs, knowledge, values, and expectations. Without a sensitivity to these contextual considerations, critics cannot effectively determine adequacy of support.

Comprehensiveness

Related to adequacy of support is an argument's overall *comprehensiveness*. Argumentation that is internally consistent and faithful to the criteria of relevance and adequacy of support may nonetheless fail to satisfy the guideline requiring comprehensiveness. For example, suppose that Karl provided internally consistent argumentation relying on well-grounded, relevant support for relevant claims. Suppose further that he provided adequate support for all of his controversial claims. It might still be possible for Karl to leave several central issues undiscussed. Such an oversight would seriously inhibit the usefulness of his argumentation to the overall decision-making process.

It is therefore important to carefully evaluate whether argumentation provides a comprehensive review of the issues and data needed to make a reasonable decision regarding the topic. Because it is never possible to adequately discuss *all* relevant issues and data, evaluation of comprehensiveness is best accomplished by weighing situational constraints against decision makers' needs. Medical practitioners quickly acquire a sensitivity to this problem.

Doctor Chen's experience illustrates the point. She was called into the emergency room to examine a young child whose liver had been seriously damaged by a bullet wound. Faced with this life-threatening emergency, Dr. Chen had to decide what type of operation to perform on her critically wounded patient. In this situation, fully comprehensive debate over the merits of various medical procedures would likely result in the child's death. In this situation, it would be reasonable to assume that comprehensiveness should be sacrificed for the preservation of the patient's life.

Similarly, in many other argumentation contexts, temporal, monetary, and other situational constraints limit the degree of argumentative comprehensiveness possible. Nonetheless, members of the composite audience expect that advocates will provide as comprehensive an analysis of a topic as the situation permits. Good evaluation of argumentation requires a determination of whether argumentation has satisfied this guideline.

Structural Coherence

Structural coherence combines structural and stylistic concerns. Arguments that move logically from one sentence to the next and from one paragraph to the next are structurally coherent. Argumentation that flows smoothly from beginning to end satisfies guidelines regarding structural coherence. Poor transitions between ideas, violations of basic principles of logic, and grammatical errors inhibit the flow of argumentation; they render arguments structurally incoherent.

The following argument illustrates structural incoherence:

▼▼▼▼▼▼

The field of medicine has saved countless lives. Much of the progress achieved in this field has been a direct result of experimentation on animals.

And I think that it is about time for us to seriously question Darwin's ideas about animal rights. His view that animal emotions and reason virtually parallel human emotions and reason are just wrong-minded and unwarranted in light of biblical evidence to the contrary.   ▼▼▼

In this example, the advocate has used the "cataloguing," or "and another thing," approach to argumentation. The second paragraph fails to follow logically from the preceding paragraph. Instead, the advocate seems to want to say, "and another thing." Also, the second paragraph contains an awkwardly constructed sentence: "His view that animal emotions and reason virtually parallel human emotions and reason are just wrong-minded and unwarranted in light of biblical evidence to the contrary." The subject of this sentence is singular (his view that . . .), yet the author uses a plural predicate (are). This example illustrates structural incoherence resulting from both poor transitions between ideas and violations of basic grammatical rules. This example also illustrates the fundamental point that evaluation of structural coherence requires critics to study the laws of reasoning and the rules of grammar and style.

▾ ▾ ▾
BASIC FALLACIES

To assist you in applying the guidelines discussed thus far, the fields of logic and rhetoric have provided lists of fallacies of argumentation. In most cases, the presence of these fallacies diminishes the quality of argumentation. When evaluating argumentation, it is therefore helpful to look for fallacies.

Formal and informal logicians, speech communication scholars, and other argumentation theorists continue to debate the nature of fallacies. The list below is not intended to represent all of the types of fallacies, nor is this list entirely uncontroversial. However, few would deny that argumentation which inadvertently contains one or more of the following fallacies falls short of the basic guidelines for good argumentation:

Fallacies of Language

- ▾ ambiguity
- ▾ vagueness
- ▾ equivocation
- ▾ obscuration

Fallacies of Evidence

- ▾ repeated assertion
- ▾ nonrepresentative instance
- ▾ insufficient instances
- ▾ invalid statistical measure
- ▾ unreliable source

Fallacies of Reasoning

- ▾ straw argument
- ▾ begging the question
- ▾ circularity
- ▾ non sequitur
- ▾ appeal to ignorance

▾ appeal to popular prejudice
▾ appeal to tradition
▾ ad hominem
▾ oversimplification
▾ hasty generalization
▾ post hoc
▾ faulty comparison

Fallacies of Language

We learned previously the important role that language plays in argumentation. We discovered, for example, that language choice affects perception. Even the most reasonable audiences respond differently to differing presentations of similar ideas. Similarly, a sensitivity to language usage can make the difference between comprehension and misunderstanding. Sensitivity to style sometimes makes the difference between maintaining open, cooperative dialogue on the one hand or resorting to hostile, destructive communication strategies on the other. In evaluating argumentation, it is helpful to look for fallacies of language.

Ambiguity   A term or expression is *ambiguous* if the audience may reasonably apply two or more distinct interpretations to it. Ambiguity may be used intentionally, as in humor. Cartoonist Mike Luckovich used ambiguity, for example, in a political cartoon published in the spring of 1989. Luckovich's cartoon responded to the political controversy resulting from allegations that House Speaker Jim Wright had violated a number of congressional rules. In April, 1989, the House Ethics Committee completed a report highly critical of Wright. Among other things, the report alleged that he had taken excessive gifts and campaign contributions from a businessperson who had "a direct interest in legislation Wright was in a position to influence." He was also charged with attempting to circumvent congressional rules regarding the maximum of outside income allowed. According to the House Ethics Committee report, Wright allegedly "peddled copies of his slender collection of homilies . . . to various groups and colleges in lieu of speaking fees at a point when he was reaching the maximum of such income allowed under House limits."[7]

Luckovich's cartoon portrays two men standing outside the congressional building in Washington, D.C. One of the men is shown holding a copy of the House Ethics Committee report. He says, "Jim Wright refuses to accept the House Ethics Committee report that says he improperly received gifts." Of course, Luckovich's readers take this to mean that Wright will not take as true what is contained in the highly critical report. But Luckovich's second

---

7.   Reported in *Newsweek,* April 24, 1989, p. 26.

character responds with, "Put it in a box, wrap it and put a bow on it. He'll accept it."[8]

Luckovich successfully uses ambiguity in this cartoon for political satire. However, ambiguity is not always intentional. Nor is it always logically acceptable. When Karl tells the audience that he "can't understand Ian's views on capital punishment," he intends the colloquial sense: "Ian's views on capital punishment are foreign and offensive to my world view." However, members of Karl's audience take him to mean, "I am unable to comprehend Ian's views." This miscommunication weakened the persuasive impact of Karl's statement and failed to meaningfully contribute to the audience's reception of it.

Context often supplies the audience with the information needed to determine which interpretation is most reasonable. However, ambiguity invites confusion and sometimes even encourages misleading interpretations. Whenever an author or writer uses a word with at least two clearly distinguishable meanings, critics need to determine whether the author or speaker has committed the fallacy of ambiguity.

Vagueness   Terms are vague when their meaning is unclear. *Vagueness* is often used to avoid risk taking in argumentation, but it usually leads to problems. For example, suppose Maya wishes to persuade her audience that they should vote for Senator Smith's bill. In her effort to avoid inciting opposition, Maya provides the following defense of the bill:

▼▼▼▼▼▼

Senator Smith's bill is wonderful in its scope. It will improve many people's lives and make America a better place to live. ▼▼▼

In this set of claims, Maya has used a number of vague terms. It is unclear, for example, what she means by "wonderful," "improve," and "better." To meaningfully consider Maya's assertions, the audience must first have a clear idea of what she means by each of these terms. As they stand, Maya's claims are too vague to be meaningful.

Equivocation   *Equivocation* is another fallacy of language. An advocate equivocates when he or she changes meanings during an argument in an effort to make an argument seem more compelling than it is.

A recent secretary of the interior once assured his audience by stating, for example, that "we should protect America's national parks and forests." Later he added, "I'll only authorize their dispersal to serve the best interests of citizens." The secretary equivocated here on his use of the terms *protect*

---

8. *Columbus Dispatch*, April 24, 1989, p. A-7.

and *national.* The audience originally thought he meant that the parks would be "held in trust for all the people." But the secretary later changed his message; he used the terms *protect* and *national* to mean "sold off only to Americans or to serve American interests."[9]

Obscuration   A fourth type of fallacy of language—*obscuration*—also inhibits the likelihood that argumentation will facilitate constructive deliberation. Argumentation that relies on overly complex sentence structure, unnecessary jargon, or other needlessly obscure terminology provides examples of obscuration. The following passage contains all three of these forms of obscuration:

▼ ▼ ▼ ▼ ▼ ▼

The determination of validity in biblical exegesis fruitfully germinates with a semantic overview and terminates with either a determination of validity or with a finding of invalidity; however, hermeneutical studies provide only a springboard for theological study. ▼ ▼ ▼

The ideas expressed in this passage could be much more clearly expressed in ordinary language. For example, the writer could have expressed the ideas more precisely as follows:

▼ ▼ ▼ ▼ ▼ ▼

To determine whether someone's interpretation of the Bible is valid, it is useful to begin with an overview of possible meanings. A finding of validity or invalidity completes the process. However, the art of interpretation is only a starting point for theological study. ▼ ▼ ▼

This rewrite avoids much of the original passage's use of jargon and complex sentence structure. As such, the rewrite will increase the likelihood that the author's ideas will meaningfully contribute to dialogue and deliberation.

Of course, in some contexts the use of jargon and other specialized terminology may actually contribute to meaningful dialogue. Medical practitioners, for example, use many technical terms when they discuss medical problems. What may appear to be obscuration to a layperson reading a medical document may in fact be precise language to an expert.

Analysis of the original passage above shows that the author probably did not deliberately employ obscuration to mislead; he or she probably has simply not yet learned to write succinctly and clearly. Sometimes, however, obscuration is used deliberately to hide a lack of knowledge, to avoid confronting issues, or to mislead the audience.

---

9.   I am indebted to John Lyne for providing this example.

Official governmental uses of "doublespeak" provide good examples. The term *peacekeepers* is used to refer to potentially lethal missiles. *Revenue enhancers* is a term for dreaded tax increases. *Low intensity conflict* is used to discuss the CIA's new theory of limited war.

Lieutenant Colonel Oliver North and Rear Admiral John Poindexter won top recognition in the 1987 doublespeak competition for their use of the term *plausible deniability* to refer to their lies and to explain their illegal behavior during the Iran-Contra affair. Poindexter earned further recognition for suggesting that he "acquiesced" in a shipment of weapons, but did not authorize the shipment. Legislation passed by Congress was referred to by Poindexter as "outside interference"!

When successful, such obscuration has the potential to jeopardize the quality of dialogue and otherwise undermine public decision making. For this reason, critics need to discover, expose, and carefully evaluate instances of obscuration.

Fallacies of Evidence

We have seen throughout this text that evidence plays an important role in every phase of good reasoning. Not surprisingly, the evaluation of evidence is also important to the process of criticizing. Useful evaluation of evidence requires an assessment of the *quality* of evidence provided, the *quantity* of evidence provided, and perhaps most importantly, an assessment of the advocate's *interpretations* and *uses of evidence*. Looking for fallacies of evidence assists each of these critical steps.

Repeated Assertion   A common fallacy of evidence is the *repeated assertion* fallacy. An advocate commits this fallacy whenever he or she relies on repetition to provide support for an unwarranted claim. This fallacy is particularly prevalent in political communication. Political advocates who lack support for their claims sometimes hope that if these claims are frequently repeated, people will begin to accept them. Critical listeners and readers realize that a claim remains unwarranted regardless of the frequency with which it is repeated.

Many advertisements also rely on the effectiveness of repetition. The audience is repeatedly told that a particular product performs better than its competitors. Without thinking, some members of the audience begin to accept the manufacturer's claim. Critical thinkers can avoid falling prey to this type of manipulation by recognizing the fallacy underlying it.

Nonrepresentative Instance   Another fallacy of evidence is the *nonrepresentative instance* fallacy. Only data that provide a reasonably accurate reflection of reality facilitate good reasoning. Instances that are not representative create distorted justifications for points of view and hence jeopardize the quality of the reasoning process. For example, the Kerns family is considering adopting a third child. In discussing this decision with them, Mavis, a family friend, informs the Kerns that adopted third children tend to have behavior problems. To support this assertion, Mavis cites four instances of families with adopted third children. In each of these instances, Mavis reports, the adopted third child has behavior problems. But upon questioning Mavis, the Kerns family learns that the selection of these four was arbitrary. Mavis picked these four families from among the troubled families she had visited in her brief time as a social worker. Clearly, this unscientific sample fails to justify Mavis's assertion. A look at a more carefully selected sample of families with adopted third children would quickly reveal that the four families cited are not representative of families with an adopted third child.

Avoidance of the nonrepresentative instance fallacy is especially important to marketing and sales practitioners. Ruth learned the significance of this fallacy when she attempted to predict how effectively Carol's new product would sell in the Midwest. Carol had asked Ruth to invest her savings in marketing the new product in three midwestern states. Ruth based her prediction of the product's midwestern marketability on the results of her survey of a small, nonrepresentative focus group. Based on these unreliable findings, Ruth decided to invest all her savings in Carol's company. The resulting miscalculation caused Ruth to lose her entire savings account.

Experts in survey research follow standard mathematical rules to avoid this type of miscalculation. These rules help researchers determine whether instances are representative. Unfortunately, such technical knowledge is not always available to participants in everyday situations of argumentation. Our search for nonrepresentative instances often depends on an application of the basic principles of reasoning discussed in this and previous chapters.

Insufficient Instances   Related to the nonrepresentative instance fallacy is the fallacy of *insufficient instances*. This fallacy occurs when an advocate generalizes from an inadequate number of instances.

Work by communication scholar Hans Jacobs illustrates this fallacy. Jacobs hoped to argue that there is more sex-role stereotypic behavior on television programming for children than on adult programming. To support his claim, Jacobs compared sex-role stereotyping on two adult programs to sex-role stereotyping on two children's programs. Yet there are more than fifty adult programs and more than thirty-five children's programs available. Results from a sample that includes only two adult and two children's programs would not provide adequate support for the scholar's generalization. Without either a significantly larger sample or a strong argument to support the reliability of his sample, Jacobs's study proves to be invalid.

Invalid Statistical Measure   The most general evidence fallacy is the *invalid statistical measure* fallacy. Biased and atypical samples, misleading graphs, and nonrepresentative averages are among the many sources of invalid statistical measure. News polls immediately following the televised 1988 presidential debates provide good examples. For these polls, people were asked to call in their reaction to the debates. Each call cost the respondent fifty cents, thereby providing access primarily to people who could afford the calls. It is easy to see how well-funded supporters of a debate participant could use this opportunity to register as many votes as possible in favor of their candidate. Given these and other validity problems, these polls do not accurately reflect public reaction to the debates.

In evaluating statistical data, it is important to distinguish different uses of the data. *How* the data are used in the argumentation often determines whether the arguer has committed a fallacy. A survey taken by a well-known group of scientists illustrates this point. The survey was called the American Defense Policy Survey. It is unclear whether the researchers collecting the information sent their questionnaire to a randomly selected group of people. If so, this aspect of their research would have been valid. However, enclosed with the questionnaire was a highly biased account of American defense policy. The letter began with the following sentence: "We are dragging Heaven into Hell." Underlined later in the letter was the following: *"We want to stop the arms race in space before it gets off the ground."* Also in the letter was the following plea: "You can talk to your relatives, your friends, and members of your community, helping to make them aware of the nuclear threat and the fact that solutions are available. And you should return the enclosed questionnaire, to let the world know that there are people who continue to care about our future."

In addition to the letter, the envelope contained a pamphlet in defense of the view that the Star Wars space-based defense program would jeopardize international peace. Also enclosed was a statement referred to as an "appeal by American scientists to ban space weapons." Thus, when the questionnaire asked, "Do you support development and deployment of a space-based anti-ballistic missile system?" it is clear that the researchers hoped the response would be "no." In this example, the survey results would not accurately reflect the general public's beliefs on the topic. Use of this survey as evidence of public sentiment toward space-based weapons would be fallacious. However, if, as their letter suggests, the surveyors simply wanted evidence to show that *there are people* who oppose space-based weapons, use of the survey results would be appropriate.[10]

Unreliable Source   Of all the fallacies of evidence, the *unreliable source* fallacy is the most dependent on context. This fallacy occurs when arguers use sources that are likely either to be particularly biased or to lack credibility *in the given context*. Often, a reliable source in one context may not be

---

10.   For a useful study of this and related types of fallacies, see Darrell Huff, *How to Lie With Statistics* (New York: W. W. Norton, 1954).

reliable in another. Recall the discussion in Chapter 4, for example, of Chief Justice Rehnquist's testimony on capital punishment. Although the chief justice would be among the most reliable sources on the question of whether capital punishment laws violate the U.S. Constitution, he is not necessarily a reliable source on the question of whether capital punishment *in fact* deters crime. A social scientist or an expert criminologist specializing in criminal deterrence would have greater reliability on this question. Similarly, a victim of a violent crime might be a reliable source on the question of who committed that crime. But he or she is likely to be seriously biased on the question of what punishment the perpetrator of the crime should receive.

Fallacies of Reasoning

We are now ready to turn to the broadest group of fallacies: fallacies of reasoning. We have previously learned that reasoning is used in every aspect of argumentation, from the discovery and evaluation of evidence, to the discovery and evaluation of underlying values, as well as the discussion of issues. Reasoning governs the generation and evaluation of every element of argumentation. Thus, evaluation of argumentation requires careful attention to fallacies of reasoning.

Straw Argument   This common fallacy is characterized by an underestimation of opposition. *Straw arguments* present weak versions of opposing views. This form of misrepresentation is often used to avoid refuting more difficult opposition arguments. However, straw arguments addressed to the composite audience are likely to weaken the arguer's effectiveness. The audience members reading or hearing the misrepresentation of their views are likely to become hostile and thereby less receptive to the arguer's reasoning. Additionally, critical listeners and readers of straw arguments may assume that the advocate's own position results from inadequate understanding of alternative points of view.

For example, Luis wants to argue against public funding of day-care centers. In his discussion of opposing views, Luis suggests that the primary reason to support public funding of day-care centers is that such funding will create badly needed jobs for day-care workers and administrators. Upon hearing this argument, Luis's audience may well assume that the reason he does not support public funding of day-care centers is that he is not familiar with the many good reasons for such funding. If he knew, for example, that public funding of day care would provide good care for the many children who are now left unattended or in homes with inadequate care, he might change his mind. Or perhaps if Luis understood that public funding of day-care centers would ultimately save taxpayers countless dollars by helping single welfare mothers get and retain jobs and by giving children (who might otherwise end up needing medical care or becoming juvenile delinquents) the care and attention they need to become productive, healthy citizens, Luis would no longer oppose public funding of day care.

But suppose that Luis's consideration of these ideas still does not lead him to believe that the public should fund day-care centers. Perhaps he believes there are better ways to achieve the goals described above. His audience will be unaware of his good reasons for disagreeing with them because his argumentation did not address these important issues. In this case, as elsewhere, straw argument weakens the value and the persuasive impact of the advocate's arguments.

Begging the Question   Another fallacy of reasoning is referred to as *begging the question.* This fallacy occurs when advocates avoid the relevant issue. In the following brief dialogue, John begs the question:

Jane: The United States should enhance its commitment to providing adequate medical care for the homeless.

John: Russia has more homeless people than the United States does.

John's claim fails to address the central issues implicit in Jane's claim. Instead, he has introduced an issue not directly relevant to Jane's position.

Circularity   Related to begging the question is *circularity.* This fallacy has aroused considerable debate among argumentation theorists. But all agree that argumentation is circular when unsupported assertions or assumptions are used to advance controversial claims.

The following argument for mandatory seatbelt laws provides a typical example of circularity:

▼▼▼▼▼▼

Mandatory seatbelt laws should be immediately passed because they are needed. Society needs to have laws that require people to wear seatbelts, even if they do not want to wear them. Therefore, we should adopt mandatory seatbelt laws. ▼▼▼

The author of this argument uses the claim that mandatory seatbelt laws are needed to support the same claim. This type of circularity fails to contribute meaningfully to dialogue.

Beardsley notes that "the most deceptive circular arguments are rather long ones; circularity is easiest to conceal when the distance between the premise and conclusion is great."[11] Not only is this type of circularity easiest to conceal to audiences, it is also sometimes easy for arguers themselves to miss.

---

11.   Monroe Beardsley, *Thinking Straight,* 4th ed. (Englewood Cliffs, N.J.: Prentice-Hall, 1975), p. 72.

Consider Erik's attempt to argue on behalf of legalizing adult access to recreational drugs. Erik wrote the following paragraph in a sincere effort to defend his position:

▼▼▼▼▼▼

Legalizing adult access to recreational drugs in this country will save money, energy, time, and many lives. It is understandable that people want to stop drug use. After all, the drug problem in this country is significant. There are literally thousands of lives lost to the ravages of drug addiction. Each day, more and more children fall prey to the drug dealer's seductive tactics. Because so many young people feel vulnerable, confused, and alone in today's complex world, it's not surprising that they are such easy prey for the dealer's campaign. It's sad too to see how many upwardly mobile people in our culture find themselves turning to drugs to escape the pain of their lonely, empty lives. Legalizing adult access to recreational drugs will address this problem. It will save time, energy, money, and many lives.   ▼▼▼

Erik was surprised when a careful reader informed him that his paragraph failed to provide support for his conclusion. Erik's insightful critic showed him that the only "support" he had given for his claim was the paragraph's opening statement. But this statement simply asserted the "argument's" conclusion. Erik quickly understood that the circular reasoning used in his paragraph failed to provide reliable assistance to readers who wished to determine whether we should legalize adult access to recreational drugs. Fortunately, the critic's comments afforded Erik the opportunity to develop a new, less circular argument.

Non Sequitur   The most all-encompassing fallacy of reasoning is non sequitur reasoning. The Latin expression *non sequitur* means "does not follow." Arguments employ the non sequitur fallacy whenever the claims they advance do not logically follow from the premises and evidence provided on their behalf. Even if we accept the premises and the evidence provided in these arguments, we would still not be obliged to accept the conclusion. The example below illustrates how this fallacy works:

▼▼▼▼▼▼

Caring for the elderly is very costly. Furthermore, every dollar expended on caring for the elderly limits by a dollar the amount of money available for other important enterprises, such as educating the young. Therefore, we should stop caring for the elderly.   ▼▼▼

It is easy to see how it would be possible to accept this advocate's premises without granting the conclusion. This is an example of an argument in which the conclusion simply does not follow from the premises; it is a non sequitur.

The majority of evidence and reasoning fallacies are examples of non sequitur reasoning. For example, the evidentiary fallacy of insufficient instances involves drawing unwarranted conclusions based on inadequate support. In this sense, the fallacy of insufficient instances is an example of non sequitur reasoning. The remaining reasoning fallacies provide further examples of non sequitur reasoning.

Appeal to Ignorance   Typically, the *appeal to ignorance* involves an unfair shift in burden of proof. The arguer supports a controversial claim by noting that the opposition is either unwilling or unable to prove the claim's unacceptability. A supporter of free access to abortions may argue that because the opposition cannot prove that life begins with conception, it follows that life does not begin with conception. Similarly, an anti-abortionist might argue that because abortion advocates cannot prove that life does not begin at conception, it follows that life does begin at conception. Neither of these advocates has directly addressed the question of when life begins. Instead, they have traded unfairly on our ignorance. Thus, neither of these advocates has assisted the audience's decision-making process.

Appeal to Popular Prejudice   Related to this fallacy is the *appeal to popular prejudice*. Too much reliance on public opinion results in this fallacy. Typically, the advocate claims that because most people believe a claim to be true, it is true. Advertisements for products and political candidates, as well as social commentaries, often appeal to popular prejudice:

- ▾ **Example 1:** This washing machine is our best seller. Therefore, you should buy this model.
- ▾ **Example 2:** The majority of the public believe he is guilty despite the jury's ruling to the contrary. Therefore, he is guilty.
- ▾ **Example 3:** The majority believe capital punishment is the best way to punish murderers. Therefore, capital punishment should remain legal in the United States.
- ▾ **Example 4:** Most people in this country waste water. Therefore, it is morally acceptable for me to waste water.
- ▾ **Example 5:** Most people get married. Therefore, you should get married.

In each of these examples, popular opinion provides the *sole* justification given to support the conclusion. Example 1 represents a type of appeal that is frequently found in the marketplace. How often have you been told that you should purchase a particular product simply because it is popular? Yet what does its popularity have to do with whether the product best meets your individual needs?

Examples 2 and 3 are also representative of a prevalent use of popular prejudice. How often have you heard people justifying their beliefs on the grounds that others agree with them? Yet history provides countless examples of the harms resulting from blind adherence to unjustified popular opinion. Popular support of slavery, child abuse, witch burning, and cockfighting are but a few examples of potentially harmful popular prejudices. Arguments that rely heavily on this type of reasoning should be carefully scrutinized.

Similarly, Example 4 represents a widely used version of the appeal to popular prejudice. How often have you heard people defending behavior they know is unacceptable on the grounds that others also engage in it? It takes little reflection to see how dangerous this type of reasoning can be.

Example 5 also represents a widely used type of appeal to popular prejudice. Acceptance of this type of appeal can lead people to behave against their better judgment, or interests, or both. Consider the example given above. Even if 99 percent of the world gets married, what does this have to do with whether marriage best meets your individual needs? How much should your decision rely on the fact that other people have found this a suitable or valuable course of action? Furthermore, what does the simple fact that many people get married tell us about whether getting married fulfilled these people's needs? In this, as in other contexts, the appeal to popular prejudice is by itself an inadequate basis for reasoned decision making.

Appeal to Tradition   Related to appeal to popular prejudice is the *appeal to tradition*. Essentially, the advocate argues that a practice is moral or a belief correct *because* it conforms with tradition: "Women have always had primary responsibility for domestic duties; therefore, men should not be expected to take responsibility for housework and child care." Socioeconomic changes and scientific discovery create circumstances that often require abandonment of such traditional views and practices.

Furthermore, traditions do not, by their mere existence, *necessarily* merit acceptance. The American South maintained a tradition of slavery that has since been exposed for its ruthlessness and immorality. Similarly, the South African government has maintained a long tradition of apartheid. The fact that this practice is traditional in no way establishes its merit. Although argument from tradition may be appropriate as a supplement to other reasons, argumentation that relies *exclusively* on this appeal falls seriously short of the guidelines for technical adequacy.

Ad Hominem   *Ad hominem* reasoning challenges claims on the basis of who made them. When Senator Jones provides compelling evidence to support the view that women earn significantly less than men for comparable jobs, an opponent ignores Senator Jones's data and accompanying reasoning and argues instead that Senator Jones is biased. Given the nature of Senator Jones's argument, her status as a source is not relevant to the issue. The opponent's ad hominem rebuttal fails to contribute to the debate over whether women earn significantly less than men for comparable jobs.

Oversimplification   Another fallacy of reasoning is *oversimplification*. Arguers commit this fallacy when they overlook potentially relevant considerations. Two of the more common forms of oversimplification are *false dilemma* and *black/white thinking*. False dilemmas oversimplify by posing arbitrarily limited options.

Corky's argument for abusing animals employs this fallacy. In support of his approach to animal training for films, Corky has argued that the only options available to him are either to chain and beat his horses or to lose his effectiveness as an animal trainer. This argument fails to consider a third option, namely, making use of the many gentle, but highly effective, methods of animal training developed by experts during the past twenty years. Adoption of this third option would prevent animal cruelty, while helping Corky effectively do his job. Ignoring this important option jeopardizes Corky's decision making on this topic.

False dilemma is perhaps one of the most common fallacies in everyday thinking. So often, we imagine that we must choose between two unappealing alternatives, when there is a third, more attractive option open to us. Jacob and Joseph's tragic experience illustrates the point. Jacob and Joseph, both fifteen years old, had been close friends since childhood. When Jacob's family moved to another community, both boys were devastated. During a reunion visit, the boys committed a double suicide, rather than be parted once again. Although an extreme case, this tragedy underscores the dangers associated with false dilemma. Jacob and Joseph's action also illustrates the importance of creativity in decision making. Had they creatively considered the alternatives available to them, Jacob and Joseph would have understood that they had more than the two alternatives—separation for life, or death together—that they originally conceived.

While inexperience and inadequate training were likely responsible for Jacob and Joseph's false perception of their circumstances, sometimes public communicators deliberately use false dilemma to achieve personal objectives.

Some politicians have been known to employ false dilemma in this way. Either we must raise taxes, they might say, or we must cut back on subsidizing medical care for the poor. This argument fails to consider other plausible alternatives, such as cutting back on another domestic or a military program, pursuing taxpayers who are delinquent in their payments to the Internal Revenue Service, redistributing tax dollars, eliminating waste in federal spending, and so on. Without public consideration of these and other alternatives, our nation is vulnerable to policy making that has potentially negative, or even harmful, consequences.

Audiences untrained in critical thinking are particularly susceptible to intentional uses of false dilemma. Advertisers, public relations consultants, and other persuasion experts in various fields make skillful use of false dilemma to create the illusion of limited options. This illusion has the potential to lead noncritical thinkers to support unqualified candidates, accept inferior services, and tolerate improper behavior.

Black/white thinking also jeopardizes decision making. This form of oversimplification arbitrarily divides ideas into two opposites, allowing no middle ground. Politicians employ this type of reasoning when they categorize policies as either all-good or all-bad. This oversimplified view ignores the many partially good and partially harmful aspects within the different political structures that form our world. Recent history provides relevant examples of the serious problems created by governmental adherence to black/white thinking. For example, much of the United States foreign policy from 1954–1976 relied on the assumption that foreign governments are either supported by Russia and hence are our enemies, or supported by the United States and hence are our friends. Experts today attribute many miscalculated foreign policy decisions during the Eisenhower, Kennedy, Johnson, and Nixon presidencies to this oversimplified view of the world.

Hasty Generalization   Another form of non sequitur reasoning is *hasty generalization.* This fallacy closely parallels several of the evidentiary fallacies. Generalizations that are unwarranted by the support provided on their behalf are considered hasty generalizations. John claims, for example, that women prefer married life to single life. He bases this claim on his interviews with seven women over a period of ten years in Eugene, Oregon. Clearly, his generalized conclusion is unwarranted given his small (and possibly biased) sample.

Hasty generalizations often result from small and biased personal samples. Carlos concludes from his exposure to three poorly behaved dogs that all dogs are poorly behaved. Levi meets two quiet Roman Catholics and concludes that all Roman Catholics are quiet.

Because we live in such a complex world, it is tempting for us to make this type of inference. If we have been exposed to only two Baptists, and both were introverted, we are inclined to assume that all Baptists are introverted. When introduced for the first time to someone from Southeast Asia, we assume that all other people from this region will share the person's traits, despite the fact that the many countries of this region have cultural norms that differ from one country to another.

Although our lives may initially feel more comfortable when we adopt these faulty generalizations, acting on them can be harmful to us, as well as to those we love. Despite the initial discomfort associated with acknowledging the limits of our knowledge and understanding, remaining open to the diversity among people of all ethnic and racial origins ultimately leads to more fulfilling and constructive personal and professional decision making. Carefully avoiding hasty generalizations in interpersonal relations, governmental policy judgments, and business decisions is well worth the effort.

Post Hoc   One common form of faulty reasoning is the fallacy of *post hoc, ergo propter hoc,* or "after the fact, therefore because of the fact." This form of non sequitur reasoning assumes that because one event occurred prior to another, the one was caused by the other. The following examples illustrate typical instances of this fallacy:

> ▾ **Example 1:** Unemployment and inflation have increased since President Lee took office. She must be doing a bad job.
> ▾ **Example 2:** Violent crime in this state has risen 14 percent since passage of the legislation prohibiting capital punishment here. Thus, passage of the bill caused the rise in violent crime.

In each of these examples, the conclusions were unwarranted given the available support. There are many possible causes, unrelated to President Lee's tenure in office, that may be attributed to the rise in unemployment and inflation. Similarly, numerous variables, unrelated to capital punishment legislation and enforcement, affect a state's amount of violent crime. These examples illustrate that, as with other fallacies of reasoning, post hoc reasoning weakens the chances that argumentation will assist reasoned deliberation.

Faulty Comparison   The last fallacy to be discussed here is the fallacy of *faulty comparison.* Arguers commit this form of non sequitur reasoning when they draw conclusions based on unwarranted comparisons. An especially clever version of this fallacy appeared on bumper stickers distributed by opponents of gun control: "Prevent forest fires; register matches," read the stickers. This admonition's comparison of match registration with handgun registration is faulty for several reasons. First, it is considerably easier to register guns than it would be to register matches. Furthermore, people generally make more benign use of matches than of handguns. Few of us feel as threatened when sharing a room with someone holding matches as with someone holding a handgun. These are but a few of the significant dissimilarities that invalidate the advocates' implied argument by comparison.

Because legal reasoning relies heavily on argument by comparison, this context provides many examples of faulty comparisons. Most commonly, a defense lawyer will compare the facts relevant to a client's case with the facts in a previous case. The lawyer will then draw the conclusion that the client's case should receive the same ruling as did the defendant in the previous case. To expose weaknesses in the analogy, opposing council will show significant differences between the facts of the two cases. Ultimately, judges and juries determine whether the defense lawyer's analogical reasoning was sound.

▼ ▼ ▼

SUMMARY: FIVE SETS OF QUESTIONS FOR EVALUATING ARGUMENT

This chapter has surveyed standards for evaluating the quality of arguments addressed to a composite audience. We have seen the importance of assessing an argument's acceptability of premises, consistency, relevance, adequacy of support, comprehensiveness, and structural coherence. Equally important is determining whether the advocate has avoided basic fallacies of language, evidence, and reasoning. The following five sets of questions encapsulate these and related basic standards of good argumentation:

1. To what degree are the arguments responsive to reasonable opposition? Has the advocate adequately anticipated alternative points of view? Does the argumentation reflect a sensitivity to the level of controversy surrounding relevant issues?

2. Is adequate support provided for controversial claims?

3. Are the arguments relevant and comprehensive?

4. Are the arguments presented as clearly and succinctly as possible? Is the argumentation structurally coherent?

5. Has the advocate avoided fallacies of reasoning?

Regardless of the context, asking these questions will help the critic determine the degree to which specific argumentation meets the rigorous standards discussed throughout this chapter. But asking these questions, like every other step in the evaluation process, requires knowledge about the relevant topic and context, understanding of the relevant issues, respect for the decision-making process, and an openness to alternative perspectives.

▼ ▼ ▼

EXERCISES

1. Record a public discussion, such as a city council meeting, a public forum, or a televised session of Congress. Next, apply the five sets of summary questions listed on this page to the discourse. Finally, write a critique of the argumentation based on your responses to these questions.

2. Evaluate the essay presented below in terms of consistency, relevance, comprehensiveness, and structural coherence:

▼▼▼▼▼▼

When a mother and father get a divorce, the children are the unfortunate victims of a child-custody choice. When this choice is not agreed on by the parents, it is up to courts to decide which parent is worthy of child custody.

The well-being of the child is and should be the most important criterion on which the courts base their decisions in child-custody cases.

Presently in child-custody cases, the judge weighs the factors that make the mother or father a good parent, but the father bears the burden of proof for worthiness of child custody. This decision stems from the attitude that the father is not capable of being a single parent over the mother because he cannot provide the love and care that the mother would provide the child. This attitude stems from a time in history when the parent's gender role was much more diverse than are present family gender roles.

But it is no longer mandatory that the mother breast-feed her baby. The bottle allows the father to feed the baby. Physically, therefore, the father can perform feminine domestic chores and feed his child, but the attitude still prevails through gender norms that the father does not openly choose to possess the caring emotional paternal requirements to raise his child.

The problem with this assumption is that emotions are a subjective feeling within a father, and a father, as a human being, is fully capable of possessing caring, emotional, parental feelings like the mother. There are many fathers who choose to accept feminine paternal gender roles and demonstrate emotional freedom.

One such feminine paternal gender role widely accepted by fathers is love for his child. The thought that men are not able to love their children because they are by nature physically stronger than women or more competitive than women is not necessarily true. My father was a very large man and I felt very much loved.

The negative masculine stereotypes such as nondemonstrativeness, childishness, and promiscuity are negative behavioral norms that are imputed on men. The problem with classifying or imputing these behaviors are changeable and a father is capable to suppress a bad behavior around his child or change it to good behavior.

I am not proposing that the mother is necessarily an inadequate parent; nor is she evolving into an inadequate parent. The evolution is occurring in the father as he adopts these motherly characteristics toward caring for his child. In court cases when the father's inadequacy as a parent is assumed, because of the assumed negative masculine norms based on gender, this is against the child's goodwill.

Therefore relieving the burden of proof from the father to show worthiness for the custody of the child will ensure a better life for the child of divorced parents because relieving the burden of proof from the father to show worthiness for child custody will ensure that the best parent gets custody. Acquired feminine paternal roles by the father let him possess "motherly" gender traits thought unique to the mother. In a courtroom, the two parents should be looked at equally, assuming the father is just as capable of success-fully raising his child as is the mother. ▼▼▼

3. Identify and name fallacies within the preceding sample.

4. Apply the standards developed in this chapter to a colleague's speech or paper. Write a summary of your evaluation.

5. Find a transcript of a well-publicized speech. Next, read reviews of the speech and record discussions about it. Critically evaluate the reviews and discussions in light of the actual transcript. Among other things, address the following questions: Are the discussants' interpretations of the text reasonable? Do their conclusions follow from their interpreta-tions? Have they omitted important parts of the text in their analyses?

6. In 1988, Jane Frances Bolding went on trial for murder. Bolding, a nurse at Prince George's Hospital outside Washington, D.C., was accused of killing three of her patients. The case against Bolding was based upon a study which showed that during a fifteen-month period, Bolding's pa-tients were 35 to 96 times more apt to suffer cardiac arrest than were patients under other nurses' care. According to a *Newsweek* report on the case, "Bolding's patients suffered 57 arrests; none of her co-workers had more than five among their patients."

   Bolding was first suspected of killing patients in 1985, when hospital officials became alarmed at the number of patients that seemed to be dying under Bolding's care. Bolding was interrogated for 22 hours, dur-ing which she admitted injecting potassium into two of her patients. However, in January of 1988, a judge ruled that police had obtained Bolding's statement under extreme duress. He would therefore not ad-mit the statement into the trial. The prosecutor was left with only the following circumstantial, statistical evidence: From January, 1984, until Bolding was fired in March, 1985, three times as many cardiac arrests were recorded on Bolding's shift than on other shifts. Bolding was the principal nurse in 65% of these cases. When Bolding's patients went into arrest, they were also more likely than others to have unexpected high levels of potassium in their blood. The Centers for Disease Control which made these findings concluded that "the biggest risk of cardiac arrest facing ICU patients was having Bolding as their nurse."[12]

   a. Do these findings provide adequate support for the prosecution's charge? Why or why not? If you were unaware of Bolding's confes-sion, and had only the CDC's findings on which to base your deci-sion, would you draw the inference that Bolding is clearly guilty of killing her patients? Would this inference be justified? Why or why not? How reliable would the CDC report be for jurors faced with this case? Why?

---

12. Mark Miller, "Murder By the Numbers," *Newsweek,* May 30, 1988, p. 58.

b. Bolding's attorneys waived the right to a jury. They decided to present their case to a judge. Why do you think they made this decision? What implications, if any, can reasonably be drawn from this decision?

7. Canon I of the American Bar Association Code of Ethics holds that "a basic tenet of the professional responsibility of lawyers is that every person in our society should have ready access to the independent professional services of a lawyer of integrity and competence." Canon 2, item 27, states that "a lawyer should not decline representation because a client or a cause is unpopular or community reaction is adverse." Furthermore, Canon 2, item 28, reads that "the personal preference of a lawyer to avoid adversary alignment against judges, other lawyers, public officials, or influential members of the community does not justify his rejection of tenured employment."

In a recent discussion with a colleague, Alicia used these ABA Code items to justify her decision to represent a person charged with selling drugs to young children. The alleged drug dealer had hinted to both Alicia and her colleague that he had in fact sold drugs to young children and that, if freed, he would be likely to continue doing so.

Alicia's colleague, Sarah, initially challenged Alicia's decision to represent this client. But when Sarah heard Alicia's defense (based on the ABA Code items cited above), the colleague concluded that Alicia had no choice but to defend the client.

a. Evaluate Alicia's justification for defending the alleged drug dealer. Do you agree with her assertion that the ABA Code items cited above justify her decision to take the case? Why or why not?

b. Identify the fallacy of reasoning on which Sarah based her conclusion. Could Sarah have drawn the same conclusion without relying on fallacious reasoning? Why or why not?

8. Jay, a criminal trial lawyer, consistently refuses to represent any client he believes is guilty of committing crimes against children. Jay cites Canon 2, Item 30, of the ABA Code (which states, among other things, that "a lawyer should decline employment if the intensity of his personal feeling, as distinguished from a community attitude, may impair his effective representation of a prospective client") to defend his refusal to represent this class of clients.

Jay's colleague, Khalid, disagrees with his reading of the ABA Code. Khalid challenges Jay's argument on the grounds that Jay's refusal to represent this class of clients violates two related ABA Code items: Canon I, Item I (cited in Exercise 7); and Canon 2, Item 29, which states, among other things, that when a lawyer is appointed by a court or otherwise directed to take a case, the lawyer "should not seek to be excused from undertaking the representation except for compelling reasons." Compelling reasons, the code goes on to say, do not include "the belief of the lawyer that the defendant" is guilty. Nor may a lawyer refuse to take a case because of the "repugnance of the subject matter of the proceeding."

a.   Which of these interpretations (Jay's or Khalid's) of the cited ABA Code Items do you find most persuasive? Why? Can you think of an alternative interpretation not compatible with either Jay's or Khalid's?

b.   Are the ABA Code Items cited in Exercises 7 and 8 consistent with one another? Why or why not?

c.   Has Jay provided persuasive support for his refusal to defend a specific class of clients? Why or why not?

d.   How persuasive do you find the basis of Khalid's objections to Jay's behavior? Why?

▼ ▼ ▼ ▼ ▼ ▼ ▼
▼ CHAPTER ▼

9

▼ ▼ ▼ ▼ ▼ ▼
▼ ▼ ▼ ▼ ▼ ▼
▼ ▼ ▼ ▼ ▼ ▼
▼ ▼ ▼ ▼ ▼ ▼
▼ ▼ ▼ ▼ ▼ ▼
▼ ▼ ▼ ▼ ▼ ▼
▼ ▼ ▼ ▼ ▼ ▼
▼ ▼ ▼ ▼ ▼ ▼
▼ ▼ ▼ ▼ ▼ ▼

Applications: Family Life Issues

Preceding chapters introduced principles and tools needed to effectively confront a wide range of personal and professional challenges. This chapter is designed to help you apply these reasoning principles and decision-making tools in a specific context. Because interaction with a reasonable and concerned audience of informed peers best assists the critical thinking process, each set of exercises is aimed at enhancing the quality of such interaction. Through a series of exercises, the chapter will help generate discussion and debate on, and personal reflection about, a number of family life topics.

Some of the exercises require performance of the fundamental tasks of discovering commonplaces and related issues. Others call for the discovery of assumptions that decision makers bring to interaction. Some of the exercises call for information gathering and analysis, whereas others focus on inference making and evaluation. But above all, the exercises interspersed throughout the chapter are designed to stimulate public dialogues and critical personal reflection about family life issues.

As we noted earlier, critical thinking requires a topic. We cannot, after all, think critically without something to think about. The following discussion highlights reasons that family life issues present special opportunities for productive critical thought.

▼ ▼ ▼

THE IMPORTANCE OF FAMILY LIFE ISSUES AND VALUES

Because our society is so firmly rooted in the preservation of individual freedoms, becoming an adult in this society involves facing an exciting, but often challenging, array of choices. People in our society are given broad freedom to decide whether to marry, stay single, or live with a partner without being married; they are free to choose whether to have children, adopt children, or not have children; and so on. In our society, adults are free to decide how to divide household responsibilities. And, although there are some public regulations intended to protect the rights of children, adults have remarkable freedom to determine how their children are raised.

Generally, people base these and other personal decisions on whatever knowledge, beliefs, and values they acquire over a lifetime. Often, peers, parents, teachers, and religious counselors provide much of the foundation for these and related family life decisions. In this technological age, people's opinions are also often influenced by the media practitioners they see and hear on television and radio. Writers' views in newspapers, magazines, books, and other print media are also known to influence people's family life beliefs and values.

These sources of influence help create the foundation for most people's family life decisions. Seldom do people carefully evaluate this foundation. In fact, for most of us, the sources of our beliefs are relatively unknown. Jane doesn't know *why* she believes that homosexual persons should not be allowed to adopt children. But she feels fairly strongly that they should not. John doesn't know who told him that men should take out the garbage and women should do the vacuuming. But he feels confident that this is the way things ought to be.

It is unusual to find someone consulting experts about these and other family life issues. How many people trying to decide whether to marry will first consult the experts on whether married people live longer than single people? Nor do people often carefully consult expert opinion on the relevant issues before deciding whether to have children.

Yet, for most of us, decisions about whether to marry or have children, how to raise children, how to develop friendships and other intimate relationships, and so on, are among the most important decisions we make. For most people, these and other family life choices more directly affect the quality of life than does virtually any other type of decision.

It is therefore especially important in the area of family life that we gain insight into our personal beliefs. What values underlie our positions on family life issues? What are the sources of these values? Are these values useful for our lives? Or do they need to be reconsidered in light of alternative perspectives?

Many people turn to religious authorities for resolution of personal issues. For them, faith in the correctness of a particular religious perspective leaves little room for questioning or doubt. A favored interpretation of biblical text serves as an authoritative guide for many of these people's intimate relationships.

Even for the most zealous believers of a particular religious faith, however, discovery and scrutiny of sources of beliefs can be a valuable process. These people will find that such an exercise provides a rare opportunity to reinforce what binds them to their beliefs. And those who come away with some questions will have the opportunity to directly confront these questions with an eye to their resolution.

But above all, discussion, debate, and personal reflection about family life issues help participants better understand the reasoning behind alternative perspectives. Cooperative argumentation with peers about these issues provides insight into other people's beliefs, values, and attitudes, thereby helping even the most ardent philosophical opponents better understand themselves and each other.

Nowhere is this more evident than in discussions about sexual identity and gender norms. Issues raised in these discussions are among the most personal, controversial, and volatile issues confronting adults within our society. Completing the first set of exercises will help you to gain a deeper understanding of these important issues.

> ▼ **Exercise 1a:** Read the following discussion about sexual identity and gender norms. As you read, identify statements that you believe are commonplaces of fact and value. Then identify the statements that you believe will (would) generate controversy.

▼ ▼ ▼
TOPIC 1: SEXUAL IDENTITY AND GENDER NORMS

Who are we? What are our appropriate sex roles? What should we expect of the men and women with whom we have relationships? What should they expect from us? These and other questions about sexual identity are among the most deeply personal and emotionally charged questions facing humankind. Adolescents facing dramatic changes in their bodies inevitably confront difficult questions about how these physical changes will affect their lives. Adults continue confronting these questions, though usually with more knowledge and stability than their adolescent counterparts. Regardless of society's other changes, questioning one's "manhood" or "womanhood" remains as serious in this society today as it was for our ancestors.

For most people, at least some of the answers to these questions are provided by parents, teachers, public communicators, peers, religious leaders, and other representatives of our society. Here, as in every other society, children are taught *norms* for social practice. *Practice or policy gender norms are standards for a man or woman's proper conduct or rules for a man or woman's morally acceptable action. Factual gender norms are commonplaces about what it means to be masculine or feminine.* Most of these norms take the form of explicit or implicit societal expectations. Regardless of their form, these expectations play a major role in shaping people's attitudes, values, and beliefs.

For most Americans, these expectations are communicated not only through the broader framework of the entire American society. They are also shaped in relation to smaller cultures within the society. Members of the Amish community, for example, share a set of norms that are distinctly different from the norms of upscale citizens in New York's Manhattan. Liberal activist pro-choice Americans living in Berkeley, California, accept a number of norms not adopted by conservative pro-life activists living in Dayton, Ohio. These differences—some trivial, others significant—influence the attitudes, beliefs, and behavior of people within these divergent groups. Similarly, members of ethnic groups within our society accept the norms associated with their cultural heritage. These group norms affect members' family life choices.

Despite these differences, however, most Americans directly or indirectly face the consequences of this nation's social, educational, and political institutions. These institutions have helped a number of norms cross this nation's ethnic and political boundaries. The section that follows will provide an overview of some of our society's shared gender norms.

The Evolution of Gender Norms

Before people had today's easy access to reliable birth control, few couples were able to plan their families. Similarly, before the development of infant formula, men were unable to "nurse" their babies. Only mothers and "wet nurses" were able to provide adequate nourishment to newborns. Coupled with the harsh realities of rural life, these basic facts of life provided strong support for believers in traditional sex-related roles. Religious beliefs about men's and women's roles were written into both the legal and moral codes that governed our society at that time. These legally encoded beliefs served as commonplaces for the society.

As with most commonplaces, these gender norms were widely accepted, with little public scrutiny. Women suckling their babies and men working the plows focused little of their intellectual energy on the relative merits of their sex-related job distribution. The majority of men and women simply accepted these gender norms. Despite examples to the contrary, it was commonly believed that men were more capable than women of doing the rigorous physical labor associated with farming. And women were generally regarded as more able than men to provide the nurturing required in raising children.

These facts of life combined with strong traditional Judeo-Christian beliefs to create sets of socially sanctioned norms for each gender. People generally believed, for example, that the woman's place was in the home. Women during this time had little official voice in political matters; they did not have the right to vote. Women had few legal protections; their husbands were legally permitted to take control of most dimensions of their lives. Similarly, men were expected to be the "breadwinners." They had little say in the distribution of domestic chores and few opportunities to nurture their young children. Nor were men socially permitted to express their emotions. They were expected to be "strong" and to protect their wives and children. These commonplaces about men's and women's roles dominated the society for a number of years.

Then came the Industrial Revolution, which helped fuel major social changes. Given a short supply of cheap labor, many shop owners encouraged young women to enter the work force. This campaign was made public during World War II as the federal government urged women to take over factory jobs vacated by men off in the trenches. Although many of the women who entered the work force in the name of patriotism were anxious to return to their homes after the war, many others found unexpected gratification in earning a salary and in being more independent. These women found it difficult to give up their jobs when the men returned at the end of the war.

To help encourage these women to return to their "rightful" places at home (and to help men get back their jobs), government and industry waged a massive public relations campaign. Films portrayed working women as unhappy, unhealthy, and sometimes even spiritually depraved. The message was clear: "Good" women stayed at home to nurture their husbands and children. To a large degree, this campaign was quite effective.

But soon there was another major social transformation. The development of readily available reliable birth control revolutionized interpersonal relationships and family life. For the first time in history, couples could plan their families. A kind of "sexual revolution" began to unfold. Men and women felt greater control over their destinies, but at the same time, they had to make difficult decisions regarding relationships and sexual issues.

Not long after reliable birth control became available, economic necessity led many homemakers back into the work force. Today, it takes two wage earners to "sustain the same middle-class lifestyle that one income could provide 20 years ago."[1] With raised economic expectations and control over childbearing schedules, dual-career households began to outnumber the traditional one-breadwinner family. So dramatic has been this change in our society that today the traditional husband-as-breadwinner and wife-as-homemaker family makes up less than 10 percent of our population. Nearly half of all married women with children under the age of one are in our country's labor force, and 71 percent of these mothers are employed full time. At the same time, major increases in the divorce rate have dramatically changed the complexion of family life. Today, one-fifth of all families with children are headed by women, and many of these families have incomes below the poverty level.

These dramatic statistics raise serious questions about men's and women's roles. But other changes have motivated people to question these roles as well. The move to an information-age economy has played an especially major role in encouraging people to question the value and appropriateness of traditional gender norms. In an information-age service economy, many (if not most) jobs require skills not associated traditionally with either sex. The apparent differences between men's and women's abilities to work plows, and the obvious differences between the sexes' abilities to breast-feed children, are inapplicable to most of today's workers. Men and women are equally capable of working computers, setting leads, writing copy, and reading news copy. And with infant formula readily available, many men eagerly nurture their infants. In short, the sex-role distinctions that played such a major role in the past now face serious challenges. Today, the very appropriateness and value of norms based on gender have become a major social issue.

Yet for most people, an infant's sexual identity continues to be of considerable importance. Obstetricians report that the question most eagerly asked by relatives and friends on learning of a child's birth is "what is it?" The answer sought, of course, is "a boy" or "a girl." Signs can be seen in storefronts or on billboards: "It's a boy!" or "It's a girl!" In short, despite other changes in our society, we remain keenly interested in a person's sexual identity.

Experiments reveal that this interest affects our interaction with newborns. When people are placed in a nursery to view a newborn wrapped in a yellow blanket, most of them spend much of their time inquiring about the infant's sex. In another experiment, adults are videotaped interacting with a newborn they are told is a girl. Later, these same adults are taped interacting with the same newborn. But this time they are told the infant is a boy. In a significant number of instances, the adults' responses to the same infant are notably different. The results of these experiments strongly suggest that our

---

1. Barbara Kantrowitz (with Elisa Williams, Jennifer Pratt, Sue Hutchinson, and Lori Rotenberk), "A Mother's Choice," *Newsweek,* March 31, 1986, p. 47.

behavior toward newborns results more from our views of the differences between males and females than from an infant's behavior.

Some scientists believe that there may also be biological factors that influence behavioral differences between males and females in our society. A few scientists contend, for example, that some differences in men's and women's hormonal makeup may influence attitudes and behavior. There are even a few scientists who believe that men's and women's brains are physiologically different and that these differences may influence the development of skills and personality traits. Neuropsychologist Sandra Witelson of McMaster University Medical School in Ontario, Canada, believes, for example, that women's brains have a larger isthmus, which is the area associated with language and speech. Some scientists believe that if Dr. Witelson's finding is valid, it would help explain women's general superiority on tests of verbal intelligence.

If we take these researchers' work seriously, we find ourselves confronting some fundamental questions: What are the essential differences between men and women? What can we predict as a result of these differences? What is entailed by the biological differences between men and women? And how many of the apparent differences between men and women can we attribute to socialization? If boys and girls are treated differently from moments after their birth, how much influence does this socialization have in creating "masculine" and "feminine" behavior?

Based on current research, it is likely that many of the apparent differences between the sexes result much more from "nurture," or socialization, than from "nature," or biology. However, in the absence of definitive answers to these issues, we are left with important personal and public choices. After all, if some of the apparent differences between the sexes are found to be attributable to biological differences, we must still decide what is entailed by this finding. Even under this scenario, we would still need to contend with the realization that socialization has some impact on perceptions, attitudes, and behavior. If instead science continues to show that many of the apparently "natural" differences between the sexes actually result from socialization, we would need to decide whether we want to work toward the elimination of norms based on gender. Should we try to raise boys and girls with few gender norms? Or should we encourage children to view themselves in terms of clearly defined masculine and feminine expectations? What can and should men and women expect from one another and from themselves in relationships?

▼ **Exercise 1b:** Previous chapters emphasized the fact that all attempts to characterize events are necessarily shaped by authors' biases. Identify biases that you believe influence the paragraphs above. Next, consider the extent to which these biases influence the resulting overview of sexual identity issues.

▾ **Exercise 1c:** Provide an alternative overview of the evolution of gender norms in this society. Identify key differences between your characterization and the preceding discussion. Finally, provide a persuasive defense of your overview.

▾ **Exercise 1d:** Review the following list of traditional gender norms. Discuss the prevalence of these norms in this society. Which, if any, of these norms do you believe continue to serve as commonplaces in our society? Which, if any, have our society abandoned?

Traditional Practice Norms for Women

Women should:

▾ take primary responsibility for domestic chores
▾ nurture their husbands and children and be sensitive to others' needs
▾ be patient, kind, loving, and giving
▾ be diplomatic and family peacekeepers
▾ be less promiscuous, less aggressive, and more passive than men
▾ be artistic and creative

Traditional Beliefs About Women

Women are naturally:

▾ capable homemakers and child rearers
▾ kind, patient, selfless, loving, gentle, nurturing, generous, giving, and good listeners
▾ more vulnerable and weaker than men
▾ poor leaders
▾ more emotional and less logical than men
▾ overly subjective
▾ more reliant on intuition than men
▾ indecisive
▾ careful and cautious, not risk takers
▾ passive
▾ more faithful and less promiscuous than men
▾ easily jealous
▾ gossipy and superficial
▾ manipulative
▾ less athletic than men
▾ better at developing and maintaining friendships than men
▾ mechanically incompetent
▾ artistic and creative

Traditional Practice Norms for Men

Men should:

▾ take care of the family (be protectors)
▾ earn enough income to support the family
▾ be aggressive

▾ be daring and adventurous
▾ be strong
▾ be competitive

Traditional Beliefs About Men

Men are naturally:

▾ strong
▾ aggressive
▾ competitive
▾ logical, mathematical, capable of objective judgment
▾ less emotional and more decisive than women
▾ reluctant to rely on intuition
▾ competent leaders
▾ good money managers
▾ risk takers
▾ athletic
▾ arrogant, selfish, possessive, and egotistical
▾ less sensitive than women
▾ not competent at domestic chores
▾ more promiscuous and less faithful than women
▾ less capable of developing and maintaining friendships than women
▾ emotionally dependent on women
▾ mechanically inclined

▾ **Exercise 1e:** Discuss the value of these norms based on gender. Which, if any, would you encourage your children to accept? Which, if any, would you like to see changed or abandoned? Do you think norms of this kind are generally beneficial or generally harmful to the quality of interpersonal relationships? What kinds of arguments and evidence would you need to support these views? What kinds of evidence would help convince you to reconsider your views on this topic?

▾ **Exercise 1f:** What are the sources of the norms listed above? Discuss television programs that you believe support some of these norms. Which television programs challenge some of these norms? What about print media? Find examples of print, radio, or television ads that you believe support the norms. How persuasive are these ads?

▾ **Exercise 1g:** Consider the discussion that follows regarding the implications of preserving traditional gender norms. Identify the claims that you believe are commonplaces. Next, identify the claims that you believe are controversial.

Issue Overview

Suppose, for the sake of discussion, that our society continues to encourage people to live in accordance with the gender norms listed above. What would be some of the likely consequences of this social endorsement?

It seems evident that most of us would like women who conform to the "feminine" gender norms. A gentle, nurturing, giving, loving person who has strong domestic skills would also be the sort of person most of us probably would want to have caring for us and our children. By the same token, however, because these people are poor leaders, more emotional than logical, poor money managers, and passive, they would probably not command respect in today's competitive marketplace. Few of us would want such people serving as senators, judges, presidents, company CEOs, or even department heads.

In contrast, men who conform to the listed masculine gender norms probably would not quickly earn most people's affection. After all, they are egotistical, selfish, more logical than emotional, aggressive, and competitive. But combining these and their other qualities, these people probably would be popular candidates for directorships of corporations or for other roles perceived as requiring strength, rationality, and aggressiveness.

Perhaps this explains why parents seldom show as much concern for an adolescent daughter's tendency toward "masculine" behavior as for an adolescent son's tendency toward "feminine" behavior. Perhaps parents believe that their "tomboy" daughters will have the means to protect themselves in the world's competitive climate. Perhaps correspondingly, parents fear that their less masculine sons will fail to command respect in any domain. For these "violators" of society's gender norms, the world can be a harsh, unaccepting place.

To help their children conform to the norms appropriate to their sex, parents purchase appropriate toys and clothing. Girls are given dolls, often with elaborate makeup cases, elegant clothes, and other feminine adornments. Girls are also given "soft" toys, such as playdough, and domestic toys, such as kitchen sets. Boys are taught to develop their aggressive instincts with guns, helmets, and crash cars. Although boys are sometimes given dolls, they are usually not encouraged to spend much time dressing these dolls in feminine clothing.

Many traditional parents encourage their boys to play football, whereas their girls are encouraged to study ballet or gymnastics. These parents urge their sons to show aggression with each other, but they teach their daughters to be passive and nurturing in relationships. In these families, boys who throw stones at ducks along the river's edge are sometimes only mildly chastised. Some traditional parents view this behavior as within the expected boundaries of "masculinity." After all, they might say, "Boys will be boys." In contrast, girls in these families are often encouraged to feed bread to the ducks and are more critically viewed if they choose to throw stones instead. On the same outing to the riverside, boys in traditional families might be encouraged to follow their adventuresome spirit along the river's edge, while their sisters are more often protected from such dangers. These boys are taken on hunting and fishing expeditions, but their sisters are taken to cooking and sewing classes. Traditional parents are often heard saying, "Come here, my son" to their young boys, whereas they avoid this type of expression when speaking with their daughters. Their boys are often allowed to fall, whereas traditional parents are more likely to jealously protect their daughters from a fall's potential hurt.

In some schools, training for adherence to gender norms continues. Books in these schools portray Jane as gentle and nurturing, Dick as strong and protective. Jane is shown caring for the children, while Dick is earning the family income. But these traditional characterizations have recently come under considerable attack; in some communities, they have become a topic of major debate.

Some people believe that teaching children norms based on gender prevents them from fully developing their individual potential. These people argue that boys who might otherwise be gentle, caring fathers and husbands are taught to suppress their nurturing qualities so that they can develop more "masculine" traits. Girls who are naturally aggressive and competitive are taught to be more "ladylike" and hence forego developing some of their natural strengths.

Worst of all, according to people opposed to teaching gender norms, these norms are arbitrary and often counterproductive to the development of fulfilling relationships. Couples who live according to these societal expectations are often unhappy. Many couples who live in accordance with these expectations base their decisions on what others tell them they should do, rather than on their own desires and needs. So Jack and Joy, for example, each face the frustrations of not fulfilling their inner desires. Joy would like to be a computer programmer, and Jack secretly desires to stay home to care for their two children. But fear of society's disapproval keeps Joy and Jack from pursuing their hidden desires. As a result, the children are left with someone who secretly resents having to stay home with them. And the family faces the daily strain of unhappy adults and children.

A world without gender norms would encourage Joy and Jack to openly discuss their secret desires. In this world, Jack would likely feel free to "admit" that he enjoys nurturing their children and that he feels the most fulfilled when he is caring for them and the home. Joy could acknowledge her desire to work outside the home and could develop her programming skills to their full potential. Without fear of societal rebuke, Joy and Jack would likely fulfill their potential and provide their children with a happier, more secure home life.

But people disagree with this view. They believe that everyone is better off when schools and families reinforce norms based on gender. According to these people, life is complicated enough without taking away the basic expectations that help couples live stable and secure lives together. When couples have to decide anew the distribution of household responsibilities, for example, they are needlessly confronted with issues that could easily be resolved through gender norms. Furthermore, when gender norms no longer guide interpersonal male-female relationships, competition rather than complementarity results. Competitive households lead to serious stress—often to divorce. And the children who live in these environments must pay the highest price.

In fact, according to the proponents of traditional gender norms, the startling statistics about divorce in our society may be largely attributable to the fact that we have been failing in our commitment to preserve traditional norms based on gender. If women would return to their rightful place in the home and men would regain their rightful place as sole breadwinner, couples would once again see marriage as the beautiful union it was intended to be. Husbands and wives would work together, rather than against each other, in the building of their unified home. And many of the social ills associated with single parenthood would disappear.

These proponents of gender norms have several observations to make about Joy and Jack as well. First, they would argue, Joy and Jack are not typical. Few men have Jack's "feminine" desires. And the development of these unnatural desires should not be encouraged because they will likely confuse Joy and Jack's children. Furthermore, if Joy and Jack really are as confused about their roles as they sound, society's adherence to norms based on gender would not prevent Joy and Jack from pursuing their own desires. They simply need to understand that their deviant feelings are different from the norm, and they should do what they can to help their own children better conform. In the long run, this will be better for everyone living in our society.

These competing perspectives about the preservation of traditional gender norms leave many questions open to debate. Some of these questions are factual. How much impact does society realistically have in shaping people's expectations of themselves and each other? What impact do these expectations have on relationships? Are norms based on gender arbitrary, or do they accurately reflect "nature"? Do gender norms help people develop stable and complementary relationships, or do they tend to stifle the development of people's potential? When children are encouraged to behave according to society's gender-based expectations, are they more likely to be well adjusted, or are they more likely to live dissatisfied lives?

Others are policy and value issues. What role should society play in the development of people's interpersonal relationships? Should parents encourage boys and girls to conform to society's gender norms? Or should they try to discover and help develop each child's individual qualities? Should educators, public officials, and other societal representatives try to encourage children to abandon gender-based expectations? Should men and women try to conform to society's gender norms? Or should couples distribute domestic responsibilities according to their own personal needs and desires?

These are but a few of the crucial issues confronting parents, public officials, and others who influence the development of interpersonal relationships. Effectively addressing these and related gender norm issues will help everyone live more fulfilling and productive personal lives.

▾ **Exercise 1h:** Discuss the issues presented in Topic 1. Where would you turn for answers to these questions? To what extent do these issues reflect the essence of the concerns addressed in the preceding discussion of gender norms? List issues that you believe are missing.

▾ **Exercise 1i:** Discuss the strengths and weaknesses of each of the competing views in the discussion above. Which perspective do you find most persuasive? Why?

▾ **Exercise 1j:** Identify the claims that you believe are commonplaces in the discussion above. Next, identify the claims that are likely to spark debate. Finally, describe the values and beliefs that you believe underlie each of the two competing perspectives. Which set of values most closely conforms to your own? What are the sources of these values?

▾ **Exercise 1k:** Identify inferences made in the discussion above. Next, evaluate the validity of these inferences.

▾ **Exercise 1l:** Develop an issues brief on the preservation of norms based on gender. After completing the brief, decide whether you support or oppose the preservation of traditional gender norms. Next, write a paper designed to persuade a composite audience to seriously consider your perspective. As you develop your arguments, carefully consider the fundamental question of whether children, adults, and relationships are better or worse off when parents, educators, leaders, and others work to preserve traditional gender norms. Finally, be sure to anticipate refutation of your controversial claims.

▾ ▾ ▾

TOPIC 2: PUBLIC POLICY AND AMERICAN FAMILY LIFE

Personal identity and gender norm issues involve all segments of our society, from the individual, to the couple, to the society as a whole. But these issues tend to dwell more in the personal realm, where the individual decides who she is or what she wishes to become. This is less true of child-rearing questions. Because children are viewed as generally powerless, they are considered vulnerable and in need of societal protection. Children are also often referred to as a society's greatest "asset," the promise of the future. And so societies tend to take special interest in the lives of their young.

Not surprisingly, our society has child-welfare regulations that are intended to prevent parental child abuse and neglect. Numerous local, state, and federal statutes regulate the education of this nation's children as well. And many laws protect children from abuse in the workplace and elsewhere. Yet we do not yet have an official "national family policy" that outlines the government's appropriate role in child care. In fact, we are the only industrialized nation without such a policy.

Many recent changes in America's family life environment have led our legislators to reconsider this nation's strong commitment to keeping government out of family life. Recently, legislators have been asked to evaluate information on American family life that has been compiled by a variety of sources. Their task will be to interpret and analyze the data and to determine what inferences should be drawn. Applying these inferences to their factual and value commonplaces, our legislators will make decisions that will affect millions of American parents and children.

▾ **Exercise 2a:** The first set of exercises in this section focuses on data available to our legislators. Look for inconsistencies among some of the data listed below. Among the conflicting data, which do you find more reliable? Why?

▾ **Exercise 2b:** Begin a search for additional data. Which of the data—those given below or those you find—are more reliable? Why?

Data on American Family Life

On women in the workplace:

▾ In 1987, women held one-half of the jobs in all of the professions (ABC News 1987 Special Report, "After the Sexual Revolution").

▾ In 1987, there were only two women among all the CEOs and presidents of America's major corporations (ABC).

▾ Among America's 16,000 corporate directors, 480 are women (ABC).

▾ There were fewer women executives at top levels in 1985 than in 1982 (ABC).

▾ In 1986, 33% of new companies were founded by women (ABC).

▾ Women earned one-third of all family income in America (ABC).

▾ Women have taken 84% of all new jobs since 1980 (ABC).

▾ 33% of working women have clerical jobs for which they earn less today (in real income) than in 1970 (ABC).

▾ 10 million American women provide their children's sole support (ABC).

▾ 61% of married couples with children are dual earners (*American Demographics* [AD], March 1988, p. 25).

▾ Both parents work in 55% of households with children under age six (AD).

▾ Married couples with children have a median income of $34,000. But women who head families with children have a median income of $11,000 (AD).

On the American family:

▾ There were 91.1 million households in the United States as of March, 1988, of which 65.1 million were families (1988 Federal Census Bureau Report [FCB]).

▾ Two-parent families are declining, slipping from 40% of all households in 1970 to 27% in 1988 (FCB).

▾ In 1988, 23% of U.S. families had children under age six (*Columbus Dispatch* [CD], August 30, 1988, p. A-5.

▾ In 1988, there were 21.9 million one-person households, up 20% from 1980 (FCB).

▾ Nearly 25% of American homes are headed by single women (ABC).

▾ There were 2.6 million unmarried couples living together in 1988, up 63% from 1980 (FCB).

▾ 20% of America's children are born to single mothers (ABC).

▾ 55% of America's children have mothers who work outside the home (ABC).

▾ From 1975–1986, the proportion of working mothers with preschool children increased from 38% to 57% (CD).

▾ Women do an average of 35 hours of housework per week, whereas men do an average of 7 hours of housework per week (ABC).

On divorce, alimony, and child support:

▾ In 1987, there were 11 million American children of divorce (ABC).

▾ More than 1 million marriages end in divorce each year (ABC).

▾ One year after divorce, women experience an average of a 73% drop in their standard of living, whereas men experience a 42% rise in their standard of living (ABC).

▾ 98% of children of divorce stay with their mothers (ABC).

▾ Less than 15% of divorced women get alimony, and the average alimony payment is under $4,000 per year (New York Task Force on Divorce [NYTF]).

▾ The average weekly child support payment per child is $34 (NYTF).

▾ 33% of divorced women with children move below the poverty line after divorce (NYTF).

▾ 42% of children of divorce get no financial support from their fathers (NYTF).

▾ 50% of children of divorce had no contact with their fathers this past year (NYTF).

On child care:

▾ More than 50 countries ensure parental access to licensed day care. The United States does not (ABC).

▾ Since 1981, federal financing of day care has been cut (ABC).

▾ Since 1981, 22 states have cut their financing of day care (ABC).

▾ 6 million American children are left in informal, unlicensed neighborhood child-care facilities (ABC).

▾ There are 9 million children currently waiting for openings in day-care centers (ABC).

▾ Child-care workers earn an average of $9,000–$12,000 per year (*Newsweek* [N], February 15, 1988, p. 57).

▾ America's corporate world has a total of 150 on-site day-care centers (ABC).

▾ 3,000 companies provide some form of support for child care (N).

▾ The average weekly cost of child care in Boston ranges from $75–$150 for a day-care center to $260–$340 for a full-time babysitter. In St. Louis the costs range from $50–$80 for day care to $165 and up for a full-time babysitter (N).

▾ Children run less risk statistically of being sexually abused in a day-care center than they do at home. (University of New Hampshire, Family Research Laboratory, Federal study for the National Center on Child Abuse and Neglect, an agency of the Department of Health and Human Services. Cited in *Columbus Dispatch*, March 22, 1988, p. A-4.)

On parental leave policies:

▾ 60% of American working women have no maternity insurance and receive no paid maternity leave (ABC).

▾ More than 60% of U.S. working women aren't guaranteed getting their jobs back after they return from maternity leave (The Economic Policy Council, a nonprofit group that studies labor management issues, as cited in *Business Week*, May 19, 1986, p. 54).

▾ More than 100 countries have laws providing paid maternity leaves for women. The United States does not (*New York Times*, September 18, 1985, p. C-6).

▾ Over 100 countries have laws providing job security for women on maternity leave. The United States does not (ABC).

▾ **Exercise 2c:** What conclusions, if any, should legislators draw from these data on women in the workplace, the American family, divorce, child care, and parental leave? Why?

▾ **Exercise 2d:** Review the following issue overview on parental leave policy. Identify assumptions of fact and value reflected in the discussion. Do you share these assumptions? Next, review the arguments given for and against a national parental leave policy. Which set of arguments do you find most persuasive? Why?

Issue Overview

The 1980s have seen growing concern over the need to provide some support for the 90 percent of American families who do not follow the traditional family model of the husband being the sole breadwinner and the wife staying home to take care of the children. In the past, little public attention was given to the fact that many American workers who wanted to stay home with their newborn infants had no job security. They were forced to choose between their jobs and their children. More recently, the fact that the vast majority of American families face difficult choices regarding their children's care has generated considerable attention to the debate over whether the United States should adopt a parental leave policy.

Proponents of such a policy note that more than 100 countries have laws that protect the job security of working parents who take time off to care for their infants. The United States is the only industrialized nation that does not provide this type of protection for its workers. Opponents respond by contending that American women have more job opportunities than do their counterparts in other nations. According to opponents of parental leave, "The United States stands to lose more economically because American women often hold higher-level positions than their foreign counterparts."[2]

Proponents of a national parental leave policy contend that workers should not have to choose between their jobs and their children. But opponents reply that forcing companies to provide parental leave would make prospective parents less desirable candidates for positions. Employers would simply avoid the problem by hiring people with grown children or those who were not likely to become parents. Proponents respond to this objection by pointing out that prospective parents currently form the most productive and significant segment of the working population. Discrimination against this major work force would be completely infeasible, if not impossible, say the proponents.

One of the most outspoken proponents of a national parental leave policy is Representative Pat Schroeder. In her book, *Champion of the Great American Family,* Schroeder explains her passionate commitment to this cause. She explains that she was working full time as a field attorney at the National Labor Relations Board in Denver when she and her husband decided to start their family. She writes:

▼▼▼▼▼▼

I didn't even bother to find out whether the NLRB had a maternity-leave policy. In 1966, the prevailing policy was "You get pregnant, you leave." If I had asked about taking maternity leave, my employers would have laughed.[3] ▼▼▼

According to Schroeder, "Popular attitudes about pregnancy have come a long way since [then], but the change in attitude did not come easily. It was not until 1984 that the American Medical Association admitted that its previous recommendation on pregnancy and work—that a woman should stop working in her sixth month—was based more on myth than on science."[4]

---

2. Michael Blumfield, "Business Balks at Parenting Bill," *Columbus Dispatch,* May 31, 1987, p. F-2.

3. Pat Schroeder, *Champion of the Great American Family* (New York: Random House, 1989), p. 45.

4. Schroeder, p. 46.

Schroeder goes on to provide a history of the parental leave debate. She points out that in 1976, the pregnancy leave issue received significant public attention as a result of the Supreme Court's ruling in *General Electric* v. *Gilbert*.[5] This case involved the allegation that GE "had discriminated against its female employees by excluding pregnancy from coverage under its disability plan."[6] The Supreme Court ruled that pregnancy is voluntary and not gender-related. Based on these premises, the Court decided that discrimination against pregnancy does not constitute sex discrimination.

On March 15, 1977, eighty-two members of Congress introduced the Pregnancy Discrimination Act (PDA) "to amend the Civil Rights Act of 1964 so that it would specifically include pregnancy."[7] The PDA became law in 1978, thereby requiring pregnancy to be treated like other disabilities. However, the PDA did not provide job security for mothers. Nor did the bill provide parental leave for fathers and mothers of newborns.

These concerns led Representative Schroeder to seek passage of a parental leave bill. However, opposition to the bill was strong. According to Schroeder, "The Chamber of Commerce and the National Association of Manufacturers joined forces with the National Federation for Independent Businesses and a coalition of trade associations to try to defeat the bill."[8] To help ensure passage of a parental leave policy, its proponents worked on writing a bill that would address many of the business community's concerns. Schroeder worked with Representatives William Clay and Marge Roukema. Together they drafted a bill, the Family and Medical Leave Act (FMLA), which exempts businesses with fewer than fifty employees. Under the compromise FMLA, employees would become eligible only after they had worked for a company for at least one year. Companies would be required to provide ten weeks of *unpaid* family leave over a two-year period. The new bill would also permit an employee to take time off to care for a seriously ill child or parent. And companies would be required to provide fifteen weeks medical leave per year to each employee. Employees taking either family leave or medical leave would have the right to return to the same position or a similar one, and their seniority, pension rights, and health-care coverage would be maintained.

Schroeder reports that by the spring of 1988, "Forty additional Democratic members and sixteen Republicans had signed on to" the FMLA.[9] According to Schroeder, the bill now had 150 cosponsors. Schroeder summarizes her views on the bill's effects:

---

5.   429 U.S. 125.

6.   Schroeder, p. 47.

7.   Schroeder, p. 48.

8.   Schroeder, p. 52.

9.   Schroeder, p. 54.

▼ ▼ ▼ ▼ ▼ ▼

If successful, the Family and Medical Leave Act will help parents bridge the gap between work and family responsibilities by encouraging employers to establish a more responsive workplace. Over 20 million women will have job protection when they become pregnant, adopt a child, or need to stay at home with a seriously ill child. Men and women will be able to care for their dependent parents. Fathers will finally be recognized as responsible parents and their rights as such will be protected. And any employee who becomes seriously ill will not face the economic disaster of losing a job at such a difficult time. If this bill becomes law, we will be able to deal directly with some conditions that create great stress on the American family. Now all we have is seminars on "How to Cope with Stress," where we tell folks to go to a spa![10] ▼ ▼ ▼

As Representative Schroeder acknowledges, however, not everyone shares her enthusiasm for the FMLA. Commentator James J. Kilpatrick joins many in opposing the bill.

▼ **Exercise 2e:** Review the following excerpts from Universal Press Syndicate Commentator James J. Kilpatrick's editorial on the FMLA.[11] Do you find Kilpatrick's arguments persuasive? Why or why not? Did Representative Schroeder adequately consider Kilpatrick's concerns in the comments provided above? Has Kilpatrick effectively addressed the concerns of those favoring passage of the FMLA?

▼ ▼ ▼ ▼ ▼ ▼

Family-Leave Bill Too Costly For Employers

Let us suppose for a moment that everything proponents say of the family-leave bill is true: The costs to employers would be generally insignificant and the benefits to working families would be highly desirable.

Granted all that, the bill remains a bad bill.

The bill, known officially as the Family and Medical Leave Act of 1989, bears the names of 139 members of the House as sponsors.

Sponsors make some self-evident points in the bill's favor: Over the past 30 or 40 years, the composition of the American work force has changed dramatically. Almost half of the labor force is female; more than half of all mothers with children under the age of 3 work outside their homes. Only 3.7 percent of our families still fit the traditional mold of mom at home with two kids and dad at work.

If we are to keep the family unit strong, the argument goes, parents must not be put to the choice of your baby or your job. When members of a family fall

---

10.   Schroeder, p. 55.

11.   *Columbus Dispatch,* February 23, 1989, p. A-13. Copyright 1989 Universal Press Syndicate. All rights reserved. Reprinted with permission.

seriously ill; someone must be able to take leave to care for them. Infants, whether newborn or adopted, need a period of close parental bonding.

Thus the bill. It would require all employers of 50 or more workers to grant up to 10 work weeks of unpaid family leave during any period of 24 months. During this period all health benefits would be continued. The absent employees would be guaranteed their old jobs, or equivalent jobs, on their return. After three years the act would apply to employers of at least 35 workers.

In the nature of things, a new bureaucracy would be created within the Department of Labor. The bill calls for the usual panoply of rules and regulations, annual reports, complaints, petitions, civil actions, administrative hearings, appeals, reviews, etc.

At this juncture, no one has more than a hazy idea of what the costs of the act would be.

At a subcommittee hearing on Feb. 7, William J. Gainer of the General Accounting Office put the annual cost to employers at $188 million, consisting chiefly of the cost of maintaining health benefits, but he had no great confidence in the figure.

The U.S. Chamber of Commerce believes the cost would be much higher.

In small enterprises especially, the temporary simultaneous absence of several employees could seriously affect productivity. Replacements would have to be recruited and trained. In the alternative, remaining workers would have to double up and do the jobs of absent colleagues.

Cost is not the main issue, though, for some small companies just getting started, it could be a real problem. The overriding objection is to the nature of one more compulsory, inflexible, federal burden upon employers. Once this bill became law, employers would have no choice; family leave would take its place with the 40-hour week and time and a half for overtime.

Employees also would lose a degree of flexibility. Many workers in their 40s and 50s have no interest at all in 10 weeks of leave to nurture a newborn or sick child. They might vastly prefer a little more paid vacation or expanded health care instead.

In a voluntary society . . . not every worker should be confined, willy-nilly, to the same wages and fringe benefits.

This is a hard bill to oppose, for its provisions are benevolent, but federally mandated benevolence carries a price. In this instance the price is too high. ▼▼▼

▼ **Exercise 2f:** Identify commonplaces of fact and value that you believe Kilpatrick and Schroeder share regarding parental leave. Do you share these commonplaces with them? Why or why not? Next, identify issues of fact and value raised by proponents and opponents of the FMLA. What are your views on these issues?

▼ **Exercise 2g:** Review the following brief presentations for and against adoption of a parental leave bill. Whose presentation do you find more persuasive? Why?

Pro: *Sally Orr, Director of Public Policy, Association of Junior Leagues*

The U.S. is the only major industrialized nation that does not guarantee parents—primarily mothers in most countries—time off to be with their children. Almost half of American women with children under 1 year old are now in the work force, and yet currently only 40 percent of American women receive some type of benefit at childbirth.

Con: *Randolph Hale, Vice-President, Industrial Relations, National Association of Manufacturers*

Such leave is a good practice where companies can afford to offer it voluntarily and employees want it. But we oppose the legislation because it would also apply to companies that can't afford to give such leave. We have to ask: How would this affect the ability of the United States to compete with the rest of the world?[12]

▾ **Exercise 2h:** Provide additional arguments that you believe would strengthen Orr's and Hale's perspectives. Given your additions, which position would you find most persuasive? Why?

▾ **Exercise 2i:** It has been argued that FMLA proponents and opponents generally agree on desired results. Do you agree with this claim? What results do you think Schroeder is seeking? What about Kilpatrick? Orr? Hale?

▾ **Exercise 2j:** Provide a summary of your understanding of the problem that led Representatives Schroeder, Clay, Roukema, and others to support versions of the Family and Medical Leave Act. How serious do you believe these problems really are? How do you believe legislators should address these problems?

▾ **Exercise 2k:** Complete an issues brief on the question of whether the U.S. Congress should pass the Family and Medical Leave Act. After completing the brief, decide whether you would support or oppose passage of the FMLA. Write a paper in defense of your position. As you prepare your arguments, be sure to carefully consider the data and arguments presented in Topic 2. Be sure too that your argumentation anticipates reasonable refutation of your controversial claims.

▾ ▾ ▾
TOPIC 3: RIGHTS OF AFFECTIONAL PREFERENCE

The topics discussed so far have covered a wide range of personal and public interests. Yet they represent only a few of the many family life concerns bridging the public and private sectors of our society. An area of growing concern centers on people's rights to freely express their affectional preferences.

---

12. From "Require Firms To Give 'Family Leave'?" *U.S. News and World Report,* July 28, 1986, p. 63.

A number of scientific studies on sexual preference, the sexual revolution, the gay rights movement, and growing public concern about AIDS have all helped generate public debate on this controversial topic. The issue overview and exercises that follow are designed to help you effectively participate in this debate.

> ▼ **Exercise 3a:** Read the following issue overview related to affectional preference. Identify commonplaces of fact and value. Next, identify claims that you believe are issues.

Issue Overview

Experts estimate that approximately 10 percent of Americans are homosexual. The actual number is difficult to determine because fear of serious negative reprisals keeps many homosexual persons from disclosing their affectional preference.

Debate continues about whether sexual preference is biological, learned, or formed as a result of both factors. Most scientists believe that a person's sexual preference is shaped early in life. Some even believe it is determined before birth. Nonetheless, some people continue to believe that sexual preference is shaped by upbringing, education, and other social factors. According to this group, homosexuality can be "cured" through a variety of therapeutic means.

In 1973, after a long and intense debate, the American Psychological Association determined that homosexuality is not a mental disorder. Previously, many mental health practitioners encouraged therapy designed to prevent and "cure" homosexuality in patients. Today, there are still practitioners who perform such therapies. However, this perspective has come under attack in the field. And the preferred approach today is to accept affectional preference as irreversible.

Some people believe that the outcome of this scientific debate is crucial to the resolution of a number of central issues. They contend that if sexual preference is determined before birth, there would be little advantage to preventing homosexuals from marrying one another, teaching in public schools, or holding other potentially influential public posts. Similarly, if sexual preference is learned, there may be grounds to continue prohibiting homosexual marriage and to continue the exclusion of homosexual persons from a wide variety of public positions.

Most experts today, however, share the technical presumption that regardless of whether sexual preference is determined by upbringing or by biological factors, it is nearly impossible to change once it has been established. According to this presumption, intensive therapy has the potential to change *behavior,* but *preference* is virtually impossible to change once it has been formed.

For many people, this position is difficult to accept at first. But the dramatic results of a simple mental exercise give credence to expert opinion on this issue. The exercise also helps heterosexual persons understand the nature and magnitude of issues related to affectional preference.

The mental exercise in question simply calls for the person to imagine living in a society in which institutions are geared to endorse homosexuality, rather than heterosexuality. To complete the exercise, try to imagine that heterosexuality is prohibited in our society. Imagine that heterosexuals in our society are not permitted to hold their loved one's hand in public. Any public display of affection between men and women is considered repugnant, and dangerous to children. Nor are heterosexuals permitted to marry. Imagine that men and women who love one another risk losing their family and friends if they openly share their feelings with their family. And imagine that the police have the right to arrest heterosexuals who choose to express their feelings through sexual intimacy with each other. Under these circumstances: (1) Do you believe most heterosexuals could "force" themselves to become homosexual? and (2) Do you believe that many people would freely "choose" to be heterosexual if they could change their sexual preference?

It has been argued that even if learning and socialization were found to affect sexual preference, people who find themselves attracted to others of their own sex should receive legal protection. Proponents of this view believe that our country was founded on a commitment to the preservation of civil liberties. Among these, they argue, is the right for consenting adults to freely express their sexuality in private, without fear of imprisonment or a worse punishment. Belief in rights of affectional preference also extends to other types of protection. Some people believe, for instance, that homosexuals should be protected from employment and housing discrimination.

But there are many who disagree with these positions. These people believe that homosexuality can and should be prevented. These opponents of the rights of affectional preference believe that society should use its institutional power to prevent homosexuality from spreading among the young, who are so vulnerable to it.

The AIDS crisis has helped spark some public support for this position. In the absence of definitive scientific knowledge about the causes of this fatal disease, many people fear having contact with possible AIDS carriers. Because homosexual men are considered especially at risk for this disease, some Americans have used the AIDS crisis to support the retention of laws that discriminate against homosexuals and help ensure their isolation from the rest of the population.

But even before AIDS became a factor in public policy debates, opposition to the rights of affectional preference formed the basis of legislative policy making. Homosexuality has been and continues to be a crime in many states, and it receives little or no legal protection in most others. In most of the nation, homosexual persons are not permitted to marry, adopt children, or teach at public schools. They may be denied jobs, housing, and insurance on the basis of their affectional preference. The United States Supreme Court has consistently upheld these and other forms of discrimination against homosexual Americans.

These strong institutional sanctions against homosexuality are reinforced in many ways throughout our society. Few television programs provide "positive" role models to young people who believe they are homosexual, and law enforcement does little to protect homosexuals who wish to publicly display their affection for one another. Further, humor at the expense of homosexuals is widely accepted. Although public expressions of racial hatred, and even some forms of sexism, are no longer socially sanctioned, public expressions of antihomosexual sentiment receive few sanctions. In some social circles, animosity toward homosexual and bisexual persons is so deep that men will react violently to being labeled a homosexual. For these people, there is almost no prospect more humiliating than the possibility of being perceived as homosexual.

For some parents, the news that a son or daughter is homosexual is almost more devastating than the news of a child's death. For some, the source of pain is the knowledge that their child will never have a "normal" life. For other parents, the anguish is the result of the fear that their child will be ostracized and discriminated against. And for yet others, the news brings as much shame as it does pain and anguish.

The controversial case of *Thompson* v. *Kowalski* dramatically highlights the intensity of feelings and the seriousness of issues associated with the debate over rights of affectional preference. Karen Thompson, a university professor in St. Cloud, Minnesota, was in her thirties when she met Sharon Kowalski. In 1979, after two years of close friendship, Karen and Sharon exchanged rings and made a lifetime commitment to be with one another. Because the community in which they lived had strong sanctions against homosexuality, Karen and Sharon kept their relationship secret, even from their families.

On November 13, 1983, Sharon was seriously injured when her car was struck by a drunk driver. Sharon stayed in a coma for five months. When she came out of the coma, she was a quadriplegic, was unable to speak, and had only partial control of her right arm and hand. With Karen's daily help, Sharon learned to communicate using a letterboard and typewriter. However, the results of tests designed to assess Sharon's ability to make decisions for herself were varied and contradictory. This created the grounds on which Sharon's loved ones would fight for control of her destiny.

In 1989, the CBS news program "West 57th" provided a forum for the people involved in this struggle.[13] In an interview with correspondent Diane Sawyer, Sharon's father, Donald Kowalski, described Sharon as "completely

---

13.   Originally broadcast February 25, 1989.

handicapped," "down-right helpless." On the same program, Dr. Keith Larson, Sharon's neurologist, described Donald Kowalski as deeply concerned with his daughter's welfare, but inclined to "act like he was entering a funeral parlor" whenever he entered Sharon's hospital room. According to Dr. Larson, Sharon "would attend to Karen much longer than anyone else."

The CBS program revealed that Sharon's father was deeply distressed at Karen's involvement in Sharon's life. In Kowalski's words, Karen "seemed to push herself forward as if she was the important one." He told Karen that if she did not "back off" from Sharon, he would prevent her from seeing Sharon at all. According to Kowalski, Karen refused to stay away. "I am family," she told him.

Karen reaffirmed her status in Sharon's life through a letter she sent to Sharon's family. In the letter, Karen told the family that she and Sharon "shared hopes and dreams." She explained that they had made a lifetime commitment to one another and that she and Sharon felt deep love for one another.

Kowalski reported being shocked by the letter. "I couldn't believe it!" he exclaimed. Kowalski summed up his feelings about the question of Sharon and Karen's relationship by saying,

▼▼▼▼▼▼

I don't feel as though I should have to believe what a schoolteacher's telling me over my daughter that I trusted all the time. . . . She never told us about any kind of a relationship. So that is what we're going to go by. We're going to believe our daughter. ▼▼▼

In the winter of 1984, Kowalski moved his daughter to a nursing home 200 miles from Karen. Two months later, Karen went to court determined to win guardianship of Sharon. Instead, the first court order named Donald Kowalski as guardian, but gave Karen equal visitation rights. When Karen exercised these rights, the Kowalskis went back to court. From 1984 to 1989, they went back to court twenty times. Kowalski expressed confusion over why they have been forced to address this issue in the courtroom. He asked, "Who comes first when there's no marriage? If you're married, that's a different story."

Of course, in Sharon and Karen's case, as with every other homosexual couple, marriage is not a legal option. If we are to accept Donald Kowalski's standard, no homosexual couple would be entitled to receive the basic rights afforded heterosexual couples.

This and related concerns led civil rights attorney Jan Goldman to become involved in the case. In 1985, Goldman interviewed Sharon. According to Goldman, Sharon answered every question directly, but slowly, with a typewriter. When asked about her relationship with Karen, Sharon wrote, "We love each other."

Yet on July 25, 1985, Donald Kowalski was given total control of Sharon's life. Within twenty-four hours, he barred Karen Thompson from seeing Sharon, he restricted visits from other friends, censored most of her mail, and moved Sharon to a nursing home. Kowalski explains that he had to take these actions to protect his daughter.

When Diane Sawyer asked Karen to summarize her reaction to these events for the "West 57th" audience, Karen said simply,

▼▼▼▼▼▼

I will always love Sharon. . . . I made a lifetime commitment to Sharon. I know that whatever she wants, I'll spend the rest of my life trying to get it for her. ▼▼▼

The case of *Thompson* v. *Kowalski* dramatically illustrates some of the serious implications that rights of affectional preference have for people's lives. Fear of losing her family's love prevented Sharon from sharing her life with her family. This secrecy helped encourage the Kowalskis to invalidate Sharon's lifetime commitment to Karen. At the same time, social sanctions and laws denied Karen and Sharon the opportunity to express their commitment through legal marriage. And because the couple was unable to marry, they were deprived of basic rights afforded heterosexual couples. Karen was denied the opportunity to nurture and care for the person to whom she had made a lifetime commitment. And Sharon was denied the love and nurturance that Karen wanted to give her. The Kowalskis have suffered great losses as well. They've endured the emotional pain of discovering that the daughter they so dearly love was afraid to share the truth about her life with them. They've also faced a painful, costly court battle over their daughter's fate. At the conclusion of the "West 57th" segment devoted to this case, Karen Thompson summed up the terrible costs associated with the struggle over Sharon's fate: "I've lost, the Kowalskis have lost, but Sharon has lost most of all."

Given prevailing attitudes and legal constraints against homosexuality, what becomes of the one in ten Americans like Sharon and Karen who must live with their homosexuality? Now that we know that homosexual adults cannot change their affectional preference, should society continue to repress these people's public expression of their most intimate feelings? What would be the social costs of permitting a wider range of expression for homosexuals? What would be the social advantages of such freedom? How might basic rights of affectional preference have changed the facts of the *Thompson* v. *Kowalski* case? Would these changes have served the Kowalskis? Sharon? Karen? What about societal interests in this case? What are the best arguments for and against trying to protect homosexual persons from job and housing discrimination? What are the arguments for and against permitting homosexual persons to marry?

These are but a few of the many issues increasingly demanding public attention. Resolution of these issues has the potential to significantly affect many institutions and traditions within our society.

▾ **Exercise 3b:** Discuss the overall value of the preceding discussion to public deliberation on rights of affectional preference. Which issues, if any, do you believe were left out of the discussion? What information would have strengthened the overall discussion? Next, discuss the biases that you believe underlie the paragraphs above. Provide your own characterization of issues related to affectional preference. What biases underlie your characterization?

▾ **Exercise 3c:** Discuss your views on the rights of affectional preference. Consider, for example, the extent to which you believe that homosexuals should have the right to privacy. Do you believe the State has (or should have) the right to prevent homosexuals from marrying one another? Why or why not? Do you believe homosexuals should be permitted to teach in public schools? Why or why not?

▾ **Exercise 3d:** Describe the sources of some of the beliefs in Exercise 3c. What is the basis of your views on homosexuality? What/who are the sources for these beliefs? How reliable are these sources? How valuable are they for shaping your personal family life views?

▾ **Exercise 3e:** Review literature on the origins and nature of sexual preference. What positions do you find most persuasive? Why? After reviewing this literature, answer the following questions about your own sexuality. How do you believe your own sexual preference was formed? How flexible is your sexual preference? How much control do you think you have over your sexual preference? Do you believe that you could change your sexual preference with counseling and therapy? Why or why not?

▾ **Exercise 3f:** Review the following commentary. Identify the claims the author appears to view as commonplaces and those the author seems to view as issues. Do you share the author's perceptions about the American public's views on this topic?

▾ ▾ ▾ ▾ ▾ ▾

Homosexual Rhetoric Needs to Be Reexamined

Homosexuals are at it again. They're trying to get even more rights than they already have. They tell us that they should be allowed to marry and that we should not discriminate against them in the workplace.

But don't let their rhetoric fool you. American homosexuals have so much political influence that they have successfully lobbied against health workers' rights to protect themselves from the scourge of AIDS. When hospital orderlies ask to be relieved of the responsibility of caring for AIDS patients, they are advised that they must not upset the homosexual lobby.

The scientific community has been particularly susceptible to homosexual influence. Despite the fact that scientists are not yet able to determine with certainty the cause of AIDS, they continue to assure the public that it is not contagious and that people cannot get the disease through casual contact.

This lobbying effort has been especially dangerous for children. Homosexuals have convinced school districts that children with AIDS should be given the opportunity to attend school with healthy children.

Yet we are told that homosexuals do not have enough rights. Anyone who has been to San Francisco knows that homosexuals are not the poor, unrepresented group they make themselves out to be. Homosexuals in San Francisco control that city's governance. They have even launched a campaign to get "spousal medical coverage" and other benefits for gay "couples" who live together.

But perhaps the greatest evidence of the homosexual community's political influence is in the area of sex education. In many school districts, children are being taught that homosexuality is an acceptable way of life. How can we protect our children from such dangerous indoctrination?

Because we are a freedom-loving society, we have been conditioned to take civil rights rhetoric seriously. It's time for us to reexamine this rhetoric and stop the gay rights movement. Our society already hangs by a tender moral thread. Let's make sure we don't go the way of the Roman Empire and lose our moral fabric altogether. ▼ ▼ ▼

▼ **Exercise 3g:** Identify the author's central arguments. What reasons does the author give (or assume) in support of the essay's central theses? Evaluate the quality of the essay's inferences. Are the premises acceptable? Is the reasoning coherent? Is it logically consistent? Has the author committed fallacies of language, reasoning, or evidence? Identify the relevant fallacies. How serious are they?

▼ **Exercise 3h:** Evaluate the persuasiveness of the commentary for a critical composite audience. Next, evaluate the persuasiveness of the commentary for a more generalized audience.

▼ **Exercise 3i:** The Supreme Court has ruled that homosexuals are not legally protected by the Constitution. They can be legally denied the right to marry one another. In most states, homosexuals are also legally denied housing, employment, insurance benefits, the right to adopt children, and the right to serve as foster parents. And, of course, they are denied all of the spousal rights associated with marriage (such as tax benefits, health benefits, access to pension funds, other insurance benefits, the right to consultation in medical emergencies, community property rights, and so on). Homosexuality is also a legally permissible ground for denying a mother or father custody of his or her children. Do you believe the commentary's author has adequately considered these facts? Are these facts relevant to your assessment of the essay's validity?

▼ **Exercise 3j:** Many people view AIDS as illustrative of the dangers associated with homosexuality. Some even view AIDS as a punishment for violating the laws of God or "nature." Studies show, however, that homosexual women have a lower percentage of AIDS cases than does any other group in the population. Discuss the significance of this fact for arguments that presume associations between AIDS and homosexuality.

▼ **Exercise 3k:** Write an issues brief on rights of affectional preference. After completing the brief, decide which arguments you find most persuasive. Write a persuasive defense of your position on the topic. As you write your arguments, be sure to carefully consider the perspectives presented above.

▼ ▼ ▼
TOPIC 4: SURROGATE MOTHERHOOD

We've dealt so far with issues both familiar to and directly relevant to most of us. Without exception, every human must contend with societal norms regarding gender. Everyone is also either directly or indirectly affected by public policies related to parental leave and child care. Similarly, because sexual identity and preference are so deeply personal, we all have a stake in the outcome of public policy debates on affectional preference.

Like affectional preference, the nature of motherhood is another topic that evokes strong emotional responses. Recently, several technological advances and societal changes have brought this topic under close public scrutiny. Surrogate motherhood—especially as publicized through the Baby M case—has helped fuel debate on this complex and emotional topic.

▼ **Exercise 4a:** Review the following issue overview. Identify commonplaces of fact and value. Then identify claims you believe will (would) spark controversy.

Issue Overview

A surrogate mother is a "woman who agrees to be inseminated by a particular man's sperm, to gestate and birth the baby, and then to terminate her involvement with the child and let the man and his wife raise the child."[14]

The facts of the Baby M case graphically illustrate the complexities of this topic. Mary Beth Whitehead was the mother of two children when she decided to serve as a surrogate parent for the Sterns. Mary Beth's husband joined her in consenting to the surrogacy arrangement.

William Stern, a biochemist, is an only child, whose mother died shortly before he and his wife Elizabeth began to pursue the surrogate mother arrangement. Elizabeth Stern, a physician, was diagnosed as having a form of multiple sclerosis. She had been told that pregnancy could worsen her condition. Because William Stern felt a strong desire to carry on his family's lineage, the Sterns preferred surrogacy to adoption.

---

14. This definition is borrowed from Ruth Hubbard's "A Birthmother is a Birthmother is a . . .," *Sojourner,* September 1987, pp. 21–22.

Upon their meeting, the Sterns and Mary Beth Whitehead all expressed great satisfaction in their arrangement. They agreed that Mary Beth would be artificially inseminated with William Stern's sperm. She would carefully guard the fetus throughout her pregnancy, and, upon the birth of the child, she would forever relinquish custody of the child to the Sterns. In return, the Sterns would pay all medical expenses and pay Mary Beth a fee of $10,000.

Throughout the pregnancy, the Sterns kept close contact with Mary Beth. She carefully protected the fetus and gave birth to a healthy girl. Upon the birth of the child, however, Mary Beth knew she would be emotionally incapable of relinquishing her child. After losing initial appeals to keep her baby, Mary Beth "kidnapped" the child. After some months, the baby was found and released to the Sterns for their custodial care. And here the legal, political, social, and ethical complexities unfold.

William Stern, the baby's biological father, demanded full custody of Baby M (named Melissa by the Sterns and Sara by the Whiteheads, the infant was named Baby M by the court in an effort to protect her privacy). Stern claimed that the contract Mary Beth signed before Baby M's birth required the mother to completely relinquish all custodial rights to the child. Mary Beth claimed that this contract could not be valid. A mother cannot, she argued, relinquish custodial rights before the birth of her child. Adoption laws, in recognition of this principle, require several days of reflection after the birth of a child before a woman can legally give the infant up for adoption. Furthermore, Whitehead argued, surrogacy contracts amount to "baby selling" and therefore cannot be upheld.

The Sterns rejected this interpretation. They argued that Mary Beth was fully aware of the contract's implications when she signed it. According to the Sterns, the surrogacy contract does not provide for the selling of a child. Surrogate mothers are paid to provide a service. And Mary Beth was refusing to meet the terms of their service agreement.

Noel Keane, an attorney who helped originally unite the Sterns and Whiteheads, recognizes the complexities of a surrogacy arrangement. "Nobody can tell you today what somebody is going to do nine months from now," he notes.[15] Given Keane's association with 140 surrogacy arrangements, his level of uncertainty on this topic attests to its complexity.

The Baby M case has been through two levels of trial, with competing outcomes. New Jersey State Superior Court Judge Harvey R. Sorkow ruled that the Stern-Whitehead surrogacy contract is legal and must be upheld. He gave the Sterns full custody of Baby M and ruled that Elizabeth Stern could legally adopt the baby.

On February 3, 1988, the New Jersey Supreme Court overruled all but the custody aspect of Judge Sorkow's decision. With an unusual 7–0 vote, the

---

15.   Barbara Kantrowitz (with Peter McKillop, Nadine Joseph, Jeanne Gordon, and Bill Turque), "Who Keeps 'Baby M'?" *Newsweek,* January 19, 1987, p. 45.

state supreme court held that Mary Beth Whitehead "is not only the natural mother, but also the legal mother, and is not to be penalized one iota because of the surrogate contract." They ruled that the surrogate contract is not only invalid; it may be criminal. The following excerpts from the court's ruling illustrate the justices' strong opposition to the surrogacy contract:

▼▼▼▼▼▼

We invalidate the surrogacy contract because it conflicts with the law and public policy of this State. While we recognize the depth of the yearning of infertile couples to have their own children, we find the payment of money to a "surrogate" mother illegal, perhaps criminal, and potentially degrading to women.

One of the surrogacy contract's basic purposes, to achieve the adoption of a child through private placement, though permitted in New Jersey, "is very much disfavored." . . . Its use of money for this purpose—and we have no doubt whatsoever that the money is being paid to obtain an adoption and not, as the Sterns argue, for the personal services of Mary Beth Whitehead—is illegal and perhaps criminal. . . . In addition to the inducement of money, there is the coercion of contract: the natural mother's irrevocable agreement, prior to birth, even prior to conception, to surrender the child to the adoptive couple. Such an agreement is totally unenforceable in private placement adoption. . . . Integral to these invalid provisions of the surrogacy contract is the related agreement, equally invalid, on the part of the natural mother to cooperate with, and not to contest, proceedings to terminate her parental rights, as well as her contractual concession, in aid of the adoption, that the child's best interest would be served by awarding custody to the natural father and his wife—all of this before she has even conceived, and, in some cases, before she has the slightest idea of what the natural father and adoptive mother are like.

This is the sale of a child, or at the very least, the sale of a mother's right to her child, the only mitigating factor being that one of the purchasers is the father.

The surrogacy contract's invalidity, resulting from its direct conflict with the above statutory provisions, is further underlined when its goals and means are measured against New Jersey's public policy. The contract's basic premise, that the natural parents can decide in advance of birth which one is to have custody of the child, bears no relationship to the settled law that the child's best interest shall determine custody.

The surrogacy contract guarantees permanent separation of the child from one of its natural parents. Our policy, however, has long been that to the extent possible, children should remain with and be brought up by both of their natural parents.

We think it is expecting something well beyond normal human capabilities to suggest that this mother should have parted with her newly born infant without a struggle. Other than survival, what stronger force is there? We do not know of, and cannot conceive of, any other case where a perfectly fit mother was expected to surrender her newly born infant, perhaps forever, and was then told she was a bad mother because she did not.

We have found that our present laws do not permit the surrogacy contract used in this case. Nowhere, however, do we find any legal prohibition against surrogacy when the surrogate mother volunteers, without any payment, to act as a surrogate and is given the right to change her mind and to assert her parental rights.

We do not underestimate the difficulties of legislating on this subject. Legislative consideration of surrogacy may also provide the opportunity to begin to focus on the overarching implications of the new reproductive biotechnology—*in vitro* fertilization, preservation of sperm and eggs, embryo implantation, and the like. . . . The problem can be addressed only when society decides what its values and objectives are in this troubling, yet promising, area.[16] ▼ ▼ ▼

Because these paragraphs appear in an official state supreme court opinion, they emphasize legal considerations. However, this decision also relies heavily on public policy regarding parent-child relationships. The justices' opinion illustrates, among other things, that surrogacy contracts raise serious social and ethical considerations. What constitutes motherhood? Are mothers and fathers equal in their roles before a baby's birth? To what extent should the differences in their roles influence society's views on a mother and father's custodial rights? Should women be permitted (or even encouraged) to use their bodies as "baby factories"? Does the State have the right to determine what women do with their bodies? What role, if any, should the State play in resolving these and related issues?

Given that approximately one of every six American couples are unable to have a child without some form of medical intervention, it's easy to understand why surrogacy is becoming such a popular option. Waiting for the availability of an adoptive child often takes up to five years, and even then there are no assurances that the child will be "normal" or healthy. Surrogacy provides the opportunity to have a child biologically linked to the father, and the power of this association should not be overlooked.

As the New Jersey Supreme Court ruling suggests, society's resolution of these issues will require careful attention to fundamental values. This association with fundamental values justifies careful and prolonged attention to the many complex dimensions of surrogacy. The very definition of parenthood in our society could be at stake.

▼ **Exercise 4b:** Identify assumptions and biases that you believe influenced the preceding issue overview. Are these assumptions warranted by critical audi-

---

16. Excerpts from "Decision by New Jersey Supreme Court in Baby M Case," *New York Times,* February 4, 1988, p. A-14.

ences reviewing the paragraphs? What about more generalized audiences? What effects did the author's biases have on the issue characterization?

▾ **Exercise 4c:** Discuss the overall value of the preceding paragraphs to deliberations on issues related to surrogate motherhood. Which issues, if any, were left out of the discussion?

▾ **Exercise 4d:** Evaluate the persuasiveness of the New Jersey Supreme Court's arguments against the validity of the surrogacy contract. To what extent do you believe the decision conforms to existing public opinion? To what extent does the decision conform to your views on the topic?

▾ **Exercise 4e:** Write arguments for and against some dimension of the surrogacy topic. As you sketch your arguments for and against a selected thesis, be sure to carefully consider discussion of the Baby M case provided above. Be sure too to carefully anticipate refutation of each of your controversial claims.

▾ **Exercise 4f:** Search for additional information on surrogate motherhood. Next, write an issues brief that highlights pro and con inferences appropriately drawn from this information.

▾ **Exercise 4g:** Washington Post Writers Group Columnist Ellen Goodman has written an editorial expressing her reaction to Judge Harvey Sorkow's original ruling in favor of the surrogacy contract.[17] Carefully review the following excerpts from the editorial. What is Goodman's overall point? Do you agree with her? Why or why not?

▾▾▾▾▾▾

Baby M's Case Won't Be Last

One sentence among the thousands in the 121-page decision read in the New Jersey courtroom remains incontrovertible: "There can be no solution satisfactory to all in this kind of case."

Not even Gilbert and Sullivan could have tied all the loose ends and confused identities of the Baby M drama into a single happy ending. So Judge Harvey Sorkow chose to do his best in the interest of the baby.

He focused precisely and exclusively on the child produced by this artificial union of Mary Beth and Bill. She would be Melissa, he ruled, daughter to the Sterns. And Mary Beth Whitehead would have no rights.

The judge called surrogacy an "alternative reproduction vehicle that appears to hold out so much hope to the childless." The end result, children for the childless, was the primary value.

But I wonder whether he heard how these words echo to many of the rest of us? An alternative reproductive vehicle? An ARV? Isn't this what has been so troubling about the whole matter? Those of us less focused on the child or the children hear the mechanistic language, and flinch at the idea that there are

---

17. *Columbus Dispatch*, April 8, 1989, p. A-9. © 1989 The Boston Globe Newspaper Company/Washington Post Writers Group. Reprinted with permission.

women ARVs—who will be recruited to manufacture children in what the judge described as a "totally personal service."

Surrogate motherhood, he suggested, was the equivalent of surrogate father-hood. But this neat legal math denies reality. A woman is more than an egg donor. Man and woman may be two halves of the genetic structure of their offspring, but their roles before birth are unequal.

This is not to suggest that, by virtue of pregnancy, every mother has a stronger claim to the newborn than any father, that the Mary Beths invariably have first rights.

But if we've learned anything even an ARV can have second thoughts.

The judge in this case appears to believe that we can write the contracts and laws to clarify human relationships. Parents such as the Sterns can have the benefits of babies like Melissa without the debits of emotional turmoil like the Whiteheads. Judges are meant to have such faith in the law. I don't share it.

The Baby M case is, and always will be, unusual. The girl is, as Sorkow wrote, "unique and at risk." She may learn about her origins from some made-for-television movie. Or a book cover, a faded clipping, a casual remark, or an appeals case.

The child will always be the most famous of her kind. But she is not alone. No law can clarify the muddy human emotions that come when we introduced hired motherhood.

The judge decided this case for the sake of the child. He admitted that there was no happy ending. But the reality is that for present and future Baby Melissas, this is no ending at all—just the beginning. ▼▼▼

- ▼ **Exercise 4h:** Identify commonplaces and issues in the excerpts from Goodman's editorial.
- ▼ **Exercise 4i:** Evaluate the persuasiveness of Goodman's comments. How persuasive are they likely to be for critical audiences? What about more generalized audiences? Why?

▼ ▼ ▼

ADDITIONAL FAMILY LIFE TOPICS

Sexual identity, gender norms, parental leave, child care, rights of affectional preference, and surrogate motherhood are but a few of the many topics that generate discussion in today's complex society. There are many other difficult choices confronting American adults.

- ▼ **Exercise 1:** Review the topics described below. Add three topics to each list.

▼▼▼▼▼▼

Personal family life: Should couples live together before they marry? What about commuter marriages? How successful are they likely to be? Should mothers of young children work or stay home with their preschool-age children? What about fathers? What should be their household and child-care responsibilities? What constitutes a family in today's society? What responsibilities do families have to their elderly members?

Public policy: Should states strengthen or loosen their divorce laws? Why? Should marriage laws be changed in any way? Should couples be forced to undergo counseling or some other form of educational process before marrying? Should schools teach sex education to young children? Should high schools provide access to birth control? Should women be permitted to have abortions on demand? Should federal or state funds be used to provide abortions to underprivileged women? What rights should fathers have in abortion decisions? Should single people be permitted to adopt children? Should parents have more control over their children's education? Who should educate our children? Using what standards? Should mothers continue to have legal presumption in child-custody cases? What rights should fathers have in these cases?

Policies related to technologies: Should doctors give parents information about a child's sex in the first-trimester of pregnancy? Should couples have access to technology that would allow them to choose a baby's sex? Should single women have access to artificial insemination by donor? Should single men have access to surrogate mothers? Should couples have access to *in vitro* fertilization? Should families have control over the medical care given their loved ones in times of medical emergency? Who should have the authority to make decisions about the care of critically ill newborns?

▼ **Exercise 2:** Select one of the topics listed above. Write an issues brief on the topic. After completing the brief, write a persuasive paper in defense of your position on the topic. Be sure your arguments carefully anticipate alternative perspectives.

INDEX

A

Abortion
  and the human fetal tissue issue, 140–141
  interplay of conventional and technical presumptions, 72
Acceptability of premises, 175–176
Adequacy of support, 182
Ad hominem argument, 195
Adler, Mortimer, 50
Advertising
  and deception, 128–129
  and the false dilemma, 196
  perceptions shaped by, 14
  and the repeated assertion fallacy, 188
Advocacy. *See also* Persuasion
  argument preparation steps, 161–164
  and deliberation, 140–142
  purpose of, 161
Aesthetic judgments, as value claims, 62–63
Affectional preference topic, 225–233. *See also* Homosexuality
AIDS example. *See also* Affectional preference topic
  implicit and explicit assumptions, 32
  and rhetorical versus mathematical probability, 84–85
Alternative perspectives
  development of for issues brief, 143, 144
  importance of anticipating, 105, 109–110
  Mill on importance of development of, 5, 102–103
Ambiguity fallacy, 185–186
Analogy, arguments by, 87–88
Analytic claim, 62*n*
Animal Welfare Act, 153
Animal welfare topic
  and acceptance of presumptions, 73
  audience and argument formulation, 101

central issue designation and characterization, 146–148
commonplaces of, 149–150
experimentation on animals, 64–66, 147–160
internal inconsistency example, 178–179
issues brief for, 153–160
legislation pending in 1989 Congress session, 148
Appeal to ignorance fallacy, 194
Appeal to popular prejudice fallacy, 194–195
Appeal to tradition fallacy, 195
Applied Science and Technology Index, 28
Appropriate circumstances, and promises, 123
Argumentation. *See also* Competitive argumentation; Cooperative argumentation
  and controversy, 47
  defined, 44
  and deliberation, 47–48
  and democracy, 50–51
  emotions and, 46–47
  Groupthink, protection against, 53–54
  and persuasion, 47
  process defined, 48
  and reasonableness, 44–45
  as a social process, 122
Argumentation context. *See* Context of argumentation
Argument evaluation. *See* Evaluation of argumentation
Arguments, as units of argumentation, 45
Art Index, 28
Aspartame example, as combative interaction, 44
Assertion, repeated assertion fallacy, 188
Assumptions. *See also* Commonplaces; Presumptions
  central role of in all communication, 30
  discovery of for issues brief, 143

W